Global Capital Markets

Global Capital Markets

A Survey of Legal and Regulatory Trends

Edited by

P.M. Vasudev

Associate Professor, Faculty of Law, Common Law Section, University of Ottawa, Canada

Susan Watson

Professor, Faculty of Law, The University of Auckland, New Zealand

Cheltenham, UK • Northampton, MA, USA

Published by
Edward Elgar Publishing Limited
The Lypiatts
15 Lansdown Road
Cheltenham
Glos GL50 2JA
UK

Edward Elgar Publishing, Inc.
William Pratt House
9 Dewey Court
Northampton
Massachusetts 01060
USA

A catalogue record for this book
is available from the British Library

Library of Congress Control Number: 2017931776

This book is available electronically in the **Elgar**online
Law subject collection
DOI 10.4337/9781786432872

ISBN 978 1 78643 286 5 (cased)
ISBN 978 1 78643 287 2 (eBook)

Typeset by Columns Design XML Ltd, Reading
Printed and bound in Great Britain by TJ International Ltd, Padstow

Contents

List of contributors   vi

Introduction   1
P.M. Vasudev and Susan Watson

PART I   INVESTORS AND THE STOCK MARKET

1   Implications of shareholder activism   17
    Anita Anand
2   Suspension of Chinese units of 'Big 4' audit firms: the question of
    moral turpitude   35
    Qingxiu Bu
3   The proposed Directive on the encouragement of long-term
    shareholder engagement in European listed companies: a critical
    appraisal   62
    Corrado Malberti

PART II   CAPITAL MARKETS DEVELOPMENT AND THE LAW

4   Revisiting corporate control-enhancing mechanisms   95
    Yu-Hsin Lin
5   Law and finance: from 'transplantation' to 'better' corporate
    governance in China   116
    Heida Donegan

PART III   CROWDFUNDING

6   The two-sided effect of crowdfunding: the visible effect on capital
    markets regulation and the unperceived effect on company law   145
    Teresa Rodríguez de las Heras Ballell
7   Regulating equity crowdfunding in India: walking a tightrope   172
    Arjya B. Majumdar and Umakanth Varottil
8   A critical examination of crowdfunding within the 'Long White
    Cloud' (New Zealand)   199
    Trish Keeper

Index   221

Contributors

Anita Anand, Professor of Law and J.R. Kimber Chair in Investor Protection and Corporate Governance, Faculty of Law, University of Toronto, Canada

Qingxiu Bu, Senior Lecturer, Sussex Law School, University of Sussex, United Kingdom

Heida Donegan, Senior Counsel and Head of China Business, Kensington Swan, Auckland, New Zealand

Trish Keeper, Senior Lecturer, School of Accounting and Commercial Law, Victoria University of Wellington, New Zealand

Yu-Hsin Lin, Assistant Professor, School of Law, City University of Hong Kong, Hong Kong SAR

Arjya B. Majumdar, Associate Professor, Jindal Global Law School, O.P. Jindal Global University, India

Corrado Malberti, Associate Professor, University of Trento, Italy; Adjunct Associate Professor, University of Luxembourg, Luxembourg

Teresa Rodríguez de las Heras Ballell, Associate Professor of Commercial Law, Universidad Carlos III de Madrid, Spain

Umakanth Varottil, Associate Professor, Faculty of Law, National University of Singapore, Singapore

Introduction

P.M. Vasudev and Susan Watson

THE CONTEXT

Capital markets are a continuous stream of activity and innovation. Constantly evolving and inherently dynamic, they offer rich material for analysis. And market activities and innovation give rise to regulatory and policy issues. Additionally, in recent decades, globalization has incentivized cross-border listings and international flows of capital. These developments add to the rich mix the capital markets offer, further catalysing the markets and making them more complex. New features also raise new regulatory challenges, among them the emergence of crowdfunding as a new method of business finance, hedge fund activism and increased use of dual-class shares as control-enhancing mechanisms in listed corporations.

To take stock of recent trends and events, and explore their regulatory and policy implications, this volume concentrates on capital market-related developments. Capital markets are a vital socio-economic institution in the contemporary world. They perform several functions: they are a repository of public savings (importantly, pension savings), a significant influence on the governance of powerful corporations that supply a variety of goods and services worldwide, and a source of finance for enterprises. Increasingly they are perceived as a barometer of general economic wellbeing. With their multiple functions, capital markets have emerged as a decisive force in the socio-economy. Promoting the markets and preserving share values are now treated as goals of public policy. Justifying the efforts that the US Federal Reserve made in the aftermath of the Credit Crisis of 2008–09, which triggered a plunge in share prices, Bernanke (2010) argued that 'higher stock prices will boost consumer wealth and help increase confidence, which can also spur spending. Increased spending will lead to higher incomes and profits that, in a virtuous circle, will further support economic expansion'. The statement accurately captures the prevalent mode of thinking about the stock market and the role of share prices as instruments for promoting general economic welfare.

In the setting described, the state of the market is treated as a key factor shaping the economic mood and affecting decision- and policy-making. It would be hard to overstate the central position that capital markets have come to occupy. These are some important reasons for making periodic global reviews of the trends in capital markets and corporate governance. *Corporate Governance after the Financial Crisis* (Edward Elgar) was published in 2012. The current volume continues with the efforts of its predecessor to map major worldwide trends and developments. The endeavour is to make a contribution to the literature on international capital markets and their regulation.

The chapters included in the volume deal with topical subjects, namely, hedge fund activism, crowdfunding, enforcement issues in cross-border listings, and the increased use of dual-class shares in recent Initial Public Offerings (IPOs) (notably from the technology sector, such as Alibaba and Facebook). Two other subjects the volume covers are recent corporate governance initiatives in the European Union and the 'law and development' story from China. The developments in the last few years offer a wealth of materials, and this underscores the importance of periodic reviews to map the events and trends. The exercise can serve a number of purposes, such as aiding scholarly research and pedagogy in academic institutions, and contributing to the discourse on topical subjects and policy issues.

The essays presented in this volume cover several major jurisdictions. In alphabetical order, they deal with Canada, China, Europe, India, New Zealand and the United States. Written by experts from the respective jurisdictions, the essays offer a nuanced analysis of the subjects, placing them in their local context.

AN OVERVIEW AND SOME THEORETICAL ISSUES

The volume explores two main themes: the trend for global convergence in capital market regulation and its nuances, and, second, the role of public regulation in fostering healthy and efficient capital markets. Globalization has spurred significant convergence, worldwide, in corporate governance and capital markets. Crowdfunding is a case in point. It has emerged as a significant source of capital for small and medium enterprises (SMEs), offering them a relatively inexpensive method of raising business finance through online platforms. Originating in its modern form in the United States, crowdfunding has swiftly spread to several other countries. In developing the regulatory model for crowd-funding, major variations are apparent among different jurisdictions.

In substance, crowdfunding operates on the same principle, which is raising business capital from retail investors through online portals. Within this seemingly homogenous space, however, regulation is shaped by different considerations in various jurisdictions, depending on local needs and any special concerns. This is evident from the three juris-dictions covered in this volume: the European Union (de las Heras Ballell, in Chapter 6), India (Majumdar and Varottil, in Chapter 7), and New Zealand (Keeper, in Chapter 8). Crowdfunding regulation in these different parts of the world, while affirming the trend of convergence, underscores the differences among jurisdictions in dealing with their local needs. To illustrate, in India investor protection concerns apparently drive the approach and the preference is for fairly stringent regulation, while in New Zealand the focus is more on facilitating fund-raising by businesses.

A second issue is about the evolution of ideas and the impact of events on the regulation of markets. The trajectory has seen changes over time, and the course of events offers valuable lessons. From the 1980s, the shareholder value maxim turned companies' focus towards capital markets and finance (see generally Porter 1997; Mitchell 2001). Widespread acceptance of shareholder value as the corporate goal encouraged stock market-centric governance (for a critique of the trend, see Stout 2012). The trends contributed to the markets attaining their present position as vital socio-economic institutions.

An important strand in the shareholder value platform (mainly, Jensen and Meckling 1976 and Easterbrook and Fischel 1991)[1] was an 'in principle' opposition to the public regulation of economic activity, in particular, corporate governance and the capital markets. Doctrinaire in approach, and drawing (with questionable accuracy) from the ideals of the American Revolution and its emphasis on liberty, shareholder value theorists railed against regulation and sought to rule it out as an option. Reflecting a spirit of rugged individualism, the theorists presented

---

[1] To be fair, a main argument of Easterbrook and Fischel (1991) against regulation related to special interest groups and their sway on the political process. They posited that 'much legislation is the outcome of the interplay of pressure groups and ... only by accident will interest group laws serve the broader public interest' (Easterbrook and Fischel 1991: 277). The complaint, which probably has greater validity in the United States, cannot be ignored. It remains a challenge for democratic institutions to overcome the influence of special interest groups and the resulting distortions in regulation.

unfettered freedom for market actors and private contracts as being the best instruments for promoting economic efficiency and achieving optimal outcomes. Regardless of merits or accuracy, they were ideas whose time had come.

The 1980s was the Reagan–Thatcher era in the United States and the United Kingdom. The erstwhile Soviet Union and China had begun to gradually step away from their totalitarian economic models, and this further supported the libertarian argument. The economic environment undermined the idea that public policy and regulation had any meaningful role in the emerging scheme of things. This was strengthened by the major events that followed: the fall of the Berlin Wall in 1989 and the disintegration of the Soviet Union in 1991. Proclaiming the 'end of history'. Fukuyama (1992) argued that humanity's long and hard march had culminated in the triumph of Western liberal democracy as the social order, over other forms of societal organization.

The 'end of history' idea found its reverberation in corporate governance and capital markets. Adopting Fukuyama's hypothesis and his phrase, Hansmann and Kraakman (2001) hailed the victory of Anglo-American shareholder primacy and shareholder value. Ironically, their article was published just before the spectacular collapse of Enron, a poster-case for shareholder value, in a heap of scandals and fraud.

Corporate governance failures, exemplified by Enron's collapse in 2001, revealed the problems with narrow approaches. In response to the failures and scandals, the Sarbanes-Oxley Act was enacted in the United States at the turn of the century. Sarbanes-Oxley inspired similar regulatory initiatives in several other jurisdictions. For example, Canada introduced certification requirements for financial statements (NI 52-109)[2] and a statutory remedy for investors against misrepresentations in continuing disclosures (Securities Act (Ontario), Part XXIII.1).[3]

With features such as mandatory audit committees and criminal consequences for financial misstatements, the Sarbanes-Oxley Act strengthened securities law intervention in corporate governance, a trend that can be traced to the Foreign Corrupt Practices Act of 1977 (FCPA).[4] The FCPA aimed to check overseas business corruption. More recently, the Dodd-Frank Wall Street Reform and Consumer Protection Act of

---

[2] NI 52-109 (Canadian Securities Administrators), Certification of Disclosure in Issuers' Annual and Interim Filings.
[3] Securities Act (Ontario), RSO 1990, c S.5.
[4] Foreign Corrupt Practices Act of 1977, Pub. L95-213, 91 Stat. 1494.

2010[5] was enacted as the public policy response to the Credit Crisis of 2008–09. It attempted to strengthen regulatory corporate governance through shareholder empowerment and enhanced executive pay disclosures. A similar approach is under consideration in Europe, as Malberti in Chapter 3 of this volume points out. The trends indicate increased use of regulation in shaping corporate practice and in ordering capital markets.

To be clear, the above is not a doctrinaire pitch for the regulation of markets. Rather, the effort is to highlight the perils of dogmatic approaches, be they pro- or anti-regulatory. At least three major features are discernible in the prevailing landscape. These are (a) greater interconnectedness among national economies and the need for ensuring reasonable order in complex arrangements; (b) suboptimal results in the absence of clear rules and appropriate regulation; and (c) the advantages of facilitative regulation.

Globalization has strengthened connections among national economies. The size and complexity of the global economic structure makes cross-jurisdictional regulation and regulatory cooperation more or less inevitable. Qingxiu Bu in Chapter 2 of this volume offers telling evidence from the experience of the US Securities and Exchange Commission (SEC) in dealing with the 'Big 4' international accounting firms (Deloitte, EY, KPMG and PwC) in investigating their audit of Chinese reverse merger companies (RMCs) listed in the US markets. In the absence of a clear regulatory framework, the SEC was challenged in accessing the audit work papers of the Chinese affiliates of the Big 4 firms, and this frustrated its efforts to examine the quality of the audit work that was done – an important exercise needed for effective investor protection in the United States where the companies were listed. Faced with these problems, SEC made persistent efforts which led to the signing of a China–United States memorandum on regulatory cooperation in 2013. The developments underscore the importance of developing appropriate regulatory machinery to manage cross-border economic collaborations that can spur growth.

Second, aside from globalization and the resulting interconnectedness, there is also recognition of the need to inculcate a reasonable degree of economic order within nations. This is particularly true of transitional economies, such as China, which have recently shifted to more diffused economic models. China, a major economy, joined the corporate stock market system of economic growth in relatively recent times – from the

---

[5]   Dodd-Frank Wall Street Reform and Consumer Protection Act of 2010, Pub. L111-203, 125 Stat. 1376.

late 1980s. Donegan in Chapter 5 explains how, starting from having only scanty laws to regulate business corporations and the capital markets, China gradually found its way through the maze. Donegan traces the country's efforts in recent decades to develop rules and regulatory mechanisms to cope with the problems that surfaced and to streamline economic activity. Significantly, China had to develop its legal and regulatory systems at the same time that its economy, as well as its relationship with mature economies around the world, was expanding at a dizzying pace.

Finally, in the present interconnected world, it is important to combine a facilitative role of regulation with its more traditional policing role and 'command and control' techniques. This is about devising mechanisms to streamline and smooth market processes and facilitating the innovations developed in the market/civil society to function beneficially, and with minimal downsides. Crowdfunding is a good example here. It originated as a civil society innovation that uses technology (through Internet portals) and brings together interested persons to provide funds for projects. The regulatory approach to crowdfunding clearly aims to streamline and smooth. It reveals a facilitative approach and sensitivity to the importance of enabling SMEs to access capital on less onerous terms. Appropriately regulated, crowdfunding can facilitate more diffused and faster economic growth.

Historically, market innovations and regulatory responses have marched alongside each other. This trend has characterized the development of capital markets and their law. The regulation of prospectuses – a market-evolved device – in Victorian England (Joint Stock Companies Registration and Regulation Act 1844),[6] and later in the federal securities legislation in the United States in the 1930s (Securities Act of 1933),[7] are illustrative. Legislation adopted a market device and made it mandatory, with rules for including sufficient disclosures in the document. Dealing with legitimate market innovations and providing appropriate pathways for them, and checking market excesses, continue to pose challenges for public policy. There is now sufficient evidence of the risks of extreme ideologies and doctrinaire approaches – a simple faith, whether in free markets or in regulation, as the panacea for all ills. If there is a lesson the events offer, it is the importance of holistic, goal-oriented methods

---

[6] Joint Stock Companies Registration and Regulation Act 1844, 7 & 8 Vict c. 110. The rule in the United Kingdom on registration of prospectuses was, however, dropped in 1847 and was not restored until 1900 (Rix 1945).

[7] Securities Act of 1933, 15 USC s. 77a.

inspired by reason and a willingness to compromise, and less by passion and ideology.

Synthetic approaches now receive greater recognition in the legal discourse. New Legal Realism (NLR) (Nourse and Shaffer 2009) offers a valuable framework for redefining and repositioning regulation in the larger economic order. NLR traces its foundations, mainly scepticism, from classical legal realism (see, for example, Cohen 1935). Nourse and Shaffer (2009) sought to expand and enrich the classical framework. NLR is presented as a response to:

> [the] challenges – of globalization, terror, and the inability of financial markets to restrain themselves, of gaping income inequality (with eight percent of gains in US net income over three decades going to one percent of the population), of societies poised as if on a hair trigger to react globally to the latest crisis, of states realizing their mutual interdependence and vulnerability, but not knowing how to address them. (Nourse and Shaffer 2009: 240)

Nourse and Shaffer (2009: 137) described NLR as 'optimistic' and posited that 'law is a world of action and our responsibility is to participate in it'. The themes and their validity are quite evident in the stories narrated in this volume from around the world. They affirm that regulation continues to have an important position in the current scheme of things, without underestimating the nuanced methods that may be needed to deal with the developments and challenges of the future.

INTRODUCTION TO THE CHAPTERS

The volume presents eight chapters, divided into three Parts. Of the three, the first Part covers, in broad terms, investors and the markets. The Part has three chapters. One explores hedge fund activism in Canada and the second discusses the problems experienced with cross-border enforcement in regard to Chinese RMCs. The third chapter critiques the initiatives recently proposed in Europe for shareholder empowerment as an instrument for improved corporate governance. Part II consists of two chapters. The first chapter explores the trend of increased use of dual-class shares in recent, high-profile IPOs and its implications, while the second traces the development of legal regulation of capital markets and corporate governance in China since the 1990s. Finally, Part III presents three essays on emerging crowdfunding regulation. They deal, respectively, with Europe, India and New Zealand.

Part I Investors and the Stock Market

Anita Anand, 'Implications of shareholder activism' (Chapter 1): from Berle and Means' (1933) paradigm of passive investors, the shareholder universe has evolved significantly over subsequent decades. Consolidation of shareholding among institutional investors has been followed by the emergence of hedge funds as significant and visible/vocal shareholders. The two classes (institutional investors and hedge funds) represent a significant concentration of public company shareholding. Many US hedge funds tend to be activist shareholders, and their presence is felt equally in Canada. Hedge funds that acquire significant minority positions in undervalued public companies, as well as traditional institutional shareholders such as pension funds, aim to maximize returns for their beneficiaries. Activism by hedge funds and traditional institutions has been on the rise.

Surveying the literature on the subject, Anand's chapter argues that activist shareholders perform a useful function in monitoring corporate managements and their activism is beneficial to all shareholders. Citing the example of Canadian Pacific Rail, the chapter also disputes a major complaint against shareholder activism, that it is too focused on the short term. In pitching for more vibrant and meaningful shareholder democracy, the chapter advocates reform of legal rules in Canada to strengthen proxy access for shareholders to nominate candidates for board elections.

Qingxiu Bu, 'Suspension of Chinese units of "Big 4" audit firms: the question of moral turpitude' (Chapter 2): the chapter explores the Chinese RMCs and their cross-border listings in the United States. In the reverse mergers, Chinese companies merged with shell companies already listed in the United States and thus avoided the regulatory scrutiny that is characteristic of IPOs. RMCs have been a popular route for Chinese companies to cross-list on US stock exchanges. Inherently, the backdoor listing subjects companies to less scrutiny than a traditional IPO. Many RMCs have been involved in accounting misrepresentations and other allegations of securities fraud, causing significant losses to investors.

The Big 4 accounting firms have played a significant role in facilitating cross-listings. These professional firms are required to apply high standards in reviewing clients' financial statements. The complaint is that their Chinese affiliates have failed to adhere to US accounting standards.

Faced with requests under the Sarbanes-Oxley Act ('SOX'),[8] the Big 4's China units refused to provide audit work papers. In doing so, the Big 4 relied on Chinese law and justified their actions in not cooperating with SEC for the investigation. Bu's chapter emphasizes the moral hazard arising from the challenges in cross-border financial reporting and auditor oversight. The chapter explains the events, in particular the persistent efforts SEC made with the Big 4, and the signing of the China–United States Memorandum of Understanding on Enforcement Cooperation (2013). Qingxiu Bu argues for international cooperation as essential for regulatory efficacy. Referring to the ambiguities that still remain, even after the China–United States Memorandum came into effect, the chapter advocates multifaceted approaches in addressing the moral hazard issue with the Big 4 firms. In particular, it argues for combining *ex ante* prevention and *ex post* sanctions with cross-jurisdictional cooperation among regulatory agencies as effective instruments to deal with globalized capital markets.

Corrado Malberti, 'The proposed Directive on the encouragement of long-term shareholder engagement in European listed companies: a critical appraisal' (Chapter 3): covering the European Union, the chapter by Corrado Malberti traces the regulatory initiatives on corporate governance announced in the aftermath of the Financial Crisis of 2008–09. In the initial phase, the reactions of the European Union to the problems raised by corporate governance were slow and were mainly addressed to the reform of the governance of financial institutions. In April 2014, however, the European Commission presented a proposal for a Directive on encouraging long-term shareholder engagement, addressed to all listed companies. The measures proposed include greater transparency on shareholder voting, proxy advisory services, and shareholder say-on-pay for director remuneration.

The chapter reviews the academic and political debate on the initiatives that were announced. It discusses questions about the adoption of the initiatives as final regulatory measures among the several jurisdictions that make up the European Union. Presenting a critical review, the chapter argues that the impact of the Commission's proposal, if finally adopted, will be modest. It will probably not achieve its intended shareholder empowerment goals. The reasons presented for the expected poor outcome are traced to (a) the lack of a satisfactory theoretical and empirical basis to support the measures proposed, and (b) the inherent weaknesses of European law in creating a single and coherent legal

---

[8]   Sarbanes-Oxley Act of 2002, Pub. L107-204, 116 Stat. 745.

framework for corporate governance. The second reason concerns the European Commission's lack of authority to compel Member States to adopt the regulations that have been proposed. The chapter concludes by pointing out this inherent weakness of European law and the problem with attempts to develop corrective legislation that are not based on empirical evidence.

Part II   Capital Markets Development and the Law

Yu-Hsin Lin, 'Revisiting corporate control-enhancing mechanisms' (Chapter 4): dual-class shares with unequal voting rights allow a select group of shareholders, usually founders/insiders, to insulate their control over corporations from threats. Terming dual-class shares and similar devices 'corporate control-enhancing mechanisms', the chapter by Yu-Hsin Lin traces the spurt in the use of dual-class shares by technology companies to the Google IPO (2004). Lin points out the high proportion (almost one-third) of Chinese tech companies listed in the United States that have adopted corporate control-enhancing mechanisms, and examines the legitimacy of the device.

The discussion of control-enhancing mechanisms also includes their perceived advantages, such as protection of human capital and preservation of competitive advantage. Yet, it is argued, the risk of expropriation by controllers is a reality for other shareholders. The discussion covers two categories of control-enhancing mechanisms, namely, participative mechanisms (mainly voting rights included in corporate charters that can be amended by shareholder vote) and non-participative mechanisms (such as shareholder agreements and pyramidal shareholdings in which non-controlling shareholders have little say). The chapter argues for greater regulation of corporate control-enhancing mechanisms in jurisdictions with weak investor protection regimes, citing the ban in South Korea on cross-shareholding among the affiliates of conglomerates (Chaebols) as an illustrative example.

Heida Donegan, 'Law and finance: from "transplantation" to "better" corporate governance in China' (Chapter 5): China's model of legal development of capital markets is the subject of the fifth chapter. Heida Donegan provides an account of the development of corporate and securities markets regulation in China since the 1990s, an important contribution to international literature on these subjects. The chapter explains how China, starting from a near-clean slate, embarked on the journey of regulatory development in a newly-evolving economic system (from centralization and government-ownership to private enterprise and a market economy), through an experimental, trial-and-error method.

Two important insights that Donegan offers in the chapter are (a) the process or order of the development of law and its relationship with economic or business growth; and (b) the issues with China adopting 'transplants' from Western jurisdictions. With regard to the order of development of law, the picture presented is one of spontaneous business activity and economic growth inspired by a vision for a better future, with little forethought about systemic implications. Then, driven by necessity, rules are developed to instil some order in the landscape. With time and experience, the rules are often abandoned in favour of new ones, or at least modified to meet evolving needs. This sequence presents, perhaps, a microcosmic example of the typical pattern in free societies where the ideas and energies of individuals and groups march freely where they may, and regulation generally occurs *ex post.*

The second issue Donegan raises is regarding the workability of 'transplants' of legal or regulatory devices from the West, such as supervisory boards and independent directors. Pointing to the absence of requisite cultural habits (mainly, familiarity) and institutions (enforcement of rights and duties through an effective system of justice), the chapter argues for acculturation of the structures and systems and better adaptation of them to local conditions and tastes. Significantly, the chapter also advances a plea for the state to step back from the economic scene, as a necessary precondition for the market institutions to develop and flourish.

Part III Crowdfunding

Teresa Rodríguez de las Heras Ballell, 'The two-sided effect of crowdfunding: the visible effect on capital markets regulation and the unperceived effect on company law' (Chapter 6): this is the first of the three chapters on crowdfunding included in Part III. The chapter covers the European Union and highlights an important aspect, namely, the need to align many rules in company or corporate law with the crowdfunding paradigm. De las Heras Ballell points out that many of the rules that have been adopted deal with typical capital markets issues, such as managing risks, protecting investor interests, preventing systemic effects and promoting transparency. The second dimension, termed 'internal', is about company law under which the enterprise seeking crowdfunding is organized.

Crowdfunding challenges several company law rules. In general, rules governing non-public companies are not designed for managing the multiple dispersed investors, atomized capital and go-public-like demands that characterize crowdfunded enterprises. Recently framed rules on crowdfunding are mainly inspired by capital market issues. Referring to European initiatives, the chapter explores the inside effect of crowdfunding and some legal strategies to tackle them. The issues include corporate governance requirements, disclosure duties, complex decision-making, exit strategies in companies facing illiquidity, finding pure investors for otherwise privately-held companies, public exposure and reputational strategies. These can be challenging for non-public companies that seek crowdfunding, as they would be exposed to unfamiliar requirements and might lack the necessary skills and systems.

Arjya B. Majumdar and Umakanth Varottil, 'Regulating equity crowdfunding in India: walking the tightrope' (Chapter 7): India is another jurisdiction exploring a journey on the crowdfunding highway. Crowdfunding is not yet a reality in this country. In this chapter, Majumdar and Varottil present a critical analysis of the Consultation Paper that the Indian regulator, the Securities and Exchange Board of India (SEBI), published in 2014 outlining the proposed roadmap. Reflecting somewhat on the theme of the previous chapter, the authors tie crowdfunding to issues under the Indian corporate statute (Companies Act 2013) and its relatively conservative approach to capital-raising by companies. Attributing the approach to the burgeoning growth that the Indian capital markets have seen in recent years, the chapter characterizes it as an effort to err on the side of caution. Majumdar and Varottil discuss a recent case (*Sahara India Real Estate Corp. Ltd* v. *Securities and Exchange Board of India*, 2013)[9] in which the Supreme Court of India ordered a high-profile listed company to refund billions of dollars to investors. Terming the impact the 'Sahara effect', the chapter critiques the tight-fisted approach proposed by the Indian regulator in dealing with crowdfunding.

Examining the Consultation Paper issued by the Indian regulator, the chapter identifies several factors likely to inhibit the growth of crowdfunding. For investors, eligibility is restricted to qualified institutional investors, high-net-worth individuals and other eligible investors with minimum income levels that are quite high. Limits are also proposed on the size of individual investments, with individual investors barred from investing more than 10 per cent of their net worth in crowdfunded enterprises. Companies seeking crowdfunding are also subject to scrutiny by the regulator. Considering the conditions, the chapter raises the question of whether the proposed rules merely retain the status quo applicable under the current rules of the Companies Act 2013 (India).

---

[9]   [2013] 1 SCC 1 (India).

Trish Keeper, 'A critical examination of crowdfunding within the "Long White Cloud"' (Chapter 8): the final chapter in the volume discusses the trends in crowdfunding and its regulation in New Zealand. The tone was set by New Zealand's recently-enacted Financial Markets Conduct Act 2013 ('FMC Act'), which aims to promote innovation and flexibility in financial markets, in addition to the traditional goal of investor protection through transparency. This is the formal justification for recognizing crowdfunding as a method of raising business finance. Under the FMC Act, New Zealand has put in place a licensing system for crowdfunding intermediaries – online platforms used for raising capital through the crowdfunding method. Keeper's chapter includes an overview of the crowdfunding sites operating in New Zealand.

Licensing is subject to compliance with the eligibility criteria prescribed for crowdfunding intermediaries. The conditions include transparency of organization, membership in an approved dispute resolution service, and self-certification by applicants' directors and senior managers. Finally, the regulator, the Financial Markets Authority (FMA), must be satisfied about the capability of applicants to provide crowdfunding service to clients. Keeper notes the rapid growth in crowdfunding in New Zealand since its introduction in 2014, but is less sanguine about the future. The chapter notes problems on all sides: low investor awareness about the unique or special features of crowdfunding; the generally liberal rules governing crowdfunded companies; and a somewhat cavalier attitude among crowdfunded companies in complying with their obligations towards investors.

CONCLUSION

The chapters presented in the volume cover several interesting and important developments in jurisdictions around the world. The discussions underscore a continuing role for regulation in the present scheme of things. Since the 2015 Ottawa Symposium, there have been significant events in the world's two largest financial markets, the United States and the United Kingdom. There was a vote in the UK for leaving the European Union (the so-called 'Brexit') and Donald Trump was elected as the next US President. Quite possibly, these political trends will shape developments in the years to come. Theresa May, who became UK Prime Minister after the Brexit vote, made a call 'to change the direction of our nation' (*Financial Times* 2016). Theresa May has emphasized business accountability, which has not been well received in some quarters, and she has been blamed for the fall in the pound's value (*ibid.*). Across the

Atlantic, there are expectations of a rollback of financial regulation in the Donald Trump era, and this has reportedly spurred a rise in the price of bank shares (Corkery 2016). In any case, the coming years promise to be eventful. The impact of the political developments on global capital markets and their regulation remains to be seen.

REFERENCES

Berle, A. and G. Means (1933), *The Modern Corporation and Private Property* (MacMillan, rev. edn 1967)

Bernanke, B. (2010), 'What the Fed did and why: supporting the recovery and sustaining price stability', *Washington Post*, 4 November

Cohen, F.S. (1935), 'Transcendental Nonsense and the Functional Approach' 35 *Columbia Law Review* 809

Corkery, M. (2016), 'Small banks cheer Trump. So, after a pause, do big ones', *New York Times*, 21 November

Easterbrook, F.H. and D.R. Fischel (1991), *The Economic Structure of Corporate Law* (Harvard University Press)

FT View (2016), 'Theresa May is taught a hard lesson by the financial markets', *Financial Times*, 7 October

Fukuyama, F. (1992), *The End of History and the Last Man* (Free Press)

Hansmann, H. and R. Kraakman (2001), 'The End of History for Corporate Law' 89 *Georgetown Law Journal* 439

Jensen, M.C. and W.H. Meckling (1976), 'Theory of the Firm: Managerial Behavior, Agency Costs, and Ownership Structure' 3 *Journal of Financial Economics* 305

Mitchell, L.E. (2001), *Corporate Irresponsibility: America's Newest Export* (Yale University Press)

Nourse, V. and G. Shaffer (2009), 'Varieties of New Legal Realism: Can a New World Order Prompt a New Legal Theory?' 95 *Cornell Law Review* 61

Porter, M.E. (1997), 'Capital Choices: Changing the Way America Invests in Industry' in D.H. Chew (ed), *Studies in International Corporate Finance and Governance Systems: A Comparison of the US, Japan and Europe* (Oxford University Press)

Rix, M.S. (1945), 'Company Law: 1844 and Today' 55 *Economic Journal* 242

Stout, L. (2012), *The Shareholder Value Myth: How Putting Shareholders First Harms Investors, Corporations, and the Public* (Berrett-Koehler)

PART I

Investors and the stock market

1. Implications of shareholder activism

Anita Anand

1.1 INTRODUCTION

Shareholder activism has become an increasingly conspicuous aspect of capital market activity. The term 'activist investor' describes an investor, often a hedge fund, which seeks to acquire significant minority positions in undervalued public companies. The investor may thereafter seek value-enhancing changes in the leadership, governance, capital structure or strategy and operations of the corporation. Such activism engages several aspects of corporate and securities law. Is the relevant law in need of amendment?

In answering this question, a starting point is Berle and Means' (1933: 6) argument that the modern corporation is one characterized by the separation of ownership and control, given that 'the position of ownership has changed from that of an active to that of a passive agent'.[1] The rise of activist shareholders over the past 25 years undermines Berle and Means' conclusion: these shareholders are anything but passive.[2] They are sophisticated, often seeking governance changes over and above those that yield a mere return on their investment.

Gilson and Gordon (2013: 863) argue that the rise of shareholder activism has led to a 'reconcentration of ownership in the hands of institutional investment intermediaries'. Yet this claim does not capture the full gamut of activist pressure. Activists may engage in one of two types of activism: offensive activism initiated by hedge funds primarily in response to poor corporate performance of potential targets, or defensive activism involving institutional activists who take on an advocacy role when they are unhappy with the corporation in which they are invested

---

[1]   For an historical analysis of Berle and Means' thesis about separation of ownership and control, see Stout (2013).

[2]   See Gilson and Gordon (2013). Stout (2013: 1178) states, 'Shareholders now have more influence over boards, and executives now are more focused on share price, than at any time in business history'.

17

(Cheffins and Armour 2011). Both offensive and defensive activists seek to participate in the governance of the corporation *ex ante*. They view shareholder participation as necessary because of the marked tendency for management to perpetuate itself in office (Kimber Report 1965).

Currently, securities and corporate law address this issue by allowing shareholder proposals and requisitions, as well as compelling corporations to provide shareholders with proxy forms and 'information circulars' prior to every annual meeting. The law also permits shareholders to put forward motions by circulating a separate or 'dissident' information circular (Securities Act (Ontario), s. 86;[3] NI 51-102 (Canada);[4] Canada Business Corporations Act, s. 150). But activists argue that these corporate law rules are insufficient; legal changes to ensure less management entrenchment and more meaningful shareholder participation in the corporation are required.

'Shareholder democracy', or the ability of shareholders to influence the corporation through their vote, is an important concept in corporate law; it underpins the legitimacy of shareholder activism. But shareholder democracy is not a static concept. Jurisdictions can experience more or less shareholder democracy depending on the substantive content of their respective corporate law statutes. Examining the relevant empirical literature, this chapter argues in favour of increased shareholder democracy in terms of shareholder representation in director nominations, in order to make the existing right to elect directors meaningful: a right to elect directors has little point if shareholders do not also have some say in choosing the candidate for whom they are voting.

Section 2 explores the concept of shareholder democracy as the main justification for increased shareholder activism. Section 3 analyses the main argument against increased shareholder democracy, namely, 'short-termism' on the part of hedge funds. Section 4 responds to the question of whether corporate law is adequate. It examines whether reform is necessary and, if so, what type of reform in particular is needed. The focus of the discussion is on proxy access. Section 5 concludes with arguments in favour of granting shareholders the right to nominate candidates for director elections.

---

[3] RSO 1990, c. S 5.
[4] NI 51-102, *Continuous Disclosure Obligations* (2012).

1.2 SHAREHOLDER DEMOCRACY

The separation of ownership and control is a characteristic of many modern public corporations (Berle and Means 1933). While shareholders, as corporations' owners,[5] may seek to maximize the value of their residual claim, managers may shirk their duties or divert corporate resources to their own benefit at the expense of shareholders (Jensen and Meckling 1976). According to Jensen and Meckling, these divergent interests can lead to agency costs: costs that shareholders incur to ensure that directors and managers do not place their own interests above the corporation's (*ibid.*; see also Bebchuk 2006b). Agency costs arise when directors' and officers' interests do not align with shareholders' interests.

Considering the potential for agency costs to arise, shareholders may be inclined to monitor the actions of directors and managers, especially since these individuals, as rational actors, may seek to entrench themselves. Some argue, contrary to empirical evidence (on this see Bebchuk and Kamar 2010; Borochin and Knopf 2016), that managers do not entrench themselves (Bainbridge 2003; Chandler 1977). However, the important point is that it is *possible* for managements to prioritize their own interests above those of corporations: as long as this possibility exists, management entrenchment remains relevant (Anand 2015).

Shareholder democracy – the idea that shareholders are able to influence corporate affairs through their vote – undermines the potential for entrenchment and agency costs. The two are inversely related. That is, the greater the shareholder democracy, the less entrenchment there will be. Thus, the question is where on the scale a legal regime is situated given the balance of power between the board of directors and shareholders (Cassim 2012). This concept can be illustrated by Figure 1.1, which we can call the 'Shareholder Democracy Scale' (SDS).

Figure 1.1   *Director primacy and shareholder democracy, as polar concepts*

---

[5]   Although it is not uncontroversial to refer to shareholders as the 'owners' of the corporation, the theoretical concerns raised by Berle and Means remain relevant (see Stout 2012).

Some believe that shareholders should have a greater voice in corporate governance in order to ensure that management and the board act in shareholders' interests. Bebchuk (2006a), for example, has advocated greater powers for shareholders to remove directors; to nominate directors on the corporate ballot; to vote by secret ballot; to initiate changes to corporate charters; and to vote on compensation. The benefit of these reforms would accrue to shareholders, of course, but would also induce 'management to act in shareholder interests without shareholders having to exercise their power to intervene' (Bebchuk 2005: 833; see also Backer 2006).

By contrast, those who favour director primacy argue for retention of powers in boards and indeed more insulated boards, believing that facilitating shareholder democracy, and thereby shareholder power, would create costs that would outweigh the purported benefits (Hayden and Bodie 2010: 2076). As Lipton and Savitt (2007: 733) argue, proposals for shareholder empowerment would:

> transfer the basic responsibility of corporate management from directors to shareholders. And … leave management and directors subservient to the whims of shareholders … no matter how inconsistent with long-term corporate performance, and no matter how destructive to the economy as a whole.

In other words, Lipton and Savitt favour less shareholder involvement in corporations so that boards can serve corporations as they are legally required to do.

The Bebchuk–Lipton debate highlights the potential for polarization when analysing shareholder democracy. However, those in each camp probably recognize that corporations can be subject to more or less democracy depending on the corporate statute. The debate is over as to where on the Shareholder Democracy Scale a jurisdiction should sit.

In practical terms, Canada's corporate law regime sits somewhere in between the two poles (see Figure 1.2), likely closer to director primacy, because Canadian corporate law grants boards the power to act in the best interests of the corporation (Canada Business Corporations Act, s. 122) but does not favour director primacy to the exclusion of shareholders' influence altogether. In particular, shareholders can make written proposals for consideration by management, requisition meetings if they hold a certain minimum percentage of votes, and bring actions for conduct that is oppressive or unfairly prejudicial to their interests (Canada Business Corporations Act, ss. 137, 143, 241). Recently proposed amendments will mandate majority voting among other reforms designed to increase shareholder participation in corporations (Innovation, Science and Economic Development Canada 2016).

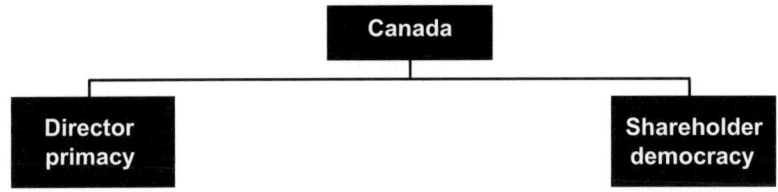

Figure 1.2   Director primacy and shareholder democracy, Canada at midway

We can argue, therefore, that Canada's legal regime supports shareholder democracy to some extent, allowing shareholders to have some influence in the governance of corporations. The important role of shareholders is most evident in recent reforms to takeover bid law under which bids are subject to a mandatory (that is, unwaivable) minimum tender condition of more than 50 per cent of all outstanding voting securities of targets, excluding those already held by the bidder and its joint actors. Bids can, therefore, only succeed with the support of a majority of independent shareholders. In essence, a bidder must obtain a majority of the shares held by others before it can take up shares (NI 62-104).[6]

By contrast, law in the United States, particularly Delaware, affords more deference to the business judgement of directors, providing them with a great deal of flexibility in making unfettered decisions (see generally Ontario Securities Commission 2013, Sch A).[7] Under Delaware law, if a court determines that a board of directors acted in good faith and in accordance with its fiduciary duties, the board is legally entitled to preserve the long-term strategic goals of the corporation. This is true even if a majority of shareholders favours an alternative approach (*Paramount Communications Inc.* v. *QVC Network Inc.*, 2011).[8] In a

---

⁶   NI 62-104, *Takeover Bids and Issuer Bids* (2016).

⁷   In the United Kingdom, the City Code on Takeovers and Mergers places many more restrictions on target boards than would apply in Canada. The Ontario Securities Commission (2013: 17) noted that the UK Code 'prohibits a target company board from taking any action during a bid, or in anticipation of a bid, that would frustrate the take-over bid or otherwise deny shareholders the opportunity to decide on its merits, unless such action is approved by target company shareholders in the face of the bid'.

⁸   637 A2d 34 (Del. 1994), Civil Action No. 5249-CC (Del.) (Ch. 2011) (QL).

takeover bid situation, for example, US boards are entitled to 'just say no' to a proposed bid and to use defensive tactics, such as poison pills, to prevent (as opposed to simply delay) a bid (Kahan and Rock 2007). Once it becomes apparent that the target company will be sold or broken up, however, the board's duty shifts to maximizing shareholder value, either by negotiating for improved bid terms or by seeking out and proposing an alternative transaction (*Revlon Inc.* v. *MacAndrews & Forbes Holdings Inc.*, 1986).[9] US law would thus fall closer to the director primacy side on the SDS (see Figure 1.3).

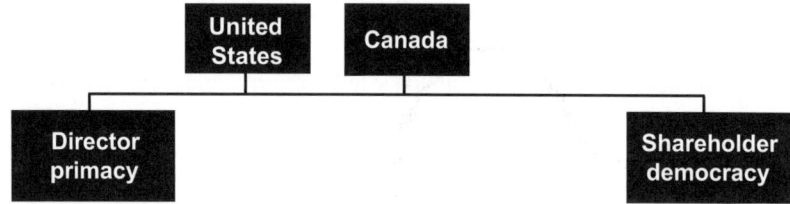

Figure 1.3   United States leaning towards director primacy

Bebchuk and Lipton would likely agree that the debate about shareholder democracy is about the extent to which we wish to carve out directorial power in favour of increased shareholder decision-making. But they disagree about where on the SDS corporate law should situate itself.

We must note that directors and other insiders are often themselves shareholders. So the implication is that the shareholders to whom the debate applies are outside shareholders who can be 'activists'; these shareholders play a particular role in corporations and serve useful purposes. It is to an analysis of these benefits that we now turn.

1.3   SHAREHOLDER ACTIVISM AND MONITORING

The Shareholder Democracy Scale illustrates that there may be more or less shareholder democracy depending on the legal regime in question. This point must be remembered when considering shareholder activism. To begin, this section discusses the monitoring role that activists play and the effect of activism on corporations. While activists monitor management, they are also criticized for having short-term focus.

---

[9]   506 A2d 173 (Del. 1986).

1.3.1 Monitoring Role

The presence of a shareholder that owns a sizeable percentage of a corporation's equity – an activist – can mitigate agency costs through two mechanisms that discipline management, namely, 'voice' and 'exit' (Edmans 2014; Hirschman 1970).[10] Of these, 'voice' involves the activist's direct intervention in the firm, often through letters to management, shareholder proposals or the exercise of control or voting rights (Edmans 2014: 24). Accordingly, managers are compelled to act in the interests of shareholders (or at least those of the activist) out of fear of replacement. 'Exit' involves the sale of the activist's shares. The sale can have the effect of driving down the firm's share price, thereby punishing management, *ex post* (*ibid.*). The threat of exit imposes *ex ante* discipline on managers.

The role that the activist plays in monitoring management and the board is central to its decision to exercise voice or exit. The larger the activist, the more readily it can absorb the cost burden of monitoring; its sizeable position in the corporation gives it added 'skin in the game' to ensure that management is held accountable (Bebchuk 2012: 47). The activist intervenes when the costs of intervention are outweighed by the private benefits of doing so.

Empirical evidence suggests that there is a positive, or at least a neutral, relationship between activists and firm value (Cronqvist and Fahlenbrach 2009; Edmans 2014; Holderness 2003). The presence of activists is associated with improved outcomes for shareholders on matters ranging from executive compensation to the facilitation of takeover bids (Bebchuk 2012). The benefits provided by the activist's monitoring flow through to other shareholders, who are able to free-ride on the large shareholder's activism.

Of course, the incentives for activists to monitor (including their willingness to internalize the costs of free-riding) vary with the size of their block (Winton 1993). Small investors can only absorb a negligible share of the firm's risk, leaving them with insufficient incentives to monitor (*ibid.*). Put another way, only large activists will monitor firms with high monitoring costs (Dhillon and Rossetto 2009). Evidence further suggests that multiple small activists are not as effective in influencing corporate decision-making as single large activists, partly because coordination costs between the small activists impede their

---

[10] For a seminal theoretical paper on the role of activists in reducing agency costs, see Shleifer and Vishny (1986).

ability to monitor the firm (Winton 1993). As such, a group of small shareholders that collectively owns a block of shares equivalent in size and right to a block owned by a single large activist will likely result in less effective monitoring (Armour *et al.* 2009).[11] It is simply more difficult to organize behaviour among a group of dispersed shareholders (Kulpa 2005), especially when shareholders have heterogeneous preferences (Armour *et al.* 2009).[12]

In short, the presence of a single activist can have a beneficial effect on the firm's governance in reducing agency costs through monitoring. At the same time, however, blocks comprised of multiple small activists may be less effective at fulfilling the role of the activist in the corporation.

1.3.2 Short-Termism

While activists play an important monitoring role in corporations, they are subject to a standard criticism, namely, 'short-termism'. This refers to the claim that they are concerned only with the short-term (as opposed to the long-term) interests of the corporation. But looking out for the short term is not necessarily inconsistent with doing the same in the long term, especially when inefficient leadership is at the helm of the corporation.

The foremost goal of an activist, and particularly a hedge fund activist, is to maximize investors' returns (Gad 2013). As unregulated entities, hedge funds search for and invest in high-yield products and projects on behalf of clients who have entrusted their money to the fund (Bennelong 2013). While hedge funds may focus on the short term to maximize their immediate returns, the focus may well coincide with the long-term interests of corporations.

The case of Canadian Pacific Railway (CP) is instructive. In 2008, CP Rail's performance began to lag behind other major North American railways. For example, by the end of 2008, CP Rail's operating ratio sat

---

[11]   Although the presence of a single large activist tends to increase shareholder monitoring of management, it is worth bearing in mind the possibility that the activist will seek to extract private benefits of control to the detriment of other shareholders.

[12]   It is worth noting, however, that the coordination issues that hinder shareholder intervention strategies actually make the threat of exit stronger, thereby allowing many small activists to have a positive impact on managerial discipline: Edmans and Manso (2010) argue that the threat of trading activity of multiple activists in the face of poor managerial performance disciplines management. Even so, wolf packs ostensibly form to intervene and agitate for change, not to passively invest and then exit.

at 80 per cent, whereas in comparison Canadian National (CN) Rail's operating ratio was only 66 per cent. In 2011, Pershing Square Capital Management, a hedge fund, formally announced that it had acquired 12 per cent of CP's shares. CP appointed two new board members and offered a board position to Bill Ackman, founder and CEO of the activist shareholder Pershing Square. Ackman rejected the offer and Pershing initiated a proxy battle, eventually proposing a slate of seven new directors. During the battle, the sitting CP board continued to support then-CEO Fred Green, whereas Pershing Square proposed Hunter Harrison, former CEO of CN. Citing the company's poor performance, CP's major shareholders publicly declared support for Pershing's director slate. Six CP board members, including Green, declined to stand for re-election. The Pershing slate was elected to the board, and Harrison was appointed CEO (Jang 2013a).

Pershing's actions served the long-term interests of CP. Even after Pershing divested about one-third of its 24 million shares (which represented a 14.2 per cent stake in CP) in October 2013, CP stock closed at CAD$147.95 a share, which was more than triple their level when Pershing began purchasing CP shares. Jang (2013b) reported:

> Harrison has led a turnaround at CP, narrowing the efficiency gap between it and rival CN. Analysts have been surprised at the pace of CP's improvements, including achieving faster average train speeds and reducing the time that locomotives are parked in rail yards.

At the time, CP's third-quarter profit was CAD$324 million, the best quarterly results in the corporation's history (*ibid.*).

The CP Rail example suggests that shareholder activism can be positive for corporations. For example, a 2010 victory by Lionsgate management over shareholder activists was followed by a share price increase of more than 100 per cent over the next two years,[13] while a victory by EnerCare Inc management also saw share price significantly increase over the next two years.[14] But we would be remiss to believe that activism has been uniformly beneficial for corporations; other proxy contest data has yielded mixed results (Atkinson *et al.* 2013). However, a

---

[13] Lionsgate enacted a poison pill provision in 2010 to discourage a shareholder's 'creeping bid'. After implementation, Lionsgate's share price increased from CAD$7.00 to CAD$14.80.

[14] In 2012 EnerCare offered to pay brokers a solicitation fee of CAD$0.05 for each share voted by a retail shareholder in favour of board re-election. EnerCare's share price improved from CAD$9.90 in April 2012 to CAD$15.85 in April 2016.

victory by the management of Baja Mining Corporation over shareholders was followed by a 99 per cent decrease in share price (share price
data from TMX Money (2013)). Meanwhile, a victory by shareholder
activists over the management of Hudbay Minerals was followed by a
subsequent share price decrease, in contrast to the example of CP above
(*ibid.*). These examples are consistent with the argument of Rose and
Sharfman (2014) that shareholder activism can provide value; however it
should be considered on a case-by-case basis.

The evidence is also mixed with respect to mergers or takeovers
following proxy contests. There have been some cases where shareholder
activists have won (or partially won) a proxy battle, but a merger or
takeover followed. For example, Biovail merged with Valeant Pharma-
ceuticals following a partial victory by shareholder activists. Pet Valu was
also involved in a merger following a victory by shareholders in a proxy
contest. This is not to say that a merger or acquisition will always occur
after a shareholder victory in a proxy contest, as the example of HudBay
Minerals, discussed earlier, demonstrates. It was not involved in an
acquisition or merger.

While shareholder activism may not be uniformly beneficial for
corporations, when it yields benefits, these accrue to all shareholders, not
only to the activist or hedge fund. Carrothers (2013) points out that the
average abnormal return at target firms in the 20 days surrounding the
disclosure of activist intentions is 7.1 per cent, and the average buy and
hold abnormal return in the 20 months after the disclosure is 23 per cent.
Similarly, Bebchuk *et al.* (2015) found a 6 per cent abnormal return in
stock price during the 40-day period straddling the announcement of an
activist campaign. This result was not offset by a subsequent long-term
decrease in stock price (*ibid.*). In short, it appears that the market as a
whole can benefit from positive responses to hedge fund activism (*ibid.*).

Consistent with the position described above, Katelouzou (2013: 504)
argues that the:

> dark side of hedge fund activism is largely a myth: activist hedge funds are
> not short-term investors ... [the] evidence makes a case for hedge fund
> activism as a value-enhancing corporate governance mechanism which could
> plausibly be corporate governance relevant.

Target share price movement following a proxy contest suggests that
shareholder activism, including the ability to assert a position that differs
from management via dissident nominees, can be good for firms.

The point here is that shareholder activists play a useful monitoring
role in target corporations and their activities can benefit shareholders at

large, not just themselves. The argument that activists are only focused on the short term is, therefore, somewhat of a diversion, especially when we consider that there are long-term benefits associated with activism.

1.4 PROXY ACCESS AND ITS DIMENSIONS

If it is the case that shareholder activism can be beneficial for corporations, the question arises as to how the law should address it. The first step in answering this question is by recognizing that the shareholders seeking to gain more power in corporations are likely to be minority shareholders unless a corporation is widely held, which is not generally the case in Canada. The discussion about reform, therefore, is largely with reference to the rights of minority shareholders.

To begin, recall that the concept of shareholder democracy contemplates that shareholders should be able to participate in the governance of corporations. Shareholder participation is believed to be necessary because of the risk of management entrenchment (Kimber Report 1965). The ultimate question, and the one debated by Bebchuk (2006b) and Lipton and Savitt (2007), is how much participation is necessary to counter the potential for entrenchment? To deal with the issue, this section explores proposals for increased 'proxy access'.

1.4.1 Proxy Access

Those who favour 'proxy access' argue that shareholders should not only be able to elect directors, but also to nominate them for election. They contend that nominees of shareholders should be placed on the same ballot as management nominees. The intended goal of this reform would be to increase the levels of independence and quality of boards of directors, while providing shareholders with a meaningful say in who is able to become a director. Thus, at issue is the nomination process available to shareholders.

One can easily concede that shareholders have statutory rights that enable them to nominate directors. Among the various shareholder rights discussed above, some of them enable shareholders to nominate directors. First, the shareholder proposal mechanism can include director nominations (Canada Business Corporations Act, s. 137(4)).[15] This is part

---

[15] For example, in *National Bank* v. *Weir* 2009 QCCS 5688, the Quebec Superior Court granted a motion by National Bank to exclude 38 proposals by a shareholder in the Management Proxy Circular under the Bank Act (SC 1991, c.

of the broader process for submitting shareholder proposals to corporations and exists independent of the securities law rules relating to proxy contests. Second, shareholders holding more than 5 per cent of the corporation's shares can also requisition a meeting to nominate a director (s. 143). But again, this can be an expensive process with no guarantee that management will accept the proposal or requisition. Also for shareholders who hold less than 5 per cent, this legislative provision is not helpful. Third, shareholders can go through the dissident proxy process, but this too is an expensive endeavour that only wealthy shareholders have utilized (CCGG Policy 2015).

While some may argue that the shareholder provisions cited above evidence a shareholder-centric bias (see, for example, Vanderpol and Waitzer 2012), we may reasonably respond that shareholders' ability to elect directors has little meaning if they do not have a definite say over which names appear on the ballot in the first place. No statutory provision exists that enables them to do that explicitly and directly (Bebchuk 2005).[16]

Some may argue that directors nominated by a shareholder will be beholden to the shareholder rather than the corporation as a whole. But this claim is unpersuasive; directors – regardless of who nominated them – have a duty to act in the best interests of the corporation (Canada Business Corporations Act, s. 122). Current directors continuously face conflicts in the course of discharging their duties, but, as fiduciaries, they are obliged by law to rise above such conflicts. To argue that directors nominated by certain shareholders would be unable to rise to the legal

---

46) proposal provisions, namely, s. 143(5)(b) and (e), which are virtually identical to the proposal provisions in s. 137(5)(b) and (e) of the Canada Business Corporations Act (RSC 1985, c. C-44). The court held that although a proposal may appear to be neutral on its face, it must be read and considered in context. The court found that in light of the timing and circumstances, it was evident that the proposals by the respondent were abusive, even though in normal circumstances these 'might be considered his rights as shareholder'. The court also noted that there was not an abundance of case law on this subject since the proposal mechanism was rarely used in Canada until recently.

[16] Supporters of 'management insulation' will counter this argument and assert that shareholders should not be given the right to nominate directors, since shareholder interests in the corporation are often short term as opposed to long term, and in general are motivated by considerations other than enhancing the corporation's long-term interests. Those concerned with the possibility of increased shareholder power may also argue that shareholder nomination power could lead to the board being 'co-opted' and represent the interests of a particular shareholder rather than the corporation as a whole.

standard required of them suggests that these directors, and directors generally, are unable to separate their personal interests from their duty to corporations. Why are shareholder nominees any different from the director population at large, many of whom are employed by or represent related parties, such as controlling shareholders or management?

Some may argue that according this right to shareholders would lead to a shareholder or a group of shareholders taking control of the board over time. Thus some type of cap seems reasonable. One proposal is to allow shareholders, for example if they hold 3–5 per cent of the corporation's outstanding shares, to have a circumscribed right, such as being able to nominate the lesser of three directors or 20 per cent of the board (CCGG 2015). Another possibility is to enable minority shareholders who have held a certain percentage of shares over a certain period of time to name at least one nominee on every slate presented to shareholders at annual shareholder meetings, with information about each of these nominees being included in proxy materials containing information on corporations' nominees.[17]

Reforms that give shareholders the ability to nominate directors by proxy should not be based solely on achieving enhanced shareholder democracy, but also on the benefits these reforms will have on corporations and corporate governance as a whole. In other words, there does not have to be a gap between those who wish to see increased shareholder democracy, on the one hand, and those who are concerned about the wellbeing of the corporation, on the other.[18] We turn now to consider some of the advantages of increased shareholder democracy for the corporation.

---

[17]   This is currently the system in Italy. See Canadian Coalition for Good Governance (2015) for other international examples. See also Skeel *et al.* (2011) for more details on the Italian system.

[18]   Bratton (2016) makes a similar point – that the existing chasm between those for and against shareholder activism is not necessary – but advances a much different reform proposal. Bratton's idea revolves around asking the question whether a 5 per cent poison pill can have policy benefits. He states, 'Some [companies] are appropriate targets for activist intervention, while others are not … company-by-company dialogue on the point would be a good thing, exploring the possibility that a 5 per cent standing pill could trigger useful informational exchanges between managers and institutional investors without simultaneously over-deterring activist intervention'.

1.4.2   Advantages of Proxy Access for the Corporation

A number of advantages result from proxy access. First, shareholder presence on the board can be an antidote to 'groupthink' norms that suppress innovation and dissent. Some argue that groupthink has been a factor in corporate scandals (for example, Enron) and helps to explain the passivity of corporate boards (Murphy 2011). It is argued that corporations need the shareholders to supply them with directors who will not hesitate to bring different viewpoints to boardroom tables. The alternative – no direct, non-discretionary inputs from shareholders into the nomination process – will do little to dispel the current apprehension regarding management and board entrenchment, and, more importantly, will do little to change prevailing corporate governance processes that at times have been at the root of corporate scandals and failures.

Second, shareholder representation can be a way to increase board independence, expertise and effective risk management. Murphy (2009: 474) argues that 'shareholder participation in corporate governance can help give the chair [of the board] the independence necessary to carry out an effective leadership role'. In addition, shareholder-nominated directors could have a depth of expertise that would allow them to possess the necessary qualifications required to serve on various committees of the board. They will be able to ally themselves with other directors who are independent of management (Murphy 2009: 472). Finally, greater shareholder participation in the nomination process could help avoid having a board that is unqualified (Murphy 2011).

Third, the evidence that shareholder activism can lead to an increase in a corporation's value suggests that formally enhancing shareholder participation in the nomination process could also be beneficial to corporations. As mentioned in section 3 above, studies demonstrate that shareholder activism has led to increases in corporate value, output and performance. Bebchuk (2013), for example, describes how target companies underperforming during the two years prior to an intervention subsequently recovered in the two years after the intervention without any evidence of adverse long-term effects. Bebchuk's finding of the positive stock price reaction to interventions in the short and long term suggests that greater shareholder representation and involvement in nominating directors could benefit corporations.

Admittedly, acknowledging the importance of shareholder democracy may divert us from the comfort sought in entrusting boards of directors with charting corporations' courses. Remember, however, that, consistent with the Shareholder Democracy Scale, shareholder democracy seeks that a balance be struck between boards of directors and shareholders. The shareholder activist movement suggests that the balance in corporate statutes is tilted too far in favour of boards. But there are legitimate arguments on both sides of the debate. Ultimately, with regard to proxy access, it is a question of making the existing right of shareholders to elect directors meaningful: what is the point of a right to elect if shareholders do not also have some say in the choice of the person for whom they are voting?

1.5 CONCLUSION

This chapter posits the Shareholder Democracy Scale as a means to understand the polarizing debate between those who argue in favour of director primacy vis-à-vis shareholder democracy. Shareholders have certain rights already under Canadian corporate law, which means that its regime does not exclusively evidence director primacy. A reform that would give greater meaning to the shareholders' right to elect directors would be granting the accompanying right to nominate directors. The two go 'hand in hand', and conferring the right would not tilt the balance away from directors to a significant degree, especially if a percentage of shareholding criterion were attached to shareholders' ability to so nominate.

REFERENCES

Anand, A. (2015), 'The Future of Poison Pills in Canada: Are Takeover Bid Reforms Needed?' 61 *McGill Law Journal* 1

Armour, J., H. Hansmann and R. Kraakman (2009), *Agency Problems, Legal Strategies and Enforcement*, Harvard John M. Olin Discussion Paper Series No. 644, available at www.law.harvard.edu/programs/olin_center/papers/pdf/Kraakman_644.pdf

Atkinson, A.J., D. Batista and B.A. Freelan (2013), '2013 Canadian Proxy Contest Study', Fasken Martineau, available at http://www.fasken.com/en/canadian-proxy-contest-study_e/

Backer, L.C. (2006), 'Direct Shareholder Democracy: Reflections on Lucian Bebchuk' 2 *Corporate Governance Law Review* 375

Bainbridge, S.M. (2003), 'Director Primacy: The Means and Ends of Corporate Governance' 97 *Northwestern University Law Review* 547

Batista, D. (2013), 'Speaking with the Enemy: How the OSC's Dialogue with Martin Lipton Threatens Those Whom the OSC is Charged with Protecting', *Lexology* (17 October), available at www.lexology.com/library/detail.aspx?g=ce491dc8-5aac-43ab-aaad-3f4bdb79dfad

Bebchuk, L. (2005), 'The Case for Increasing Shareholder Power' 118 *Harvard Law Review* 833

— (2006a), 'Investors must have power, not just figures on pay', *Financial Times*, 27 July

— (2006b), *The Myth of the Shareholder Franchise*, Harvard John M. Olin Discussion Paper Series No. 567, available at http://lsr.nellco.org/cgi/viewcontent.cgi?article=1353&context=harvard_olin

— (2012), 'The Law and Economics of Activist Disclosure' 2 *Harvard Business Law Review* 39

— (2013), 'The Myth that Insulating Boards Serves Long-Term Value' 113 *Columbia Law Review* 1637

Bebchuk, L., B. Alon and W. Jiang (2015), 'The Long-term Effects of Hedge Fund Activism' 115 *Columbia Law Review* 1085

Bebchuk, L. and E. Kamar (2010), *Bundling and Entrenchment*, Harvard John M. Olin Discussion Paper Series No. 659, available at www.law.harvard.edu/programs/olin_center/papers/pdf/Bebchuk_659.pdf

Bennelong (2013), 'Debunking Hedge Fund Myths', Century Private Wealth, available at www.centuryprivatewealth.com.au/news/view/debunking_hedge_fund_myths

Berle, A. and G. Means (1933), *The Modern Corporation and Private Property* (MacMillan, rev edn 1967)

Borochin, P. and J.D. Knopf (2016), 'Do Managers Seek Control and Entrenchment?' (7 October), available at http://papers.ssrn.com/sol3/papers.cfm?abstract_id=2670918

Bratton, W.W. (2016), 'Hedge Fund Activism, Poison Pills and the Jurisprudence of Threat', CLS Blue Sky Blog, Columbia Law School (6 October), available at http://clsbluesky.law.columbia.edu/2016/10/06/hedge-fund-activism-poison-pills-and-the-jurisprudence-of-threat/

Canadian Coalition for Good Governance (CCGG) (2015), 'Shareholder Involvement in the Director Nomination Process: Enhanced Engagement and Proxy Access', available at www.ccgg.ca/site/ccgg/assets/pdf/proxy_access_finalv.35.docx_630.pdf

Carrothers, A. (2013), 'Friends or Foes? Activist Hedge Funds and Other Institutional Investors', McMaster University deGroote School of Business, available at www.degroote.mcmaster.ca/articles/friends-or-foes-activist-hedge-funds-and-other-institutional-investors/

Cassim, F.H.I. (2012), 'The Division and Balance of Power between the Board of Directors and the Shareholders: The Removal of Directors' 29 *Banking and Finance Law Review* 151

Chandler, A.D. (1977), *The Visible Hand: The Managerial Revolution in American Business* (Harvard University Press)

Cheffins, B.R. and J. Armour (2011), 'The Past, Present, and Future of Shareholder Activism by Hedge Funds' 37 *Journal of Corporation Law* 51

Cronqvist, H. and R. Fahlenbrach (2009), 'Large Shareholders and Corporate Policies' 22 *Review of Financial Studies* 3941

Dhillon, A. and S. Rossetto (2009), *Corporate Control and Multiple Large Shareholders*, University of Warwick Working Paper, available at www2.warwick.ac.uk/fac/soc/economics/staff/academic/dhillon/wp/submission16nov09.pdf

Edmans, A. (2014), *Activists and Corp Governance*, European Corporate Governance Institute Finance Working Paper No. 385, available at http://papers.ssrn.com/sol3/papers.cfm?abstract_id=2285781

Edmans, A. and G. Manso (2010), 'Governance Through Trading Intervention: A Theory of Multiple Activists' 24 *Review of Financial Studies* 2395

Gad, S. (2013), 'What are Hedge Funds?', Forbes, available at www.forbes.com/sites/investopedia/2013/10/22/what-are-hedge-funds/

Gilson, R. and J. Gordon (2013), 'The Agency Costs of Agency Capitalism: Activist Investors and the Revaluation of Governance Rights' *Columbia Law Review* 863

Hayden, G. and M.T. Bodie (2010), 'Shareholder Democracy and the Curious Turn toward Board Primacy' 51 *William and Mary Law Review* 2071

Hirschman, A.O. (1970), *Exit, Voice and Loyalty* (Harvard University Press)

Holderness, C.G. (2003), 'A Survey of Activists and Corporate Control' 9 *Economic Policy Review* 51

Innovation, Science and Economic Development Canada (2016), 'The Government of Canada Introduces a Bill to Promote Corporate Transparency and Diversity' (28 September), available at http://m.marketwired.com/press-release/government-canada-introduces-bill-promote-corporate-transparency-diversity-2162359.htm

Jang, B. (2013a), 'As Harrison takes CP's top job, Ackman's coup is complete', *Globe and Mail*, 29 June, available at www.theglobeandmail.com/globe-investor/as-harrison-takes-cps-top-job-ackmans-coup-is-complete/article4379406/

— (2013b), 'Activist investor Ackman unloads $835-million CP stake', *Globe and Mail*, 29 October, available at www.theglobeandmail.com/report-on-business/ackman-unloads-835-million-cp-stake/article15065221/

Jensen, M. and W. Meckling (1976), 'Theory of the Firm: Managerial Behavior, Agency Costs and Ownership Structure' 3 *Journal of Financial Economics* 305

Kahan, M. and E.B. Rock (2007), 'Hedge Funds in Corporate Governance and Corporate Control' 155 *University of Pennsylvania Law Review* 1021

Katelouzou, D. (2013), 'Myths and Realities of Hedge Fund Activism: Some Empirical Evidence' 7 *Virginia Law and Business Review* 459

Kimber Report (1965), *Report of the Attorney-General's Committee on Securities Legislation in Ontario* (Queen's Printer)

Kulpa, A. (2005), 'The Wolf in Shareholder's Clothing' 6 *UC Davis Business Law Journal* 4

Lipton, M. and W. Savitt (2007), 'The Many Myths of Lucian Bebchuk' 93 *Virginia Law Review* 733

Murphy, M. (2009), 'Restoring Trust in Corporate America: Toward a Republican Theory of Corporate Legitimacy' 5 *New York University Journal of Law and Business* 415

— (2011), 'Assuring Responsible Risk Management in Banking: The Corporate Governance Dimension' 36 *Delaware Journal of Corporate Law* 121

Ontario Securities Commission (2013), 'Notice and Request for Comment: Proposed NI 62-105 Security Holder Rights Plans, Proposed Companion Policy 62-105CP, and Proposed Consequential Amendments', NI 62-105, available at www.osc.gov.on.ca/documents/en/Securities-Category6/ni_2013 0314_62-105_security-holder-rights-plan.pdf

Rose, P. and B. Sharfman (2014), 'Shareholder Activism as a Corrective Mechanism in Corporate Governance' *Brigham Young University Law Review* 1015

Shleifer, A. and R.W. Vishny (1986), 'Large Shareholders and Corporate Control' 94 *Journal of Political Economy* 461

Skeel Jr, D.A., V. Chahar, A. Clark *et al.* (2011), 'Inside-Out Corporate Governance' 37 *Journal of Corporation Law* 147

Stout, L. (2012), *The Shareholder Value Myth* (Berret-Koehler Publishing)

— (2013), 'On the Rise of Shareholder Primacy, Signs of Its Fall, and the Return of Managerialism (In the Closet)' 36 *Seattle University Law Review* 1169

The Panel on Takeovers and Mergers (2008), 'The City Code on Takeovers and Mergers', available at www.thetakeoverpanel.org.uk/wp-content/uploads/2008/11/code.pdf?v=120916

TMX Money (2013), 'Share Price Data', available at www.tmxmoney.com/en/index.html

Vanderpol, S. and E.J. Waitzer (2012), 'Addressing the Tension between Directors' Duties and Shareholder Rights: A Tale of Two Regimes' 50 *Osgoode Hall Law Journal* 177

Winton, A. (1993), 'Limitation of Liability and Ownership Structure of the Firm' 48 *Journal of Finance* 487

2. Suspension of Chinese units of 'Big 4' audit firms: the question of moral turpitude

Qingxiu Bu

2.1 INTRODUCTION

Cross-border listings make business increasingly global. Other than Initial Public Offerings (IPOs), reverse mergers have been a popular vehicle for Chinese companies to cross-list on US stock exchanges. Listing through reverse mergers subjects companies to less scrutiny than traditional IPOs. Many reverse merger companies (RMCs) have been involved in accounting misrepresentations and other securities fraud. The Big 4 accounting firms (Deloitte, EY, KPMG and PwC), which played a significant role in facilitating the cross-listing of Chinese companies in the United States, are supposed to apply high standards in reviewing the Chinese companies' financial statements. There were allegations that the Chinese affiliates of the Big 4 failed to adhere to US accounting standards. Faced with requests under the Sarbanes-Oxley Act of 2002, s. 106 ('SOX 106')[1] for foreign audit work papers, the Big 4's China units refused to cooperate with the US Securities and Exchange Commission (SEC)'s investigations into accounting problems with Chinese companies. The SEC Administrative Law Judge ruled that the Big 4's Chinese units should be suspended from auditing companies that are publicly traded in the United States (*In the matter of BDO China Dahua CPA Co. Ltd et al.* 2014).[2]

---

[1] Sarbanes-Oxley Act of 2002, Pub. L107-204, 116 Stat. 745 ('SOX').

[2] *In the matter of BDO China Dahua CPA Co. Ltd, Ernst & Young Hua Ming LLP, KPMG Huazhen (Special General Partnership), Deloitte Touche Tohmatsu Certified Public Accountants Ltd, PricewaterhouseCoopers Zhong Tian CPAs Ltd,* Securities and Exchange Commission (US) Administrative Proceeding File Nos 3-14872, 3-15116, 22 January 2014. The proceeding also included BDO

This chapter addresses the challenges of cross-border financial reporting and audit oversight, and the resulting moral hazard. Section 2 of this chapter provides an overview of the global landscape of audit practice and financial reporting. Section 3 examines the deadlock where SEC and the Public Company Accounting Oversight Board (PCAOB) could not play an effective oversight role, and the grounds on which the Big 4 accounting firms refused to comply with SOX 106 requests with regard to the RMC audits. Section 4 discusses the decision to suspend the Big 4's Chinese affiliates and their refusal to provide documents, which supports the theory of moral hazard. Despite efforts for improvement, the Dodd-Frank Wall Street Reform and Consumer Protection Act (Dodd-Frank Act) does not create a private action avenue to check the Big 4's moral hazard. Section 5 explores how multi-jurisdictional cooperation can aid in dealing with the issues, and in countering moral hazard. Section 6 concludes with advocating multi-jurisdictional cooperation as a valuable tool to promote market integrity.

2.2 GLOBAL LANDSCAPE OF AUDIT AND FINANCIAL REPORTING, AND MORAL HAZARD

2.2.1 Global Audit and Financial Reporting Landscape

High quality, independent audits are essential for investor protection (Franzel 2012). As systemically important intermediaries, auditors' most valuable asset is their reputation, the harm of which could threaten their viability (Markoff 2013; *DiLeo* v. *Ernst & Young*, 1990).[3] Gatekeepers' reputations have a direct bearing on the reliability of financial statements (Cunningham 2006) and reputations are an incentive for them to detect accounting deceptions (Watts and Zimmerman 1983). The Big 4 firms employ over 700,000 people and generate annual revenues of over US$100 billion (Hudson *et al.* 2014). They operate globally and enjoy reputations for performing higher quality corporate audits than smaller firms. The oligopoly in the large-company audit market limits the alternatives for multinational companies (Cunningham 2006). A result is

---

Dahua, the Chinese affiliate of BDO International, in addition to those of the Big 4 firms. BDO Dahua was omitted from the suspension order because, by this time, BDO International and Dahua had terminated their relationship and Dahua CPA had stopped servicing US-listed clients. As such, BDO Dahua was merely censured for its conduct.

3   901 F 2d 624, [629] (7th Cir. 1990).

moral hazard, which can impair audit quality and compromise financial statement reliability (*ibid.*).

As watchdogs, the Big 4 must ensure high-quality audits – consistently and globally – to promote the safety and soundness of financial markets. Big 4 accounting firms are key players in an array of cross-border transactions, and reports about their role raise legal and ethical concerns.

The Big 4 operate under the laws of different political and regulatory jurisdictions. They were the major auditors in Chinese IPOs and RMCs. Precipitated by the Global Financial Crisis and the international reach of the Dodd-Frank Act, never before have global financial markets been subject to the high level of regulation as they are now (Buxbaum 2006). For instance, s. 404 of the Sarbanes-Oxley Act requires auditors to report on companies' assessment of internal controls over financial reporting. Section 929 of the Dodd-Frank Act[4] is an elastic provision that creates unparalleled enforcement risks for auditors. The Dodd-Frank Act expands SOX provisions, placing auditors under the jurisdiction of US courts and requiring them to produce to the SEC and PCAOB audit work papers 'and all other documents of the firm related to' audits or interim reviews of any issuer (Dodd-Frank Act, s. 929J). Enormous challenges remain despite the increased regulation of global financial institutions (Baxter 2014).

2.2.2 Moral Hazard: Hypothetical Threats over the Integrity of Audits Standards?

The problem of moral hazard arises if the Big 4 believe they are 'too big to fail' and act on the basis that enforcement agencies will not take damaging action that could result in a firm leaving the market (House of Lords 2010). Given the high level of concentration in the audit industry, the departure of any of the Big 4 firms would have serious consequences for large public companies, and potential systemic consequences raise substantial policy concerns (Cunningham 2006). In particular, the lack of alternatives for clients is a direct concern because smaller firms would lack the scale and skills to audit the Big 4's clients (House of Lords 2010). Hypothetically, no other auditing firms could adequately replace them. Prentice (2006: 786) observed:

---

[4] Dodd-Frank Wall Street Reform and Consumer Protection Act, ss. 929J, 929M, codified at 15 USC ss. 77o(b) and 80a-48(b), 929N codified at 15 USC s. 80b-9(f), 929O codified at 15 USC s. 78t(e).

> Reputational constraints fail to restrain large accounting firms, both because large firms have a huge competitive advantage over second-tier firms that is difficult to squander and because as a group, large firms are lumped together such that one firm does not profit much from behaving better than its competitors.

It has been argued that any possible collapse or even suspension among the big accounting firms could leave many Chinese companies scrambling for new auditors and complicate the audits of some US multinational companies in respect of their Chinese operations (Rapoport 2014a). China-based issuers' trade on US exchanges would be compromised, their market capitalization would plummet, and investors would be harmed (*In the matter of BDO et al.*, 2014).

Perceptions about consequences can encourage greater risk-taking than markets would tolerate (Baker 1996). Once an institution is thus insured (in a sense), it has an incentive to take on more risk. The moral hazard problem is particularly severe in auditing where a loss could have industry-wide repercussions (Cunningham 2006). There is, in general, legal and regulatory forbearance among public authorities in several jurisdictions. Liability is lowered either by statute or through the enforcement route. Preventing the failure of an institution that is deemed too big to fail explains the US government's decision not to pursue criminal indictment against KPMG (*SEC* v. *KPMG LLP*, 2006).[5] 'Liability limitation agreements' (LLAs) for auditors that are permitted under the UK Companies Act 2006[6] (ss. 534–8) can similarly shield audit firms. Some EU Member States' statutes enable reducing auditor liability through proportionate liability or liability caps (Doralt *et al.* 2008).[7]

The elements outlined above potentially increase the moral hazard for auditors and cushion the consequences of bad behaviour. The philosophy of 'too big to fail' does not adequately consider the victims at the end of the capital market chain, namely, investors. The reasoning explains how the economics of moral hazard have been deployed in a fashion that favours the interests of the Big 4 over investors. The paradoxical

---

[5]   412 F Supp. 2d 349, [372]–[373] (SDNY 2006).

[6]   Companies Act 2006 (UK) (c. 46).

[7]   The EU Member States' limited liability regimes for auditors include the cap, proportionality and LLAs. They are either in the form of a cap on the level of possible liability claims (Austria, Belgium, Germany), through to a system of proportionate liability whereby auditors are liable only for the damages caused directly as a result of their negligent behaviour (Spain), or by allowing auditors to establish LLAs with their clients (United Kingdom).

justification legitimizes the abandonment of legal rules (Baker 1996) to achieve a plausible public interest objective. Given the increasingly interwoven capital markets across the world, the moral hazard problem may systematically jeopardize efforts to protect the legitimate interests of shareholders. The costly trade-off is against the pursuit of high quality global governance. The Big 4 must take on greater responsibility because they are most in control of loss-causing behaviour and can also be counted upon to respond rationally to incentives (Baker 1996).

2.3 PUBLIC COMPANY ACCOUNTING OVERSIGHT BOARD: GATEKEEPER OF GATEKEEPERS

Chinese companies often bypass the stringent scrutiny of an IPO process by using defunct shell US companies that are listed on an exchange. They arrange for the shell to acquire the Chinese company. Big audit firms have facilitated the process by representing these companies and certifying their financial statements. Section 929J of the Dodd-Frank Act enables SEC/PCAOB to obtain foreign audit work papers for investigations. PCAOB, as the overseer of the audit of public companies subject to US securities laws, has sought audit work papers for its investigations of Chinese companies that are suspected of being involved in accounting misrepresentations and inaccurate disclosures. James Doty (2011) pointed out the reality in his testimony to Congress, observing that PCAOB was 'unable to conduct inspections in China, based primarily on assertions by the Chinese of national sovereignty issues'. Another risk that auditors face is securities class actions following accounting debacles.

2.3.1 Chinese Reverse Mergers and Accounting Problems

As pointed out, many Chinese companies gained access to US capital markets through reverse mergers. The reverse merger method helps companies avoid the higher costs and rigours of traditional IPOs. Listing in the United States enhances firm value (Litvak 2007), given the legal and reputational bonding effects of US law (Siegel 2005). Chinese RMCs agree to abide by US laws when they gain access to US financial markets. Investors who buy securities from them pay a higher price based on the cross-listing's reputational value (Ringe and Hellgardt 2011). Through cross-listing, foreign issuers subject themselves to the stricter US regime; one that presents serious litigation risks and substantial regulatory oversight (Zuber 2014).

RMC auditors must file reports regarding the effectiveness of the companies' internal controls (SOX, s. 404). RMCs must make accurate disclosures about their financial condition, or risk violating US securities regulations. Relatively lax accounting and audit standards in China make it a challenge for several RMCs to prepare financial records accurately according to US accounting standards. Shareholders in the United States have been victims of RMCs' accounting problems (McMahon 2013). As a result of inaccurate financial statements, SEC has even delisted some RMCs and sought audit work papers from their audit firms (Siegel and Wang 2013).

(a)   RMC malfeasance and shareholder litigation
Dozens of RMCs selling their shares in the US markets have been accused of fraud by investors and the SEC. Many of them have had significant accounting deficiencies, and a surge in lawsuit filings has deepened investors' mistrust (Kolker 2011). The events reflect the difficulties of RMCs in adapting to the burdens and responsibilities involved with a US listing. These problems have caused the companies' stocks to plunge, costing US investors billions of dollars, at least on paper. A major issue has been discrepancies between earnings reported to the SEC, on the one hand, and to the China State Administration for Industry and Commerce (SAIC), on the other. The differences in the reported figures may be due to the RMCs seeking to avoid tax in China and/or different accounting conventions and standards (Steinman 2014). Accounting inconsistencies have raised red flags and inflicted losses on investors, in addition to breaching anti-fraud rules that prohibit the use of manipulative or deceptive devices in purchase/sale of securities (17 CFR s. 240.10b-5 (2013)).

(b)   Shareholder litigation: challenges and hurdles before plaintiffs
Chinese reverse mergers present two significant challenges, namely, the quality of audits and the ability of plaintiffs to enforce securities laws. Given the lack of reliable remedial avenues, US shareholders are unable to seek recourse against fraud (Zuber 2014). Investors have legitimate concerns about how to recover losses when financial disclosures turn out to be fraudulent (Aguilar 2011). Among other legal barriers, gathering evidence can be difficult when the individuals concerned often reside in China.[8] With nearly all of the relevant papers being physically located in

---

[8]   Regardless of a valid cause of action, service of documents via the Hague Service Convention (Convention on the Service Abroad of Judicial and Extrajudicial Documents in Civil or Commercial Matters, Hague Conference on Private

China, it can be difficult for plaintiffs to bear the burden of proof because US courts are unable to compel defendants to hand over necessary documents (McMahon 2013). RMCs also tend to move assets that could satisfy a judgment outside jurisdictions accessible to US investors (Kolker 2011). Last, but not least, remedies obtained in the United States may not be enforceable (Aguilar 2011). Chinese law recognizes certain judgments awarded in the United States, but bureaucratic and cultural barriers have stymied efforts by US plaintiffs to enforce judgments in China (Kolker 2011).

Deficiencies in financial disclosures raise the question as to whether auditors must be imputed with a duty of care to shareholders and potential investors for their certification of accounts (Farrar *et al.* 2010). There is always a significant obstacle to establishing accessory liability (Davies 2011). Knowingly assisting a tort does not necessarily lead to liability, which may represent a gap in the law (Talley 2006).[9] Notably, s. 929P(b) of the Dodd-Frank Act confines the jurisdictions of US courts to actions brought by the SEC. It does not cover private civil actions. Therefore, lawsuits are not an option for shareholders and they may need to turn to regulators (Zuber 2014). This reaffirms the long-standing debate about the efficacy of *ex ante* prevention by enforcement agencies as against *ex post* judicial remedy in protecting investors. Undoubtedly, both are equally valuable and complementary in promoting capital market integrity and enhancing investor protection.

2.3.2   PCAOB's Reach and Limits

PCAOB supervises accounting firms that audit public companies. Firms registered with the PCAOB are legally obliged to provide audit papers and, potentially, testimony, if requested. PCAOB can institute disciplinary proceedings if a registered public accounting firm or its associated persons fail 'to comply with an accounting board demand' (PCAOB

International Law, 1969) is unrealistic. For instance, the Court in *SEC* v. *Deloitte Touche Tohmatsu CPA Ltd, Shanghai* (2014) could not enforce a subpoena because SEC failed to properly serve the Order to Show Cause under Federal Rule of Civil Procedure 4(F) and the Hague Convention. Rosier (2015) submitted to the United States–China Economic and Security Review Commission that, 'Service of process on a Chinese defendant via the Hague Service Convention is lengthy, bureaucratically burdensome, and generally unreliable'.

[9]   See also US Supreme Court decision in *Stoneridge Investment Partners, LLC* v. *Scientific-Atlanta* 552 US 148 (2008) (parties who merely assist another in violating s. 10(b), which prohibits manipulative or deceptive devices in the sale of securities, are not liable under s. 10(b)).

Rules, s. 5110(a)(1)). Some weaknesses undermine PCAOB's enforcement when foreign jurisdictions are involved, as the Chinese RMC episode revealed. The agency could not obtain the detailed financial information it needed to prove fraud. There were also procedural challenges in gaining access to the RMC's audit papers.

(a) PCAOB's mission and the reality in China

To trade on a US exchange, a company must be audited each year by a firm licensed in the United States. Without audited financial statements, companies cannot stay listed on US exchanges. PCAOB inspects smaller registered firms located inside the United States every three years; this policy is under review by the SEC (SEC 2016). PCAOB's mission is to protect the interest of investors and further the public interest in the preparation of informative, accurate and independent audit reports for public companies (PCAOB Mission and Vision 2016). PCAOB is also responsible for setting accounting principles, ensuring compliance, and disciplining those that fail to meet PCAOB requirements (SOX, s. 103). Although auditor independence and audit quality have been strengthened by the Sarbanes–Oxley Act, PCAOB has raised concerns that some US accounting firms may not have performed sufficient due diligence in accordance with PCAOB standards (PCAOB 2011).

There are 48 foreign registered audit firms in China, and another 52 in Hong Kong (Ferguson 2012). General lack of auditor independence undermines efforts to improve internal governance (Yang *et al.* 2003). Weaknesses in China's audit practice prevent internal audits from serving as effective deterrents. In addition, China's accounting standards deviate considerably from international ones (Chen *et al.* 2015). American auditors cannot open offices in China and must operate through Chinese affiliates. They have to rely on papers prepared by affiliates in China (Lubman 2012).

As a consequence, for the RMCs significant portions of audit were signed off by a US firm but the audit was actually conducted by an agency that cannot be inspected by the PCAOB. US firms may have to hand out audit work to Chinese affiliates without being able to verify the accuracy of the work done. These issues also apply to the Big 4's Chinese affiliates. An audit report could be signed by a member of the Big 4 firms, but might not reveal the extent of their participation (Ferguson 2012). This has exposed the inability of the Big 4 to impose common standards on their China units. The quality of work performed by the affiliates was investigated by SEC (*In the matter of BDO et al.*, 2014).

(b) SOX 106 requests and the sovereignty issue

PCAOB endeavours to prevent financial fraud, *ex ante,* and its methods include inspection of auditors. In inspecting the Chinese affiliates of Big 4 firms, PCAOB encountered significant hurdles and challenges. The Chinese government is hostile to intervention in what it views as domestic affairs that raise issues of sovereignty (Stephens 2011). Without a formal system in place, PCAOB lacks access to audit firms in China, and this prevents inspection and ensuring there is compliance with the Sarbanes-Oxley Act, SEC requirements, and its own standards. There are complaints that China provides no meaningful assistance in cross-border investigations.[10] The China Securities Regulatory Commission (CSRC), which is also the chief regulator of accounting firms, has long rejected PCAOB requests to inspect US-registered and China-based auditors on the ground that it would infringe China's national sovereignty (Barber 2013). Under state secrecy laws,[11] the concern about sovereignty makes it difficult for PCAOB to adequately review the work of Chinese auditors who sign off on the books of RMCs. This prevents PCAOB from evaluating the auditors' quality control procedures. The situation is serious for investor protection and the public interest. In dealing with issues of financial integrity, sovereignty ought not to be used to shield inadequate financial transparency (Lubman 2012). International comity per se under this circumstance may not bar enforcement of the SOX 106 requests (Bather and Burnaby 2006).

To improve preventive cross-border quality controls, PCAOB has requested permissions to conduct joint inspections with Chinese regulators (Gillis 2014). SEC also made concerted efforts to obtain information from Chinese audit firms (Black 2013). The audit firms' refusal to share working papers resulted in SEC initiating legal proceedings. SEC filed a motion seeking to subpoena papers from Deloitte Touche Tohmatsu CPA Ltd, Shanghai (*SEC* v. *Deloitte,* 2011)[12] and brought administrative enforcement actions against the Chinese affiliates of the Big 4 (SEC

---

[10]   *SEC* v. *Deloitte Touche Tohmatsu CPA Ltd* No 1:11-mc-00512-GK-DAR (DDC, 3 December 2012). The CSRC failed to provide any meaningful assistance in response to 21 requests for cooperation made by SEC since 2009.

[11]   The State Secrets Law was revised on 29 April 2010 and became effective on 1 October 2010.

[12]   *SEC* v. *Deloitte Touche Tohmatsu CPA Ltd* Civil Action No 1:11-MC-00512 (DDC, filed 8 September 2011).

Administrative Proceeding 2012,[13] culminating in *In the matter of BDO et al.*, 2014).

2.4 SUSPENSION OF BIG 4'S CHINA UNITS: DEFENCE OF 'BETWEEN A ROCK AND A HARD PLACE'

The Big 4 firms performed audit work for the majority of RMCs that have a substantial portion of their operations in China. In the *BDO* case, SEC alleged that the Big 4's Chinese affiliates conducted deficient audits and enabled accounting frauds to go undetected. They were charged with violating securities laws for refusing to furnish audit papers for PCAOB inspection. The SEC Administrative Law Judge ruled that the Chinese units had 'wilfully violated' US laws and should be suspended from auditing firms that are publicly traded in the US markets (*In the matter of BDO et al.*, 2014). The decision seems critical to SEC's ability to investigate potential securities law violations and protect investors.

2.4.1 *SEC v. Deloitte Touche Tohmatsu CPA Ltd* (2011)

Even before initiating the administrative proceeding against the Big 4 (and BDO) in 2012, SEC had brought a motion in the Federal District Court in Washington DC, against Deloitte in 2011, to subpoena audit documents. Deloitte Touche Tohmatsu CPA Ltd, Shanghai (DTT) had acted as the auditor of Longtop Financial Technologies Ltd since the company listed its shares on the New York Stock Exchange in 2007 through an IPO. SEC was concerned with Deloitte's quality control over its Shanghai-based affiliate. To avoid violating Chinese laws on disclosing information, Deloitte resisted demands from SEC for its records (Henning 2011). In September 2011, SEC filed a subpoena enforcement action to force Deloitte's Chinese affiliate to turn over Longtop audit papers (*SEC v. Deloitte*, 2011).[14] Judge Deborah Robinson ordered DTT

---

[13]   'SEC Charges China Affiliates of Big Four Accounting Firms with Violating US Securities Laws in Refusing to Produce Documents' (3 December 2012), available at www.sec.gov/News/PressRelease/Detail/PressRelease/136517 1486452#.U-3ummPLKM0.

[14]   SEC also included Deloitte Touche Tohmatsu Shanghai in the SEC Administrative Proceeding (2012) it initiated against the other large accounting firms for their refusal to furnish documents, charging them with violation of the US Securities Exchange Act and the Sarbanes-Oxley Act.

Shanghai to explain why the firm should not be required to comply with the SEC subpoena.

DTT Shanghai argued that turning over the audit paper would subject it to legal risk because China's State Secrets Law treats the documents as akin to state secrets (art. 25). DTT Shanghai further contended that producing the audit work papers would allow China to 'dissolve the firm entirely and to seek prison sentences up to life in prison for any Deloitte partners and employees who participated in the violation' (Chovanec 2012). DTT Shanghai appeared to have been caught in the middle of conflicting requirements and found itself between a rock and a hard place with regard to possible cross-border liability exposure (Betman and Law 2013).

If the court ordered DTT Shanghai to turn over the records and it refused, it could result in a criminal misdemeanour conviction punishable by a fine (15 USC s. 78u(c)). The firm could also face suspension or revocation of registration by PCAOB as an auditor in the United States for violating the agency's rules (Nagy 2005). On 27 January 2014, SEC moved to dismiss the case, stating that a diplomatic resolution had been reached with the CSRC. Under the resolution, the Chinese regulator agreed to the production of most of the audit papers SEC had requested (*SEC* v. *Deloitte*, 2014).[15] This was the first time that SEC had brought an enforcement action against an overseas firm for failing to comply with a SOX 106 request and successfully resolved the issue through cross-border enforcement cooperation. The case underscores SEC's aggressive approach towards corporate gatekeepers and its determination to obtain work papers from RMC auditors. Hopefully, the case will have a strong deterrent effect on other China-based accounting firms.

2.4.2   The Big 4's State of Mind: Judicial Nature of the Refusal

SEC's dispute with the Chinese units of the Big 4, culminating in the Administrative Law Judge's ruling *In the matter of BDO et al.* (2014), had its roots in a wave of alleged accounting improprieties by RMCs. The investigations led SEC to initiate administrative proceeding against the Big 4's affiliates in December 2012, arguing that US law compelled them to comply with such requests (Rapoport 2014b). In this case, SEC was both the prosecutor and enforcer of the Sarbanes-Oxley Act, while the Big 4's Chinese affiliates were *de facto* defendants (Filip *et al.* 2014).

---

[15]   *SEC* v. *Deloitte Touche Tohmatsu CPA Ltd* 11 Misc 512 (GK) (DDC, 27 January 2014).

The action resulted from the audit firms' refusal to cooperate in SEC investigations. As noted, the SEC Administrative Law Judge held that the audit firms breached US law when they refused to furnish audit work papers to aid SEC in investigating the RMCs. SEC alleged that, in auditing the RMCs, the firms failed to 'exercise professional scepticism and due professional care' applicable under PCAOB Auditing Standard AU 230 (as in force then).

PCAOB has the authority to revoke audit firms' registrations and SEC can impose a practice bar. On 22 January 2014, the Big 4's China units were suspended for six months. Administrative Law Judge Elliot levied sanctions against them for withholding audit documents requested by SEC in the course of enforcement investigations (SEC Rules of Practice, r. 102(e)). The Administrative Law Judge's ruling focused on a narrow legal question, namely, whether the Big 4's refusal to produce audit papers on the plea about restrictions under Chinese Secrecy Law amounted to a 'wilful refusal to comply' with the SOX 106 request made by SEC. Yet, in substance, the ruling reflects the tension arising from the long-running dispute over SEC's access to information and the approach of the CSRC.

(a)   Refusal to produce audit work papers: was it 'wilful'?

Section 106 of the Sarbanes-Oxley Act requires foreign accounting firms to produce audit papers to SEC/PCAOB. It is unlawful to wilfully refuse to comply with any request made by SEC/PCAOB (SOX, s. 106(e)). In declining to comply with SOX 106 requests, the big accounting firms were, plausibly, driven by concerns over potentially draconian Chinese law (*In the matter of BDO et al.*, 2014, at 106). Primarily, Administrative Law Judge Elliot's inquiry turned on whether the Big 4's conduct constituted 'wilful refusal to comply'.

Refusal in the context of SOX 106(e) requests should be evaluated against the standard set by the US Supreme Court in *Société Internationale* v. *Rogers* (1958),[16] a case involving the refusal to furnish Swiss banking documents on the ground that doing so would violate Swiss law. A knowing failure to produce documents in response to a SOX 106 request constitutes 'wilful refusal to comply', which means choosing not to act after receiving a request requiring action (SEC Rules of Practice, r. 102(e)(1)(iii)). Each of the Big 4 defendants chose not to comply with the SOX 106 request, therefore constituting the violation (SEC 2014).

---

[16]   *Société Internationale Pour Participations Industrielle et Commerciales SA* v. *Rogers* 357 US 197, [207] (1958).

Thus, the 'failure to comply' was equated with a 'refusal to comply'. If any other standard were applied, regulated entities would have a perverse incentive to be less cooperative than they should be (*In the matter of BDO et al.*, 2014, at 93).

Second, the Securities Exchange Act is explicit that it is unlawful to use or employ, under certain circumstances, any manipulative or deceptive device or contrivance in contravention of SEC regulations (15 USC s. 78j(b)). The sanctions under s. 105(c)(5) of the Sarbanes-Oxley Act are divided into those requiring proof of a particular state of mind and those requiring no such proof (15 USC s. 7215(c)(4), (5)). The former might be roughly characterized as more than wilfulness, as that term is used in the Securities Exchange Act, and less than *scienter* (Dunn 1998). The presence of *scienter* can be the decisive factor in imposing a bar (Walker 1979). Nevertheless, the question of exactly what state of mind satisfies the *scienter* requirement of s. 10b-5 is left unaddressed (*Makor Issues and Rights* v. *Tellabs, Inc.*, 2006).[17]

Wilfulness under the Securities Exchange Act means 'intentionally committing the act which constitutes the violation' (*SEC* v. *Wonsover*, 2000).[18] The Big 4 had no intent to defraud, nor were they reckless (Barber 2013). There had been no extreme departure from the standard of ordinary care. In this regard, *scienter* is not limited to intent to defraud, which must be viewed through a wider lens (*In the matter of BDO et al.*, 2014, at 106). Knowing or intentional misconduct in general qualifies as *scienter*. This standard is consistent with the relevant SOX provisions, such as s. 105(c)(7), about the effect of suspension of accounting firms after disciplinary proceedings, and s. 107(d)(3), which deals with censure of PCAOB board members and removal from office.

Wilfulness need not be an element of unlawful conduct for which courts can impose civil penalties, but it is sometimes an element of a particular administrative sanction (see, for example, 15 USC s. 78u(d)(3)). A defendant may simply argue 'good faith' to rebut a showing of wilfulness. A factor worth noting is that the failure to provide a required report constitutes a wilful violation even without a knowledge requirement (Novak 2013). In this regard, the wilfulness or good faith can hardly affect the fact of non-compliance (Murley 1982). Even so, the Big 4's refusal to submit audit papers may still be open to criticism and even penal action. Arguably, their focus was on business development in

---

[17]   437 F 3d 588, [601] (7th Cir. 2006).
[18]   205 F 3d 408, [414] (DC Cir. 2000).

China and insufficient attention was paid to issues such as onerous Chinese laws and their implications for compliance with US laws.

(b) Lack of good faith

The Big 4 accounting firms argued that 'wilful refusal' requires consciousness of wrongdoing or a lack of good faith. But the SEC Administrative Law Judge held that a good faith effort to obey the law means a good faith effort to obey all law, not just the law that one wishes to follow (*In the matter of BDO et al.*, 2014, at 105). Good faith in this context would mean that the Big 4 had 'attempted all that a reasonable man would have undertaken in the circumstances to comply with' the SOX 106 requests, applying the standard in *Société Internationale* v. *Rogers* (1958). Wilfulness requires notice that a request had been made, followed by a choice to comply or not comply (*In the matter of BDO et al.*, 2014, at 92). The Big 4 knew they had received SOX 106 requests. Their decision not to provide the requested documents to the SEC constituted a 'wilful refusal'. The motive for the choice was irrelevant, so long as the Big 4 knew of the request and chose not to comply with it. In this vein, bad faith need not be demonstrated, and good faith was not a defence (*ibid.*: 41).

In *Arthur Andersen LLP* v. *United States* (2005),[19] the US Supreme Court held that 'knowingly' and 'corruptly' have distinct meanings that must each be given effect, so a conviction requires proof both of consciousness of wrongdoing, that is, knowledge, and of wrongful intent, i.e. corruption (18 USC s. 1512(b)(2)). Criminal wilfulness generally requires a bad purpose or knowledge that one's conduct violates the law, which is inconsistent with good faith (*Bryan* v. *United States*, 1998).[20] Wilfulness in some criminal contexts may be negated by subjective good faith (*Cheek* v. *United States*, 1991).[21] However, there is no wilfulness requirement for imposition of civil penalties by a district court. Proof of wilfulness, sometimes required in SEC administrative proceedings, is generally not required in civil proceedings (Glaser 2014). Generally in civil cases, wilfulness merely 'differentiates between deliberate and unwitting conduct' (*Bryan* v. *United States*, 1998). Therefore, it would not be justified to evaluate the Big 4's omission with regard to SOX 106 requests with standards governing criminal wilfulness.

---

[19]   544 US 696 (2005).
[20]   524 US 184, [191]–[192] (1998).
[21]   498 US 192, [202] (1991).

2.4.3   Statutory Approaches: Dodd-Frank Act

Prior to the enactment of the Dodd-Frank Act, which took effect on 22 July 2010, disgorgement and civil penalties pursuant to the Securities Exchange Act were authorized only in the case of wilful misconduct (15 USC s. 78u-2(a)(1), (e) (2006)). Section 929P of the Dodd-Frank Act amended the Securities Exchange Act by making civil penalties available in cease-and-desist proceedings without any need to show wilfulness (15 USC s. 77h-1(g)(1) (2010)). Section 929P(b) extends the jurisdictional reach of US anti-fraud securities laws to transactions occurring outside the United States that involve only foreign investors, as well as conduct occurring outside the United States that has a foreseeable effect within the United States (Ringe and Hellgardt 2011). Under s. 929O, SEC can impose aiding and abetting liability on persons who 'recklessly' provide substantial assistance to persons violating the Securities Exchange Act (15 USC s. 78t). The Dodd-Frank Act (s. 929M), for the first time, establishes liability for persons who aid and abet violations of the Securities Act of 1933.

The Dodd-Frank Act has enhanced SEC's ability to obtain audit work papers in investigating Chinese RMCs. It imposes additional requirements continuing from SOX 106 (Cox 2013). The Dodd-Frank Act strengthens SEC's ability to levy monetary penalties in aiding and abetting cases under the Investment Advisers Act (Dodd-Frank Act, s. 929N), thereby closing a gap and conferring authority that SEC previously lacked (*SEC* v. *Bolla*, 2008).[22] It eases SEC's burden in aiding and abetting cases by lowering the state-of-mind requirement to recklessness, effectively overruling court decisions that had required proof of actual knowledge (Dodd-Frank Act, s. 929O).

2.4.4   Invalid Defence: Between a Rock and a Hard Place

The Big 4 argued that they would run afoul of Chinese state secrecy laws if they provided audit work papers to US law enforcers. The Sarbanes-Oxley Act, s. 106 requires non-US auditors to abide by the Act and PCAOB rules in the same manner and to the same extent as US auditors. Compliance with SOX 106 requests would result in a criminal conviction in China because Chinese law forbids disclosure of state secrets. The auditors seemed to face the proverbial immovable object, namely, the Chinese State Secrecy Law, in dealing with SEC's subpoena powers

---

[22]   550 F Supp 2d 54 (DDC, 2008).

(Barber 2013). This, however, was not accepted as an affirmative defence for not producing audit work papers (SEC Administrative Proceeding 2012). US courts, typically, enforce subpoenas despite conflicting foreign laws and companies that do not comply with subpoenas face potentially harsh consequences (see, for example, *Wultz* v. *Bank of China*, 2012).[23] According to Zuber (2014), weak rule of law in China has resulted in the general lack of enforcement of Chinese accounting standards. Young (2014) argued that the plea of the Big 4 about avoiding breach of the Chinese State Secrecy Law was just an excuse to avoid handing over records that could incriminate the firms for financial fraud or negligence.

SEC's position is that foreign firms auditing US issuers should not be permitted to shield themselves from regulatory scrutiny to the detriment of US investors (SEC Administrative Proceeding 2012). As registered US public accounting firms, they should meet their US legal obligations. The Administrative Law Judge censured the Big 4's Chinese affiliates and ordered their suspension (SEC Rules of Practice, r. 102(e)(1)(iii)). This ruling is a dramatic development in a longstanding dispute arising from the tension between the requirements under the Chinese Secrecy Law and SOX 106. In making the lengthy order, SEC Administrative Law Judge Elliot considered the nature of the Big 4's actions, the likelihood of future violations, and the need for a strong deterrent effect, with particular regard to the public interest. It is apparent that the judge also gave serious consideration to the potential market effects of practice bar.

2.4.5   A Settlement Between the SEC and the Big 4

To settle the SEC Administrative Proceeding (2012), the Big 4 agreed to pay a total penalty of US$2 million and provide the required documents (SEC Settlement 2015).[24] Under the terms of settlement, SEC maintained its supervision authority but suspension was lifted to avoid substantial negative collateral consequences. Antonia Chion of the SEC Enforcement Division observed, 'the settlement is an important milestone in the SEC's ability to obtain documents from China … The settlement provides a path forward for obtaining productions and enhanced future cooperation from the Big Four firms' (cited in SEC Settlement 2015). The settlement includes a mechanism to restart proceedings if the Big 4 failed to cooperate in the future. Yet the fundamental potential for conflict remains

---

23   No. 11 Civ 1266-SAS, 2012 WL 5378961, 3–8 (SDNY, 29 October 2012).
24   'SEC Imposes Sanctions Against China-Based Members of Big Four Accounting Networks for Refusing to Produce Documents' (6 February 2015), available at www.sec.gov/news/pressrelease/2015-25.html#.VPm41fmsV8E.

unresolved. The settlement does not target the ultimate source of the problem, namely, the issue of whether compliance with the Sarbanes-Oxley Act would violate China's state secrecy laws.

2.5 DEVELOPING AN EFFECTIVE REGULATORY FRAMEWORK

Cross-border regulatory cooperation and sharing information is vital in the common mission to improve the protection of investors, who rely on auditors to assure that the financial reports are transparent, complete, and fairly stated (Ferguson 2012). SEC/PCAOB inspections are an integral part of the mission to improve audit quality. Audit work papers are a critical source of substantial information. When PCAOB investigates potential misstatements, reviewing the audit papers is a fundamental component of the integral process to ensure the quality of audits. Filing an enforcement action against audit firms may be an effective option for the SEC in its attempt to deter fraudulent conduct (Zuber 2014). It would be better to use it as a last resort. The SEC Administrative Law Judge's decision appeared to point the way toward a US–Chinese diplomatic compromise, as both countries would suffer more if the Big 4's suspension was affirmed. After all, effective cooperation is essential to ensure audit quality and investor protection (Franzel 2012). The SEC engaged in diplomatic discussions with its Chinese counterpart in efforts to expand enforcement cooperation between the two jurisdictions.

2.5.1 Sanctions vis-à-vis Compliance: Which is More Viable for Neutralizing Moral Hazard?

On purely technical grounds, the economics of moral hazard are incomplete because they assume that sanctioning the Big 4 accounting firms would destabilize financial markets and adversely affect the audit of major multinationals. This economic interpretation ignores potential alternatives and also the issue of how tightened governance would minimize the cost of loss. An optimal solution to systemic risk in the concentrated audit market and the resulting moral hazard is to reduce concentration by increasing choice in the market. This would require policies to encourage the emergence of more firms that are capable of auditing large multinational companies. Allegations of fraud and questionable audit standards of the Big 4's China units have shaken investors' confidence.

An overriding concern must be to protect the integrity of SEC's processes. Effective and robust enforcement remains a critical tool in protecting investors and advancing the public interest. SEC's suspension of the Big 4 is indicative of some frustration with the progress made in this regard. It is essential to neutralize the moral hazard and rebuild auditors' impaired reputations for integrity (Cunningham 2006).

(a) Reassessing the classical theory of 'too big to fail'

The 'too big to fail' philosophy may create a risk of moral hazard that discourages enforcement agencies from taking appropriate action in cases involving the Big 4. Supporters of the approach might argue that practice bar or suspension would have negative collateral consequences on the market, including substantial costs to issuers, preventing China-based issuers from trading on US exchanges and consequent harm to investors. It could complicate the audits of various RMCs, as well as American firms operating in China. The Big 4's dire predictions about investor losses, delisting and loss of market capitalization, generally predicated on a lack of adequate substitute auditors, are unrealistic and unpersuasive (*In the matter of BDO et al.*, 2014, at 108–9).

Consequences for investors ought to be a determining factor in evaluating the sanctions in the public interest. Furthermore, China-based US issuers may engage adequate substitutes for the Big 4. Reportedly, some smaller accounting firms with bases in China and the United States have produced audit work papers without raising issues regarding state secrets and even without formal SOX 106 requests (Francine 2014). This is very different from the conduct of the Big 4. With them, possibly, there might be issues of differentiation of governance in China and the United States characterized by the different auditing standards and applicable legal duties. Partnoy (2004) advocated stricter auditor liability through an *ex ante* formula for damages, as a method to raise the stakes for auditors for their audit failure.

(b) *Ex ante* prevention vis-à-vis *ex post* sanction

To maintain the integrity of financial markets and assure the accuracy of issuers' disclosures, it is indispensable to reshape the incentives for gatekeepers. *Ex ante* moral hazard is the theoretical basis for PCAOB to reduce the Big 4's incentive to breach the law. Any isolated approach is unlikely to be an effective avenue for redress. The current enforcement climate underscores the need for effective corporate compliance programmes, which have become a part of the statutory and regulatory landscape (PCAOB Strategic Plan 2014).

There is a strong public interest in ensuring that issuers make adequate financial disclosures. It is essential to allow SEC and investors to have more information before a company's shares are traded on US stock exchanges. SEC introduced new procedures that focus on quality and integrity as absolute priorities. Under SEC's updated listing rules, RMCs are subject to a year-long 'seasoning period' before listing on a US exchange (SEC 2011). The seasoning period is intended to provide greater assurance that the company's financial reports are reliable. It enables auditors to fully inspect a company's records and allows for regulatory and market scrutiny of RMCs. More stringent listing requirements toughen the standards that Chinese companies must meet to become listed. The preventive measures should root out, or at least reduce, the likelihood of fraud by RMCs. Rigorous listing standards can effectively complement other methods such as political leverage and judicial enforcement.

Recognizing that obstacles to inspection continue, PCAOB strengthened its rules for inspections of audit firms outside the United States. SEC filed enforcement actions against several audit firms in addition to delisting some RMCs for fraudulent or delinquent filings (Zuber 2014). For the first time, PCAOB rejected the registration of a Chinese auditing firm, Zhonglei CPA Co., primarily because PCAOB was unable to inspect the firm's work for companies based in China. The decision signals that allowing inspections of auditors' papers is necessary to ensure continued access for Chinese issuers to the US capital markets (Goldberger and Krabill 2011).

Chinese audit firms could be barred from vetting the accounts of US-listed companies because of regulatory stand-offs, which could in turn lead to significant trade disputes (Jones 2011). The breadth of gatekeeper prosecutions reflects the aggressive governmental decision in the United States to use individual prosecutions to deter corporate misconduct. Such preventive measures can encourage the development of internal mechanisms in firms to improve quality of audits and check fraud, only to the extent the enforcement agencies can credibly threaten to prosecute. *Ex post* moral hazard is the theoretical basis for SEC to minimize the cost of recovery of losses. The suspension orders it secured against the Big 4 could presumably have a strong general deterrent effect on other Chinese accounting firms. *Ex post* punitive sanctions, without adequate and effective preventive solutions, *ex ante,* may not sufficiently protect investors.

2.5.2   Memorandum of Understanding: Symbolism or a Breakthrough?

China has an economic incentive to ensure that the US capital markets and investors remain comfortable with Chinese issuers, including RMCs, so foreign capital continues to flow into the country. The spate of questionable practices by Chinese RMCs has considerably tempered investments and may prompt quicker action from the Chinese government to stem the heightened concerns of Western market participants. Reviewing audit documents is fundamental to investigating potential misconduct and ensuring the quality of audit work. In general SEC has broad investigation powers, but it has little control over Chinese entities and assets in China.

The question for China and the United States is how to address conflict-of-law issues and conduct inspections in ways that respect national sovereignty and the legitimate regulatory goals of both countries. It is essential to establish a channel of cooperation between US and Chinese regulators, with specific reference to audit papers. The ultimate purpose is to accomplish the goal of having quality audits and protecting investors, without subjecting the Big 4 to unnecessary burdens or conflicting requirements.

(a)   Memorandum of Understanding between PCAOB and CSRC

A Multilateral Memorandum of Understanding (MMoU) was developed by the International Organization of Securities Commission (IOSCO) in 2002 to facilitate information-sharing and cooperation (IOSCO 2002). Under the MMoU, a signatory can request assistance from regulators in member countries in investigating securities law violations. SEC was an early signatory to the MMoU. The CSRC joined IOSCO in 1995 and signed the MMoU in 2007 (CSRC 2007). In principle, the MMoU can enhance international enforcement cooperation, but the long-standing stand-off between the United States and China suggests that the mechanism does not work well. This is largely due to the non-binding nature of multilateral enforcement.

Bilaterally, United States–China cooperation has focused on developing an effective cross-border audit oversight system to ensure market integrity and investor protection. In May 2013, PCAOB concluded a Memorandum of Understanding (MoU) on enforcement cooperation with the CSRC and the Chinese Ministry of Finance (MoF) (MoU 2013).[25] The United States–China MoU is intended to resolve the tension between

---

[25]   United States–China Memorandum of Understanding on Enforcement Cooperation (MoU) (2013), available at https://pcaobus.org/International/Documents/MOU_China.pdf.

the Big 4's competing obligations under US and Chinese laws. It 'establishes a cooperative framework between the parties for the production and exchange of audit documents relevant to investigations in both countries' and, to that end, 'provides a mechanism for the parties to request and receive from each other assistance in obtaining documents and information in furtherance of their investigative duties' (*ibid.*). In principle, the MoU can help PCAOB obtain information if advance notice is given to the CSRC and the Chinese MoF.

(b) Promising but not guaranteed

The United States–China MoU (2013) represents a breakthrough towards more collaborative assistance between the two countries with respect to securities enforcement. Enhanced cooperation can promote investor confidence by improving the accuracy and reliability of audits (MoU, art. 1). It could lead to incremental change. Cross-border cooperation will help Chinese companies prosper in a globalized marketplace and access international capital. There is a reasonable likelihood of less violation in the future, because under the MoU framework auditors consider themselves able to produce audit work papers directly to PCAOB.

The MoU provides that Chinese regulators and PCAOB will assist each other in obtaining materials related to investigations of auditors. The agreement allows audit documents to be shared. In principle, it could provide PCAOB fraud investigators access to the work papers of the Big 4's China units. This represents significant progress in US–Chinese auditor oversight and paves the way for cross-border enforcement assistance between the two jurisdictions. The MoU may even lead to greater transparency and better corporate governance in China, and facilitate more effective regulatory monitoring of Chinese auditors.

Ideally, the MoU could give PCAOB the ability to seek a range of information and documents from audit firms: audit work papers, documents on an audit firm's quality control systems, and documents defining the nature and scope of services provided by the firms. The MoU may present a path for PCAOB/SEC to obtain documents without placing audit firms at risk of violating Chinese law. Yet it is too early to be optimistic with regard to the efficacy of the MoU, due to some inherent uncertainties.

First, Chinese regulators may refuse to produce documents where production would violate Chinese law. The MoU explicitly provides (art. 3(b)(i)):

A request for assistance may be denied on an exceptional basis by the Requested Party: (i) where the request would require the Requested Party to act in a manner that would violate domestic law.

A contentious issue that remains is whether the production of audit papers via CSRC/Chinese MoF would shield the Big 4's Chinese units from liability under the Chinese State Secrecy Law. It would appear that CSRC still has the same grounds for refusing requests from PCAOB for audit papers as it did prior to the MoU. This is the Big 4's primary defence for refusal to submit the requested papers, and a positive interpretation would be that production of papers becomes lawful with CSRC's authorization. Chinese laws strictly prohibit the disclosure of certain documents, subject of course to flexible notions about the public interest.

Second, the United States–China MoU does not permit PCAOB to carry out its obligations under the Sarbanes-Oxley Act and conduct the required periodic inspections of registered auditors of China-based issuers. To strengthen the reliability and accuracy of audit reports and protect investors and the public interest, it is essential to secure a physical inspection so that PCAOB can regularly monitor and evaluate auditors' performance. Under the MoU, PCAOB is allowed periodic observational visits to China but it still has no permission to conduct on-the-ground inspections of Chinese audit firms, which PCAOB views as a critical part of its oversight function and investigative role. Visitation rights apply only to enforcement cases and not routine inspections of auditor firms (Lynch 2014). This partial progress only enables investors to find out how they have been defrauded *ex post*, and does not provide a viable approach for fraud prevention *ex ante*.

Third, the MoU explicitly asserts that it creates no legal obligations (art. 1(b)). As mentioned above, China retains the right to reject requests for documents in some circumstances. In addition, any possible assistance must be consistent with domestic laws. It appears broadly subjective as to whether effective cooperation could be achieved given such discretion.

The above barriers and uncertainties raise questions as to whether the United States and China have meaningfully resolved the conflict-of-law issue. Their MoU does not enable uniform and substantive review of audits. It can only sporadically help SEC get the documents it seeks. To a great extent, the MoU appears to be an ad hoc rather than systemic resolution of the issue about cooperation, more so if the law remains unchanged in this regard. Notably, Chinese statutory changes are subordinate to political reform. It would be unrealistic to seek meaningful reform without changing the ideological perception that PCAOB inspection would pose a threat to China's national security. It remains to be seen whether this MoU will result in more meaningful access to auditors' documents.

2.6 CONCLUSION

To recapitulate, a large number of Chinese companies gained listings on US stock exchanges through reverse mergers which subjected them to less scrutiny than traditional IPOs. Many Chinese RMCs were found to have been involved in accounting misrepresentations and securities fraud. Obtaining audit firms' work papers is critical to PCAOB's ability to adequately protect investors from the dangers of accounting fraud. Procedural challenges and hurdles make it unlikely that *ex post* solutions, by themselves, will be an adequate method. The Big 4, perceiving that regulators would not tolerate a reduction in their numbers, face a moral hazard amounting to turpitude. Audit work papers constitute the best contemporaneous documentary evidence of the financial state of issuers, and SEC had to launch administrative proceedings when faced with the Big 4's failure to furnish documents.

Robust enforcement against wrongdoing and penal action against guilty audit firms is necessary to maintain the integrity of the capital market. It is essential to adopt multifaceted approaches to address the moral hazard issue of the Big 4 firms. Combining *ex ante* prevention and *ex post* sanctions, along with active bilateral executive cooperation, can provide a more reliable method to neutralize the moral hazard issue of auditors.

REFERENCES

Aguilar, L. (SEC Commissioner) (2011), 'Facilitating Real Capital Formation' (4 April), available at www.sec.gov/news/speech/2011/spch040411laa.htm

Baker, T. (1996), 'On the Genealogy of Moral Hazard' 75 *Texas Law Review* 237

Barber, P. (2013), 'Bull in the China Market: The Gap between Investor Expectations and Auditor Liability for Chinese Financial Statement Frauds' 24 *Duke Journal of Comparative and International Law* 349

Bather, A. and P. Burnaby (2006), 'The Public Company Accounting Oversight Board: National and International Implications' 21 *Managerial Auditing Journal* 657

Baxter, L. (2014), *Extraterritorial Impacts of Recent Financial Regulation Reforms: A Complex World of Global Finance* (28 August), available at http://scholarship.law.duke.edu/faculty_scholarship/3355

Betman, R. and L. Law (2013), 'The (Too) Long Arm of the S.E.C.: When a Foreign Employee of a U.S.-Based Multinational Financial Services Client is Threatened with a Subpoena' 10 *Berkeley Business Law Journal* 1

Black, N. (2013), 'Crouching Tiger, Hiding Auditor' 1 *Cornell International Law Journal Online* 162

Buxbaum, H. (2006), 'Transnational Regulatory Litigation' 46 *Virginia Journal of International Law* 251

Chen, Y. *et al.* (2015), 'GAAP Difference or Accounting Fraud? Evidence from Chinese Reverse Mergers Delisted from U.S. Market' 7 *Journal of Forensic and Investigative Accounting* 122

Chovanec, P. (2012), 'Clash of the Balance Sheets' *Foreign Policy*, 10 December

Cox, J. (2013), 'Strengthening Financial Reporting: An Essay on Expanding the Auditor's Opinion Letter' 81 *George Washington Law Review* 1036

CSRC (2007), 'The CSRC Signs IOSCO Multilateral MoU' (12 April), available at www.csrc.gov.cn/pub/csrc_en/affairs/AffairsIOSCO/200708/t20070810_710 93.html

Cunningham, L. (2006), 'Too Big to Fail: Moral Hazard in Auditing and the Need to Restructure the Industry before It Unravels' 106 *Columbia Law Review* 1698

Davies, P. (2011), 'Accessory Liability for Assisting Torts' 70 *Cambridge Law Journal* 353

Doralt, W. *et al.* (2008), 'Auditor's Liability and its Impact on the European Financial Markets' 67 *Cambridge Law Journal* 62

Doty, J. (2011), 'Testimony Concerning the Role of the Accounting Profession in Preventing Another Financial Crisis' (US Senate Committee on Banking, Housing and Urban Affairs, Subcommittee on Securities, Insurance, and Investment, 6 April), available at https://pcaobus.org/News/Speech/Pages/ 04062011_DotyTestimony.aspx

Dunn, M. (1998), 'Pleading Scienter after the Private Securities Litigation Reform Act: or, A Textualist Revenge' 84 *Cornell Law Review* 193

Farrar, J. *et al.* (2010), 'Auditor Liability to Third Parties after Sarbanes-Oxley: An International Comparison of Regulatory and Legal Reforms' 19 *Journal of International Accounting, Auditing and Taxation* 66

Ferguson, L. (2012), 'Investor Protection through Audit Oversight' (21 September), available at http://pcaobus.org/News/Speech/Pages/09212012_Ferguson CalState.aspx

Filip, M. *et al.* (2014), 'SEC Bars Chinese Units of Big Four Accounting Firms', available at www.kirkland.com/siteFiles/Publications/Alert_012914.pdf

Fornelli, C. (2013), 'Testimony Before the US-China Economic and Security Review Commission on China's Financial Conditions and Their Impacts on US Interests' (7 March), available at www.uscc.gov/sites/default/files/3.7.13_ Fornelli_Testimony.pdf

Francine (2014), 'One Way or Another: The SEC versus the Chinese Big Four Firms' (25 January), available at http://retheauditors.com/2014/01/25/one-way-or-another-the-sec-versus-the-chinese-big-four-firms/

Franzel, J.M. (2012), 'Protecting Investors through Independent, High Quality Audits' (Public Company Accounting Oversight Board, 14 October), available at http://pcaobus.org/News/Speech/Pages/10142012_FranzelNACD.aspx

Gillis, P. (2014), *The Big Four and the Development of the Accounting Profession in China* (Emerald Group Publishing)

Glaser, S. (2014), 'Statutes of Limitations for Equitable and Remedial Relief in SEC Enforcement Actions' 4 *Harvard Business Law Review* 129

Goldberger, N. and L. Krabill (2011), 'Crouching Tiger, Hidden Fraud' 3 *Financial Fraud Law Report* 714

Henning, P. (2011), 'Deloitte's quandary: defy the SEC or China', *New York Times*, 20 October

House of Lords (2010), 'Auditors: Market Concentration and Their Role', available at www.parliament.uk/documents/lords-committees/economic-affairs/auditors/auditorswe1.pdf

Hudson, M., S. Chavkin and B. Mos (2014), 'Big 4 Audit Firms Play Big Role in Offshore Murk', International Consortium of Investigative Journalists (5 November), available at www.icij.org/project/luxembourg-leaks/big-4-audit-firms-play-big-role-offshore-murk

IOSCO (2002), 'Multilateral Memorandum of Understanding Concerning Consultation and Cooperation and the Exchange of Information', available at www.iosco.org/about/?subsection=mmou

Jones, A. (2011), 'China and US in standoff over auditors', *Financial Times*, 6 November

Kolker, C. (2011), 'U.S. lawsuits against China companies face hurdles', *Reuters*, 14 February, available at www.reuters.com/article/china-lawsuits-idUSN14292 11020110214

Lipton, M. *et al.* (2008), 'Risk Management and the Board of Directors' (November), available at http://corpgov.law.harvard.edu/wp-content/uploads/2008/11/risk-management-and-the-board-of-directors.pdf

Litvak, K. (2007), 'Sarbanes-Oxley and the Cross-Listing Premium' 105 *Michigan Law Review* 1857

Lubman, S. (2012), 'Unpacking the law around the Chinese reverse takeover mess', *Wall Street Journal*, 24 January

Lynch, S. (2014), 'US audit watchdog nearing China deal to inspect audit firms', *Reuters*, 5 February

Markoff, G. (2013), 'Arthur Andersen and the Myth of the Corporate Death Penalty: Corporate Criminal Convictions in the Twenty-First Century' 15 *University of Pennsylvania Journal of Business Law* 797

McMahon, D. (2013), 'Rare victory for U.S. investor in Chinese reverse merger company', *Wall Street Journal*, China Real Time, 23 January

Mircovich, S. (2014), 'SEC suspends Chinese units of "Big Four" accountants over audit secrecy', *Reuters*, 23 January

Murley, T.S. (1982), 'Compelling Production of Documents in Violation of Foreign Law: An Examination and Re-evaluation of the American Position' 50 *Fordham Law Review* 877

Nagy, D. (2005), 'Playing Peekaboo with Constitutional Law: The PCAOB and Its Public/Private Status' 80 *Notre Dame Law Review* 975

NASDAQ (2011), 'Additional Listing Requirements for Reverse Merger Companies', Exchange Act Release No. 65708, 2011WL 5434020 (8 November)

Novak, S. (2013), 'What to Do When a Client Has an Undisclosed Foreign Account' *Journal of Accountancy*, 1 December

NYSE Additional Listing Requirements for Reverse Merger Companies (2011), Exchange Act Release No. 65709, 2011WL 5434021 (8 November)

Partnoy, F. (2004), 'Strict Liability for Gatekeepers: A Reply to Professor Coffee' 84 *Boston University Law Review* 365

PCAOB (2010), 'Staff Audit Practice Alert No. 6, Auditor Considerations Regarding Using the Work of Other Auditors and Engaging Assistants from Outside the Firm' (12 July)

— (2011), 'Activity Summary and Audit Implications for Reverse Mergers Involving Companies from the China Region: 1 January 2007 through 31 March 2010' (15 March), available at http://pcaobus.org/Research/Documents/Chinese_Reverse_Merger_Research_Note.pdf

— (2014), 'Strategic Plan: Improving the Quality of the Audit for the Protection and Benefit of Investors 2014–2018' (26 November), available at https://pcaobus.org/About/Administration/Documents/Strategic%20Plans/2014-2018.pdf

— (2016), 'Mission and Vision', available at https://pcaobus.org/About/History/Pages/default.aspx

Prentice, R. (2006), 'The Inevitability of a Strong SEC' 91 *Cornell Law Review* 775

Rapoport, M. (2014a), 'SEC, Big Four Chinese affiliates make progress in talks over documents', *Wall Street Journal*, 22 October

— (2014b), 'Judge suspends Chinese units of Big Four auditors—ruling bars firms from audit work for six months', *Wall Street Journal*, 23 January

Ringe, W.-G. and A. Hellgardt (2011), 'The International Dimension of Issuer Liability: Liability and Choice of Law from a Transatlantic Perspective' 31 *Oxford Journal of Legal Studies* 23

Rosier, K. (2015), 'China's Great Legal Firewall: Extraterritoriality of Chinese Firms in the United States' (5 May), available at www.uscc.gov/sites/default/files/Research/Extraterritoriality%20of%20Chinese%20Firms_Research%20Report_0.pdf

SEC (2011), 'SEC Approves New Rules to Toughen Listing Standards for Reverse Merger Companies' (9 November), available at www.sec.gov/news/press/2011/2011-235.htm

— (2012), 'SEC Charges Deloitte & Touche in Shanghai with Violating US Securities Laws in Refusal to Produce Documents' (9 May), available at www.sec.gov/News/PressRelease/Detail/PressRelease/1365171488960

— (2013), 'The Investor's Advocate: How the SEC Protects Investors, Maintains Market Integrity, and Facilitates Capital Formation' (10 June), available at www.sec.gov/about/whatwedo.shtml#.VKhk9dKsUow

— (2014), 'Securities Exchange Act of 1934 Release No. 72140' (9 May), available at www.sec.gov/litigation/opinions/2014/34-72140.pdf

— (2016), 'Public Company Accounting Oversight Board; Notice of Filing of Proposed Amendments to Board Rules Relating to Inspections' (Release No. 34-77558; File No. PCAOB-2007-04, 7 April), available at www.sec.gov/rules/pcaob/2016/34-77558.pdf

Siegel, J. (2005), 'Can Foreign Firms Bond Themselves Effectively by Renting US Securities Laws?' 75 *Journal of Financial Economics* 319

Siegel, J. and Y. Wang (2013), *Cross-Border Reverse Mergers: Causes and Consequences*, Harvard Business School Strategy Unit Working Paper No. 12-089 (24 September)

Steinman, J. (2014), 'Reversing the Tide: A Targeted Approach to the Regulation of Chinese Reverse Mergers in the United States' 34 *Northwestern Journal of International Law and Business,* The Ambassador, 1

Stephens, P. (2011), 'A story of Brics without mortar', *Financial Times*, 24 November

Talley, E. (2006), 'Cataclysmic Liability Risk among Big Four Auditors' 106 *Columbia Law Review* 1641

Walker, C. (1979), 'Accountants' Liability: The Scienter Standard under Section 10b and Rule 10-5 of the Securities Exchange Act of 1934' 63 *Marquette Law Review* 243

Watts, R. and J. Zimmerman (1983), 'Agency Problems, Auditing, and the Theory of the Firm: Some Evidence' 26 *Journal of Law and Economics* 613

Yang, L. *et al.* (2003), 'Auditor Independence Issues in China' 29 *Managerial Finance* 57

Young, D. (2014), 'China auditors, U.S. in dangerous game of brinksmanship', *Forbes*, 27 January

Yuk, P.K. (2012), 'Big Four, China and the SEC: a game of chicken', *Financial Times*, 3 December

Zuber, K. (2014), 'Breaking Down a Great Wall: Chinese Reverse Mergers and Regulatory Efforts to Increase Accounting Transparency' 102 *Georgetown Law Journal* 1307

3. The proposed Directive on the encouragement of long-term shareholder engagement in European listed companies: a critical appraisal

Corrado Malberti

3.1 INTRODUCTION

In the aftermath of the Financial Crisis of 2008–09, the reactions of the European Union (EU) to the problems raised by corporate governance were slow and principally addressed to the reform of the governance of financial institutions. Only in April 2014 did the European Commission present a proposal for a Directive on the encouragement of long-term shareholder engagement addressed to all listed companies. This proposal, among other measures, is intended to grant to general meetings the right to vote on related-party transactions and remuneration policies.

The Commission's proposal has been criticized by legal commentators as being based on wrong theoretical assumptions about the virtues of shareholder engagement and unlikely to be effective in achieving its intended goals. In spite of these first reactions, the draft versions of the Directive currently under discussion before European institutions do not completely challenge the soundness of the strategy pursued by the Commission, and they simply try to further limit the scope and the impact of the proposed measures.

In this chapter I argue that, considering the evolution of the academic and political debate, the expected impact of the Commission's proposal, if it is finally adopted, will be modest and will probably not achieve its intended shareholder empowerment goals. The chapter begins with a review of the recent history of the initiatives of the EU relating to corporate governance. It also describes the measures proposed by the Commission in the recently published draft Directive on encouraging long-term shareholder engagement. Particular attention is devoted to provisions concerning related-party transactions and remuneration policies. Section 3 investigates the first academic reactions to the Commission's initiative and the criticisms raised by legal commentators.

Section 4 explores the possibility that the reasons that make it difficult to achieve an authentic harmonization of European national laws are rooted in the lack of a satisfactory theoretical and empirical background to support the adoption of the measures proposed, and in some features of the institutional framework of the EU. This section also examines the inherent weaknesses in European law and the risks they pose for the proposed corrective legislation, which again is not supported by empirical evidence. Section 5 concludes the chapter.

3.2 RECENT EUROPEAN DEBATE ON CORPORATE GOVERNANCE

3.2.1 First Reactions in the European Union to the Financial Crisis

The recent initiatives undertaken in Europe in the domain of corporate governance aim at the problems that allegedly became evident during the Financial Crisis. The starting point of this evolution was the De Larosière Report (DLR 2009), which, however, devoted only a few remarks to corporate governance. The focus of the Report was on the governance of financial institutions and two issues were considered to be most problematic: (a) the lack of expertise of boards and senior managements in dealing with risks associated with financial products (DLR 2009: 32); and (b) the misguided remuneration and incentive schemes, which exacerbated risk-taking and short-termism (DLR 2009: 30).

To address the first set of problems, the De Larosière Report suggested measures to improve risk management (DLR 2009: 32). With regard to remuneration schemes, the Report recommended making sure that compensation incentives were 'better aligned with shareholder interests and long-term firm-wide profitability' of financial institutions, by ensuring that the assessment of bonuses be made in a multi-year framework and that bonuses reflect the actual performance of directors and managers (DLR 2009: 31).

A few days after the publication of the De Larosière Report, the European Commission also made available the Communication entitled 'Driving European Recovery', which further explored some of the shortcomings of corporate governance that became evident during the Financial Crisis. In a few words, the Commission proposed to take action in the domain of directors' remuneration, not only for financial institutions but also for listed companies (European Commission 2009). Also in this case the stated goal of these measures was 'to avoid short-term excessive risk-taking' (DLR 2009: 17).

This initial reflection on the possible corporate governance implications of the experience gathered during the Financial Crisis finally resulted in the publication of two Recommendations of the Commission on remuneration policies: one addressed to financial institutions (Recommendation 2009/384/EC) and the other to listed companies (Recommendation 2009/385/EC). These two documents complemented two other previous Recommendations on remuneration policies issued in 2004 (Recommendation 2004/913/EC)[1] and 2005 (Recommendation 2005/162/EC),[2] respectively.

Though addressed to two different types of entities, the two Recommendations shared many points in common. First, both documents gave particular emphasis to the necessity of better disclosing information concerning remuneration schemes (Recommendation 2009/384/EC, section 3;[3] Recommendation 2009/385/EC, para. 5).[4] Second, both Recommendations included detailed rules on the structure of these schemes. Among other things, they suggested a balance between the variable and non-variable parts of the remuneration as well as a deferral of the variable part (Recommendation 2009/384/EC, para. 4; Recommendation 2009/385/EC, paras 3–4).

Interestingly, the Recommendation discussing the remuneration of directors in listed companies also mentioned some measures that were already included in the first Recommendation of 2004 (Recommendation 2004/913/EC). The 2004 Recommendation invited Member States to require (a) a remuneration statement to be submitted to a vote in the general meeting, either mandatory or advisory (DLR 2009: para. 4.2);[5]

---

[1] Commission Recommendation 2004/913/EC of 14 December 2004 fostering an appropriate regime for the remuneration of directors of listed companies [2004] OJ L385/55.

[2] Commission Recommendation 2005/162/EC of 15 February 2005 on the role of non-executive or supervisory directors of listed companies and on the committees of the (supervisory) board [2005] OJ L52/51.

[3] Commission Recommendation 2009/384/EC of 30 April 2009 on remuneration policies in the financial services sector [2009] OJ L120/22.

[4] Commission Recommendation 2009/385/EC of 30 April 2009 complementing Recommendations 2004/913/EC and 2005/162/EC as regards the regime for the remuneration of directors of listed companies [2009] OJ L120/28.

[5] However, this Recommendation also provided that a Member State could only impose a requirement to vote on the remuneration statement if shareholders

and (b) the prior approval of the annual general meeting for remuneration schemes, whether directors were 'remunerated in shares, share options or any other right to acquire shares or ... on the basis of share price movements' (DLR 2009: para. 6.1). Continuing from this framework, the 2009 Recommendation further advised Member States to encourage shareholders, above all institutional shareholders, to attend general meetings and, where appropriate, use their voting rights concerning directors' remuneration (Recommendation 2009/385/EC, para. 6.1).

Even in these first actions following the Financial Crisis, it was evident that the measures adopted by the European Commission were distinctively aimed at two different types of entities: on the one hand, financial institutions and, on the other, listed companies. Another important aspect of this early debate concerning strategies to address the problems raised by the Financial Crisis is that, even if it was clearly acknowledged that the issues raised by the governance of financial institutions had implications that were different from those of listed companies, the solutions considered appropriate to solve the problems in the former were frequently believed to be also suitable for improving the governance of the latter.

However, from a practical standpoint, the European Commission did not consider this first attempt at reform to be particularly successful. In fact, European Recommendations are not binding on EU Member States, and the Commission felt that the Member States put the effectiveness of the suggested measures at risk by not adopting them promptly and uniformly (European Commission 2010a and 2010b).

3.2.2 Debate on the Governance of Financial Institutions

(a) Public consultation 2010

In the scenario described, the European Commission decided to further explore the possibility of improving the governance of European companies by separating the discussion on the measures addressed to financial institutions from the initiatives addressed to listed companies,

---

representing at least 25 per cent of the votes attending the annual meeting requested it.

and it gave priority to the former. Therefore in June 2010, the Commission launched a public consultation on governance in financial institutions and remuneration policies (European Commission 2010c),[6] which highlighted several problems in financial institutions.

More precisely, as indicated by the European Commission (European Commission 2010c), these problems were: (a) conflicts of interest; (b) defective implementation of corporate governance principles; (c) the inability of boards to effectively supervise and take action; (d) the inability to properly address risk management; and (e) the position of shareholders who might have short-term investment horizons and few incentives to effectively monitor managers and directors.

The measures proposed to solve these issues were diverse. Among other things, they concerned (a) the composition and structure of the board; (b) the potential role of shareholders and institutional investors in the governance of financial institutions, with particular attention to strategies facilitating the identification of shareholders; (c) the enhancement of the consistency and effectiveness of EU actions on directors' remuneration;[7] (d) the possibility of adopting initiatives to prevent and fight conflicts of interest in financial markets; and (e) the improvement of the effectiveness of risk management.

Stakeholders' reactions to the Commission's envisioned actions were not particularly positive and, in some cases, even sceptical (European Commission 2010e). Without entering into the details of the reactions to each measure (for further details on these reactions, see Malberti 2013), it is worth noting that the initiatives concerning conflicts of interest, remuneration policies and the potential role of shareholders were not always well received. More precisely, with regard to shareholders' engagement, the respondents to the consultation were generally in favour of a mandatory disclosure of institutional investors' voting practices. They also favoured compulsory adhesion of institutional investors to national or international codes of best practice and the creation of mechanisms to facilitate the identification of shareholders and cross-border voting. In contrast, the respondents did not support the adoption of any further action in the domain of remuneration policies. It was

---

[6]   For further details on the measures proposed in this consultation, see also the Commission Staff Working Document accompanying the Green Paper (European Commission 2010d).

[7]   Although this consultation concerned financial institutions, it also explored the available strategies to enhance the consistency and effectiveness of European measures dealing with remuneration, not only of financial institutions, but, more broadly, of listed companies.

believed that, in light of the existing Recommendations, the ongoing review of the Capital Requirements Directive at that time, and since the effects of the implementation of these measures were still to be evaluated, no additional initiatives were needed. Finally, the reactions to the possibility of reinforcing the legal framework concerning the prevention of conflicts of interest were mixed. However, the prevailing opinion urged better coordination and alignment, at the European level, of the rules dealing with this issue.

(b) Rules on remuneration policies in Capital Requirements Directive III

The long debate on the governance of European financial institutions finally produced some tangible results with the adoption of the Capital Requirements Directive III (CRD III) in 2010 (Directive 2010/76/EU)[8] and the Capital Requirements Directive IV/Capital Requirements Regulation (CRD IV/CRR) in 2013 (Directive 2013/36/EU[9] and Regulation (EU) 575/2013,[10] respectively). These pieces of legislation reshaped the existing framework provided by the earlier capital requirement Directives (Directives 2006/48/EC[11] and 2006/49/EC[12] (collectively, CRD I), and Directive 2009/111/EC[13] (CRD II)).

CRD III, addressed to credit institutions, enacted new rules on remuneration policies. These measures concerned the role and duties of

---

[8]   European Parliament and Council Directive 2010/76/EU of 24 November 2010 amending Directives 2006/48/EC and 2006/49/EC as regards capital requirements for the trading book and for re-securitizations, and the supervisory review of remuneration policies [2010] OJ L329/3.

[9]   European Parliament and Council Directive 2013/36/EU of 26 June 2013 on access to the activity of credit institutions and the prudential supervision of credit institutions and investment firms, amending Directive 2002/87/EC and repealing Directives 2006/48/EC and 2006/49/EC [2013] OJ L176/338.

[10]   European Parliament and Council Regulation (EU) 575/2013 of 26 June 2013 on prudential requirements for credit institutions and investment firms and amending Regulation (EU) 648/2012 [2013] OJ L176/1.

[11]   European Parliament and Council Directive 2006/48/EC of 14 June 2006 relating to the taking up and pursuit of the business of credit institutions (recast) [2006] OJ L177/1.

[12]   European Parliament and Council Directive 2006/49/EC of 14 June 2006 on the capital adequacy of investment firms and credit institutions (recast) [2006] OJ L177/201.

[13]   European Parliament and Council Directive 2009/111/EC of 16 September 2009 amending Directives 2006/48/EC, 2006/49/EC and 2007/64/EC as regards banks affiliated to central institutions, certain own funds items, large exposures, supervisory arrangements, and crisis management [2009] OJ L302/97.

remuneration committees, and the structure and disclosure of the remuneration policies of persons whose activities have a material impact on
the institutions' risk profile. With particular regard to the latter set of
measures, it was provided that remuneration policies had to promote
'sound and effective risk management', could not 'encourage risk-taking
that exceeds the level of tolerated risk of the credit institution', and
should pursue the 'long-term interests of the credit institution' (Directive
2006/48/EC, Annex V, section 11, para. 23(a) and (b), as amended by
CRD III).[14]

The boards of financial institutions were required to provide, at least
on a yearly basis, a review of the general principles of the remuneration
policy and they were also responsible for implementing these principles
(para. 23(c) and (d)). The issues of the deferral of payments and the
balance between the variable and non-variable parts of remuneration
were finally addressed: credit institutions were required to 'set the
appropriate ratios between the fixed and the variable component of the
total remuneration' (para. 23(l)), and they were also required to pay at
least 50 per cent of the awarded bonuses with shares or other instruments
subject to a retention policy (para. 23(o)).

In addition, the payment of 'performance-based components of remuneration [was to be] spread over a period which [had to take] account
of the underlying business cycle of the credit institution and its business
risks' (para. 23(h)). CRD III also provided that at least 40 per cent of the
variable component of the remuneration had to be deferred over a period
of not less than three to five years and had to be correctly aligned with
the nature of the business, its risks, and the activities of the person in
question (para. 23(p)). In addition, if the variable part of the remuneration was particularly high, payment of at least 60 per cent of the variable
remuneration had to be deferred (*ibid.*). Member States were required to
enact legislation to reduce the total variable remuneration in case of the
subdued or negative financial performance of credit institutions, 'taking
into account both current remuneration and reductions in payouts of
amounts previously earned, including through malus or clawback
arrangements' (para. 23(q)).

On disclosure of remuneration policies, CRD III required Member
States to ensure that credit institutions were subject to extensive reporting
obligations for personnel whose activity could have an impact on their
risk profile (Directive 2006/48/EC, Annex XII, Part 2, para. 15, as

---

[14] More broadly, on the rules on remuneration in CRD III, see Ferran 2012:
15.

amended by CRD III). In this framework, particular emphasis was given to disclosing information about the decision-making process adopted for determining the remuneration policy, the link between pay and performance, and the structure of remuneration schemes (*ibid.*).

The approach in CRD III deserves attention for several reasons. First, among the different areas of intervention that were under discussion at that time to improve the governance of financial institutions, the greatest attention was given to remuneration policies. Second, the strategy adopted was to regulate both the substantive and disclosure aspects of remuneration policies. Third, these measures were introduced not by issuing a Recommendation, but by enacting a European Directive, which is a binding legislative measure addressed to the Member States of the EU.

CRD III was an important milestone in the regulation of the governance of European companies, yet it concerned only a few, although very important, entities. In addition, this legislation principally focused on the problem of bad incentives created by imprudent remuneration policies. Moreover, some flexibility was still granted to Member States in implementing this Directive in their national legislation. In any case, CRD III was quickly replaced by CRD IV/CRR, which was finally enacted in 2013 after lengthy negotiations.

(c) Measures concerning corporate governance in CRD IV/CRR
The measures concerning corporate governance in CRD IV/CRR followed in the footsteps of CRD III, even if their scope was surely broader. The CRD IV/CRR framework, as in CRD III, did not affect the governance of all listed companies, but was addressed only to credit institutions and financial firms. Moreover, the provisions on remuneration policies remained a key aspect of this legislation. However, CRD IV/CRR also dealt with other aspects of corporate governance, such as the structure of the management body, and enhanced the scope and nature of the disclosure obligations for financial institutions.

Starting with this last aspect of CRD IV/CRR, a fundamental change concerned the nature of the provisions devoted to disclosure. In CRD III, these rules were included in an Annex to the Directive. In CRD IV/CRR they became, and currently still are, a part of the CRR, which, being a Regulation, has direct effect and does not need to be transposed by the Member States. The information on remuneration policies to be made available by credit institutions and financial firms closely follows the approach adopted in CRD III, with some adjustments mainly due to the modifications made to the rules on the structure of remuneration introduced by CRD IV, examined below (Regulation (EU) 575/2013, art.

450(1)). An important innovation was the obligation to disclose the number of individuals being remunerated more than 1 million euros (art. 450(1)(i)).

On the structure of the boards of directors, CRR also imposed disclosure obligations with regard to (a) multiple directorships held by members of the managing body; (b) recruitment policies and actual knowledge, skills and expertise; (c) policies on diversity with regard to the selection of members of the management body; and (d) information regarding risk management and risk profile of the institution (Regulation (EU) 575/2013, art. 435(2)).

The substantive part of the corporate governance measures in CRD IV/CRR was included in art. 88 onwards of CRD IV. They define the duties of the management body (Directive 2013/36/EU, art. 88(1)); impose a separation of the functions of the chairman of the management body from the chief executive officer; and, in certain cases, require the appointment of a nomination committee (art. 88(2)). There are also rules on the composition of the management body. They impose limitations on directors' multiple mandates and require directors to be of good repute and meet knowledge, skill and experience requirements (art. 91(1)). Management bodies should promote diversity (art. 91(10)), with special attention to gender diversity (recital (60) and art. 88(2)(a)).

With regard to substantive rules on remuneration policies, the framework of CRD III was largely confirmed (compare Directive 2013/36/EU, arts 92, 94 and Directive 2006/48/EC, Annex V, section 11, para. 23 as amended by CRD III). Yet some relevant aspects of the rules were made stricter. For example, a cap has been introduced to the variable component of the remuneration, which is not allowed to exceed 100 per cent of the fixed component of the remuneration. However, if some strict conditions are satisfied and with the approval of the shareholders, Member States can allow an increase of this ratio to 200 per cent (Directive 2013/36/EU, art. 94(1)(g)(ii)). Another important modification concerns the requirement of CRD IV that '[u]p to 100% of the total variable remuneration' must be made 'subject to malus or clawback arrangements'. In addition, credit institutions and financial firms are also required to 'set specific criteria for the application of malus and clawback' with regard to situations in which the member of the staff 'participated in or was responsible for conduct which resulted in significant losses to the institution' or 'failed to meet appropriate standards of fitness and propriety' (Directive 2013/36/EU, art. 94(1)(n)). To conclude, CRD IV/CRR also highlights that risk management has other dimensions, different from that of the remuneration policy (Directive 2013/36/EU, art. 76).

3.2.3 Debate on the Governance of Listed Companies

(a) Green Paper 2011

While the discussions on the review of the Capital Requirements Directives were still ongoing, the European Commission also started exploring the reform of the governance of all listed companies. In April 2011, it published the consultation on the EU corporate governance framework (European Commission 2011a). This document was principally focused on three possible areas of intervention: (a) the structure and functioning of boards of directors; (b) the role of shareholders; and (c) the effectiveness of the 'comply or explain' principle.

With regard to the 'comply or explain' principle, the Commission asked if the 'explain' part needed to be reinforced, and if it was desirable to give monitoring authorities the power to verify if the information published was sufficiently informative and comprehensive. The proposals related to boards were more articulate. They concerned the structure of this corporate body, and covered issues such as enhancement of board diversity, limitations on multiple mandates, and mandatory separation of the functions and duties of the chairpersons of boards from chief executive officers. Other tentative proposals related to risk management. Importantly, the problem of remuneration was also addressed: the possibility of mandating disclosure of individual directors' remuneration and, more in general, of the remuneration policies of companies, was evaluated, and the possibility of putting these policies to a binding vote of the shareholders was also explored (European Commission 2011a: 9).

The proposals related to the role of shareholders focused on the problem of short-termism, and they can be divided among those (a) directed to institutional investors, asset managers and proxy advisors; (b) aimed at facilitating the identification of shareholders; and concerning enhancement of the protection of minority shareholders by allowing them to better represent their interests (for example, by appointing some members of boards) or by introducing a European framework on related-party transactions (European Commission 2011a: 11).

The reactions of the stakeholders to the strategies proposed by the Commission were generally not positive (compare European Commission 2011b). In particular, it was felt that many of the solutions that were under discussion for dealing with the governance problems of financial institutions were simply replicated for listed companies while the problems of the latter type of companies were different from the former (Davies *et al.* 2011: 4).

With regard to remuneration policies, most respondents supported an enhancement of disclosure obligations (European Commission 2011b:

10). Requiring a shareholder vote on remuneration policies was seen less favourably and, in any case, the majority of the participants in the consultation preferred an advisory vote (*ibid.*). The respondents also supported improving the rules on shareholder identification and favoured mutual recognition among Member States of national identification systems (European Commission 2011b: 15). Also, the idea of requiring proxy advisors to be more transparent received a positive reaction (European Commission 2011b: 14).

The part of the consultation that was not warmly received was that devoted to minority shareholders. The proposals on appointment of directors representing minority shareholders and on related-party transactions were criticized. It was believed that the safeguards already in place were sufficient, and that any further action could result in a potential increase in the distorted and abusive use of these tools of corporate governance (European Commission 2011b: 16).

(b)   Action Plan on European company law and corporate governance 2012

The next step in the debate on the governance of listed companies took place in 2012 when the Commission published the new Action Plan on European company law and corporate governance (European Commission 2012). It evoked many of the corporate governance strategies that were discussed in the consultation on the EU corporate governance framework. More precisely, the Action Plan envisaged the possibility of amending the Shareholder Rights Directive (Directive 2007/36/EC)[15] and introducing legislation aimed at (a) disclosing the voting and engagement policies and voting records of institutional investors; (b) improving transparency on remuneration policies for directors; (c) recognizing shareholders' right to vote on remuneration policies; and (d) improving shareholders' control over related-party transactions (European Commission 2012: 8). In another part, the Action Plan also mentioned a planned initiative to improve shareholder identification (European Commission 2012: 7). Interestingly, all measures regarding the structure of boards and risk management, to which the consultation on the EU corporate governance framework gave great attention, were only mentioned with respect to the initiative to strengthen disclosure requirements on board diversity and risk management (European Commission 2012: 6).

---

[15]   European Parliament and Council Directive 2007/36/EC of 11 July 2007 on the exercise of certain rights of shareholders in listed companies [2007] OJ L184/17.

(c) 2014 proposal to revise the Shareholder Rights Directive

The efforts to improve the governance of listed companies finally materialized in 2014. On 9 April, only a few weeks before the election of the new European Parliament and a few months before the end of his mandate, Commissioner Barnier, among several initiatives in the domain of company law and corporate governance, presented a proposal to revise the Shareholder Rights Directive (European Commission 2014a). The Commission highlighted five issues that needed action: (a) the insufficient engagement of institutional investors and asset managers; (b) the inadequate transparency of proxy advisors; (c) the difficult and costly exercise of investor rights; (d) the insufficient links between pay and performance of directors; and (e) the lack of shareholder oversight of related-party transactions. All these problems were articulated in detail in the explanatory memorandum (European Commission 2014a) and the impact assessment (European Commission 2014b) accompanying the proposal to amend the Shareholder Rights Directive.

The problem of insufficient engagement of institutional investors and asset managers has been addressed by requiring them to develop a policy on shareholder engagement to be disclosed to the public. In case institutional investors and asset managers decide not to develop such a policy or to disclose it, they must provide a reasoned explanation for the decision (European Commission 2014a, art. 1, amending Directive 2007/36/EC by inserting arts 3f(3) and (4)). The policy should also include strategies to manage actual and potential conflicts of interest with regard to shareholder engagement (European Commission 2014a, amending Directive 2007/36/EC by inserting art. 3f(2)). More generally, it has also been proposed to strengthen the disclosure obligations imposed on institutional investors and asset managers with regard to their investment strategies in view of the medium-to-long-term performance of their assets (European Commission 2014a, amending Directive 2007/36/EC by inserting art. 3g).

With regard to the lack of transparency of proxy advisors, the proposal would require Member States to 'adopt and implement adequate measures to guarantee that their voting recommendations are accurate and reliable, based on a thorough analysis of all the information that is available to them' (European Commission 2014a, amending Directive 2007/36/EC by inserting art. 3i(1)). In addition, the Commission also proposed imposing on proxy advisors several obligations concerning disclosure of their activities (European Commission 2014a, amending Directive 2007/36/EC by inserting art. 3i(2)) and identification and disclosure of actual and potential conflicts of interest (European Commission 2014a, amending Directive 2007/36/EC by inserting art. 3i(3)).

The issue of the difficulties and costs investors face when attempting to exercise the rights flowing from their securities is addressed with an elaborate set of provisions. If adopted, the proposal would grant to companies the right to identify shareholders, eventually also through the chain of intermediaries, but exclusively for the purpose of facilitating the exercise of shareholder rights (European Commission 2014a, amending Directive 2007/36/EC by inserting art. 3a). Intermediaries would also be required to facilitate the exercise of shareholder rights, including the right to take part and vote in general meetings (European Commission 2014a, amending Directive 2007/36/EC by inserting art. 3c). In addition, if companies decide not to directly communicate with shareholders, and if the information is necessary to exercise a right of the shareholders or the information is directed to all shareholders of a specific class, it must be transmitted without undue delay by the intermediaries to the shareholders. Moreover, the Commission also proposes to require intermediaries to transmit information that is received from the shareholders and addressed to companies concerning the exercise of rights flowing from the shares (European Commission 2014a, amending Directive 2007/36/EC by inserting art. 3b).

The most debated measures proposed by the Commission in the revision of the Shareholder Rights Directive concern remuneration policy and related-party transactions. With regard to the first area of intervention, the proposed modifications would require Member States to oblige companies to prepare a report providing a detailed 'overview of the remuneration, including all benefits in whatever form, granted to individual directors … in the last financial year' (European Commission 2014a, amending Directive 2007/36/EC by inserting art. 9b(1)).

Another provision of the draft Directive would grant shareholders the right to vote on the remuneration policy of directors (European Commission 2014a, amending Directive 2007/36/EC by inserting art. 9a(1)) and on the remuneration report mentioned above (European Commission 2014a, amending Directive 2007/36/EC by inserting art. 9b(3)). More specifically, the policy must indicate the relative proportion of the fixed and variable parts of the remuneration and provide detailed indications on the structure of variable remuneration. In addition, the remuneration policy must illustrate how it contributes to the long-term interest and sustainability of the company. Unless exceptional circumstances occur, it must also describe 'the ratio between the average remuneration of directors and the average remuneration of full time [*sic*] employees of the company other than directors', and explain why the ratio is considered appropriate (European Commission 2014a, amending Directive 2007/ 36/EC by inserting art. 9a(3)).

While the shareholder vote on the remuneration report would take place every year at the annual general meeting, the vote on the remuneration policy would take place at least every three years. The vote on the remuneration policy would be binding and companies could pay remuneration to their directors only in accordance with an approved policy (European Commission 2014a, amending Directive 2007/36/EC by inserting art. 9a(1)). In contrast, the consequence of a vote against the approval of the remuneration report would simply be an obligation for the company to explain in the following remuneration report whether or not that vote of the shareholders had been taken into account (European Commission 2014a, amending Directive 2007/36/EC by inserting art. 9b(3)).

Provisions on related-party transactions, with several exemptions and qualifications, would require companies to publicly announce transactions with related parties that, at the moment of their conclusion, represent more than 1 per cent of companies' assets. This announcement would also be accompanied by 'a report from an independent third party assessing whether or not [the transaction] is on market terms and confirming that [it] is fair and reasonable from the perspective of the shareholders' (European Commission 2014a, amending Directive 2007/36/EC by inserting art. 9c(1)). In addition, transactions representing more than 5 per cent of the company's assets, or which could have a significant impact on profits or on turnover, would be subject to prior approval by the general meeting (European Commission 2014a, amending Directive 2007/36/EC by inserting art. 9c(2)).

In addition to the measures detailed above, the European Commission has also undertaken other initiatives to address the corporate governance problems highlighted by the Financial Crisis. For example, the issues about board structure were addressed in another initiative of the Commission, which focused only on disclosure (European Commission 2013, and now Directive 2014/95/EU).[16] Similarly, the review of the 'comply or explain' approach is not mentioned in the Shareholder Rights Directive. As indicated in the 2012 Action Plan, the Commission adopted a softer approach and published only a non-binding Recommendation.

---

[16] European Parliament and Council Directive 2014/95/EU of 22 October 2014 amending Directive 2013/34/EU as regards disclosure of non-financial and diversity information by certain large undertakings and groups [2014] OJ L330/1.

3.3 SHAREHOLDER RIGHTS DIRECTIVE: FIRST REACTIONS TO THE PROPOSALS

The interventions addressed by the proposed revision of the Shareholder Rights Directive have already given rise to interesting reactions. Until now, the debate has principally focused on the soundness of the strategies adopted by the Commission. In general, legal commentators have showed scepticism about the measures proposed.

3.3.1 Institutional Investors and Asset Managers

Starting with the proposals concerning the engagement of institutional investors and asset managers, improving the disclosure of the policies on shareholder engagement was supported by commentators even before the presentation of the 2012 Action Plan (Antunes *et al.* 2013: 311). However, since the publication of the proposed revision of the Share-holder Rights Directive, it has been highlighted that measures similar to those recommended by the Commission already existed in the United States and they failed to achieve their intended goals. This suggests it would be difficult to expect that European initiatives would perform better than their US counterparts (Rock 2015: 12).

Scholars have argued that it would be too burdensome to require institutional investors and asset managers to disclose voting policies with regard to each company in which they hold shares (Böckli *et al.* 2015: 3). It has been commented that the initiative on engagement policies should take the form of a Recommendation, rather than a Directive (Böckli *et al.* 2015: 4). Other criticisms have concerned (a) the failure to recognize the presence of blockholders in the governance of European companies; (b) the dubious link between an increase in activism and the improvement of corporate governance; (c) the risk of undermining existing incentives to engage shareholders in activism; and (d) the difficulties of relying on a time horizon engagement criterion as a metric of good or bad corporate governance (Strand 2015b: 36).

3.3.2 Proxy Advisors

With regard to the measures addressed to proxy advisors, it was suggested in the consultation on the EU corporate governance framework that proxy advisors' activities required 'coordinating efforts at the EU and national level in such areas as disclosure of conflicts of interest, information on voting policies and individual follow up in case of contested meetings' (Davies *et al.* 2011: 18). However, a few months before the publication of the 2012 Action Plan, other company law experts were more cautious about taking any action in this domain. They recommended that the Commission avoid intervening in this field, collect more data, and wait for the outcome of the discussions concerning the self-regulation of this industry, before deciding if additional actions were really needed (Antunes *et al.* 2013: 314).

After the publication of the proposal to revise the Shareholder Rights Directive, a cautious approach has also been supported by the same experts who, in the consultation on European corporate governance framework, advocated additional efforts at the European and national level. In fact, this group of experts concluded that 'it would be preferable to further continue to address this matter in accordance merely with industry codes of conduct, as has been proposed by ESMA after extensive consultation' (Böckli *et al.* 2015: 5). Concerns about the lack of reliable data and information on how the proxy advisor industry operates in the EU has also been voiced by other scholars (Strand 2015b: 50), who have emphasized that, in light of the little information available, it is difficult to conclude that proxy advisors offering voting recommendations are plagued by dangerous short-termism (*ibid.*). In this context, it has been highlighted that the alleged existence of problems deriving from the potential or actual conflicts of interest of proxy advisors has found little support in the literature (Strand 2015b: 51).

3.3.3 Identification of Shareholders

The initiatives concerning the identification of shareholders are considered to be an important aspect of the strategies available to improve the governance of companies. For example, the Report by the Reflection Group argued that facilitating the vote of shareholders in general meetings should be considered a priority for the advancement of European company law (Antunes *et al.* 2011: 50). Another group of company law experts, in the context of the consultation on the EU corporate governance framework, recommended that shareholders should be able 'to take part in the general meeting and cast their votes independently from any intervention of the securities depositary system' (Davies *et al.* 2011: 19). In addition, support for measures to improve the communication between companies and shareholders was further reiterated by the members of the Reflection Group at the time of the consultation on the 2012 Action Plan (see Antunes *et al.* 2013: 310), who concluded that '[a]lthough the nature of the initiative is yet unknown, we strongly support the principle that a company should be able to identify its shareholders').

Taking into account their widespread favour, the measures presented by the Commission ought to have been received warmly by scholars and experts. However, the first reactions have not been enthusiastic. Remarkably, an important group of scholars that previously considered important to take action in this field has now concluded that the initiatives proposed by the Commission are only a 'suboptimal mechanism to facilitate shareholder voting' (Böckli *et al.* 2015: 6).

The criticisms of the draft Directive are many: first, the possible advantages deriving from the facilitation of the exercise of shareholder rights must be confronted with the possibility – which is likely in Europe – that a company has a concentrated ownership. In these situations, it has been argued that it would be difficult to expect an improvement in the activism of small shareholders, even if the exercise of their rights was to be made easier (Böckli *et al.* 2015: 7; Strand 2015a: 41). A second issue is the costs associated with shareholder identification. This could be particularly relevant if measured against the potential advantages from such identification, which might often be limited (Böckli *et al.* 2015: 7, arguing that '[a] full identification of all shareholders as is proposed would result in considerable costs'; compare Strand 2015b: 54). A third problem is the possibility that the cumbersome identification process might not result in an actual identification of some important shareholders, who could deliberately decide to hide their identity behind legal structures or other legal arrangements (Böckli *et al.* 2015: 8), or who could simply be inaccurately identified by the intermediaries (Strand 2015b: 55).

Finally, the fact that 'the rights to be established under the Directive are vested in companies, not their shareholders' (Böckli *et al.* 2015: 6) could also result in having companies that 'use the shareholder identification information to make engagement more, not less, difficult' (*ibid.*), and to limit the possibility of shareholders having access to their rights when they need them (Böckli *et al.* 2015: 7). From this perspective, it must also be highlighted that the Directive does not give the shareholders the ability to identify each other, which could be crucial when facilitating the formation of coalitions among shareholders (Strand 2015b: 56).

3.3.4 Insufficient Link between Pay and Performance of Directors

As mentioned above, since the beginning of the debate on corporate governance following the Financial Crisis, the problems about the insufficient link between pay and performance had been at the centre of discussions. Both the CRD III and the CRD IV/CRR devoted attention to these issues. With regard to listed companies, several points were already raised at the time of the consultation on the EU corporate governance framework. More precisely, at that time it was recognized that strengthening the disclosure of remuneration policies could improve corporate governance in companies with both dispersed and concentrated ownership (Davies *et al.* 2011: 10). Also, the introduction of a remuneration report was considered to be a promising strategy to address these issues (Davies *et al.* 2011: 11).

However, even at this early stage, there were criticisms about the virtues of the approval of remuneration policies and remuneration reports by general meetings (Davies *et al.* 2011: 12). Doubts on the benefits of introducing a 'say on pay' at the European level were also expressed by the members of the Reflection Group on the Future of EU Company Law in their contribution to the consultation that preceded the 2012 Action Plan. Even if the possibility of requiring a binding shareholder vote on remuneration policies was not ruled out, these experts recommended that the Commission gather additional information on this matter before taking action (Antunes *et al.* 2013: 312).

After the publication of the Commission's proposal, the problem of the mandatory and binding nature of the vote of the general meeting on the remuneration policy remained a sensitive issue (in addition, the disclosures in the remuneration report received some criticism; see Johnston and Morrow 2014: 8). For example, it was said that the Commission, in ruling out more interventionist approaches to pay, may be relying on widespread, but misguided, economic assumptions (Johnston and Morrow 2014: 9).

It has also been argued that the mandatory and binding 'say on pay' rules proposed by the Commission simply rely on unproven assumptions (Strand 2015b: 41). In particular, it has been questioned whether there is a problem with executive compensation and whether this problem can be solved by granting to shareholders the right to vote on remuneration policies (see Strand 2015b: 42, for further details on the literature supporting these claims). In addition, it has also been suggested that other aspects of remuneration policies, such as the structure of the compensation, are addressed only marginally by the new draft Directive, while these aspects could probably play a more important role in improving the governance of companies (Strand 2015b: 45).

3.3.5   Related-Party Transactions

To conclude this review of the reactions to the revision of the Share-holder Rights Directive, it is necessary to analyse the rules on related-party transactions. Interestingly, already in the context of the consultation on the EU corporate governance framework, it was recognized that a problem existed in this area and it was suggested that the Commission adopt a Recommendation to deal with this issue (Davies *et al.* 2011: 21).

Similarly, the members of the Reflection Group showed interest in the adoption of an initiative in this area in their contribution to the consult-ation on the 2012 Action Plan. The Reflection Group discussed the possibility of adopting either substantive requirements or disclosure requirements with regard to related-party transactions (Antunes *et al.* 2013: 312). However, it also maintained a cautious approach and suggested a careful assessment of the matter (Antunes *et al.* 2013: 313).

After the publication of the draft Directive, Luca Enriques published an interesting analysis of the proposed rules on related-party transactions (Enriques 2015). He concluded that, to ensure their effectiveness, these rules should rely on a good enforcement system (Enriques 2015: 32). From this perspective, Therese Strand examined the problem of the enforcement of related-party transactions in the proposal for the revision of the Shareholder Rights Directive. She concluded that the lack of effective rules for enforcement should be considered an important loophole in the Commission's initiative (Strand 2015b: 49).

Furthermore, Luca Enriques also argued that the Commission's pro-posal presents several problems: being under-inclusive, providing weak safeguards, and being inflexible. With regard to the first point, he argued that the proposed quantitative requirements are not particularly reliable and potentially subject to manipulation (Enriques 2015: 27; a concern also shared by Strand 2015b: 47). In addition, the scope of the Directive seems to be limited only to transactions with related parties and not to transactions in which related parties might have an interest (Enriques 2015: 28). Finally, it also seems that the proposed legislation would not be applicable to transactions concluded by the subsidiaries of companies subject to the rules on related-party transactions (*ibid.*).

The criticisms about the rules to regulate related-party transactions also concern the poorly outlined content of the fairness opinion and the disclosure obligations imposed on companies (Enriques 2015: 29). In addition, the approval of the general meeting could only be a weak protection, as it is uncertain to what extent shareholders can be disinter-ested and effective in evaluating these transactions (Enriques 2015: 30; compare Strand 2015a: 34). Moreover, the approval of the transactions comes at the end of a negotiation process, the details of which Member States are free to leave to interested parties (Enriques 2015: 30), and affiliates of the related party are not expressly prevented from voting in favour of the transaction (*ibid.*).

Finally, the rules proposed by the Commission are inflexible because they do not recognize the possibility of taking advantage of alternative arrangements that could exist or be used in Member States to deal with the problems raised by related-party transactions (*ibid.*). In addition, the exemption regime does not appear to be sufficiently flexible (*ibid.*; see also Strand 2015a: 33, who argues that the exemption regime is too narrow).

3.4 REVISING THE SHAREHOLDER RIGHTS DIRECTIVE: A CRITICAL APPRAISAL

3.4.1 Are the Commission Proposals a Serious Effort?

In light of the reactions to the proposals for revising the Shareholder Rights Directive, it is reasonable to question whether these reforms are sufficiently fine-tuned and well-suited to reach their intended goal, which is improving the corporate governance of European listed companies. As pointed out above, the proposed measures have been criticized on several grounds. Criticisms include that they (a) would be burdensome for institutional investors and asset managers; (b) would be costly for companies; (c) do not take into account the specific features of the European financial markets; (d) are based on wrong theoretical assumptions; (e) are not founded on reliable empirical evidence; (f) fail to design rules that could achieve the specific goals set in the Directive; (g) support rules that, in practice, could work against their intended goals; (h) are dangerous for the continuance of healthy governance practices that currently exist; (i) are too reliant on inflexible mandatory regulation; (j) favour suboptimal regulatory strategies; (k) are overreaching; and (l) are under-inclusive.

Certainly, the evaluations are subject to qualifications and should be understood in the specific context of each measure that has been proposed by the Commission. However, the negative reactions show the limits of the approach followed by the European institutions in dealing with the corporate governance problems raised by the Financial Crisis. In addition to the predictable controversies such an important piece of legislation could give rise to – because of political reasons, or simply for its legislative drafting technique – it is worth noting that many of the criticisms of the proposed revisions of the Shareholder Rights Directive rely on empirical evidence which, quite often, does not support the solutions presented by the Commission.

In a paper published after the enactment of the Sarbanes-Oxley Act of 2002,[17] Roberta Romano (2004) famously argued against the adoption of legislation that was not supported by solid empirical evidence. More precisely, she argued that 'finance and accounting literature provides a metric for evaluating the effectiveness of the legislation, by facilitating identification of whether specific pieces of the legislation can be most accurately characterized as efficacious reforms or as quack corporate governance' (Romano 2004: 8). Since then, many other scholars have examined legislation applying a similar criterion, and labelled as 'quack corporate governance' any initiative that is not validated by empirical evidence (see, for example, Enriques and Zetzsche 2015).

It is also worth noting that the comments and suggestions of Romano (2004) were directed to European institutions and Member States that, at that time, were considering the possibility of adopting legislation in response to the Enron-era European financial scandals such as Parmalat. Romano (2004: 12) observed:

> [I]n reacting to Parmalat's collapse the European Commission appears to be drawing a mistaken inference from the US experience, and ... the member states, and European Parliament members, should press the Commission to proceed with great care on its proposed initiatives so as to avoid the US Congress's public policy blunder.

In recent years the 'quack corporate governance' narrative has gained some momentum also in the EU, principally as a reaction to the initiatives undertaken in the aftermath of the Financial Crisis. Not surprisingly, validation of legislation in light of the empirical evidence has become a key aspect of the European corporate governance debate (see, for example, Paredes 2010). For example, it has been questioned whether the design of a single supervisory mechanism could be considered a quack initiative (Tröger 2014). Also the rules on remuneration policy mandated by CRD III and CRD IV/CRR have been challenged in light of empirical evidence (Ferrarini 2015). Finally, the rules in CRD IV/CRR on board composition, functioning and members' liability have been criticized as examples of quack corporate governance (Enriques and Zetzsche 2015).

---

[17]   Sarbanes-Oxley Act of 2002, Pub. L107–204, 116 Stat. 745.

Many of the solutions elaborated by the European Commission in the revision of the Shareholder Rights Directive could be – and actually have been – challenged for their empirical soundness. Therefore, this initiative could give more than one reason to support the rhetoric of the quack corporate governance enthusiasts. To corroborate this conclusion, further arguments can be found in Commissioner Barnier's words, who, in presenting the proposal, stated:

> The last years have shown time and time again how short-termism damages European companies and the economy. Sound corporate governance can help to change that. Today's proposals will encourage shareholders to engage more with the companies they invest in, and to take a longer-term perspective of their investment. To do that, they need to have the rights to exercise proper control over management, including with a binding 'say on pay'. (European Commission 2014c)

In light of these remarks, even without being overly confident about the virtues of empirical evidence, the suspicion that at least some of the measures proposed have been adopted simply as a reaction to the Financial Crisis, without carefully evaluating their consequences and implications, is legitimate.[18] A cursory analysis of the criticisms of the Commission's initiatives confirms this suspicion without even considering the comments concerning the lack of empirical evidence. In fact, commentators have also questioned the desirability of the proposed measures based on their technical formulation as well as practical consequences. This can probably also be interpreted as another sign of the perceived need for the European Commission to take action in the domain of corporate governance.

3.4.2 Will the Revision of the Shareholder Rights Directive be Trivial?

(a) Intrinsic weaknesses in European company law
Regardless of whether the solutions proposed in the revision of the Shareholder Rights Directive are considered questionable and/or not well-grounded in empirical evidence, it is still unclear if they will have a significant impact on the corporate governance of European companies. In fact, this initiative is, just as the original Shareholder Rights Directive was, a measure aimed at promoting the freedom of establishment. Therefore, it should be considered, as with any other piece of European

---

[18]   Romano 2004: 2 argued that quack corporate governance measures can be characterized as being 'recycled ideas advocated for quite some time by corporate governance entrepreneurs'.

legislation addressed to listed companies, subject to the triviality criticisms that have been advanced towards European company law more broadly (Enriques 2006). From this perspective, the possibility that the Directive will not be strongly enforced against Member States is plausible (Enriques 2006: 12). This may also lead to domestic interpretations by Member States that could be difficult to reconcile with those of other national jurisdictions or with the intended goals of the European legislation (Enriques 2006: 16). Moreover, the very nature of the Directive itself, which is addressed to Member States and not to individuals, works against the effectiveness of the initiative: if a Member State decides not to faithfully implement a Directive and the Commission does not intervene to discipline it (compare Enriques 2006: 16), the chances that an incorrect implementation will be challenged are limited.

In addition, some problems that may result in the triviality of European company law, such as recourse to optional rules and unimportant provisions, or the adoption of rules that can easily be avoided, also partially affect this proposal (Enriques 2006; 23). As mentioned before, it has been argued that the rules on the identification of shareholders may have only limited effect and the rules on related-party transactions could be subject to manipulation.

(b) European Council debate

It should be highlighted that in the discussions currently taking place at the European Council and the European Parliament, the initial Commission proposal is undergoing significant changes. For example, the text currently under discussion at the Council (Council of the European Union 2015a) would allow Member States to limit the scope of shareholder identification to those holding more than 0.5 per cent shares or voting rights. In addition, the scope of the disclosure obligation imposed on proxy advisors has been narrowed.

With regard to remuneration policies, even if the vote of the general meeting is binding, Member States may still make this vote advisory in nature, with a condition that in the event of a negative vote, a revised policy must be submitted to a vote at the next general meeting. For the advisory vote on the remuneration report, for companies with an average market capitalization of less than 200 million euros, Member States may provide that, as an alternative to the vote, the remuneration report of the last financial year is submitted for discussion in the annual general meeting as a separate agenda item.

With regard to related-party transactions, the original quantitative thresholds of 1 per cent and 5 per cent of assets have disappeared and been replaced by a materiality test, which remains quantitative in nature;

however, its precise form will be determined by each Member State. Moreover, Member States will be allowed to grant the right to approve a related-party transaction not necessarily to the general meeting, but to the company's administrative or supervisory body. Finally, the exemptions have been extended and clarified.

(c) Debate at the European Parliament

The version of the Directive under discussion at the European Parliament at the time of writing[19] reconsiders some important aspects of the Commission's initial proposal.[20] With regard to the rules on related-party transactions, the Parliament's new text abandons the asset thresholds originally provided in the draft Directive. In addition, the European Parliament's version would allow Member States to give the power to approve material transactions not only to the general meeting, but also to the administrative or supervisory body of the company.

The European Parliament has also introduced new parts into the proposal that, at the time of writing, are hotly debated at the political level. Proposed amendments to Directive 2013/34/EU and Directive 2004/109/EC will introduce a country-by-country tax-reporting requirement for large undertakings and public-interest entities (see Council of the European Union 2015b: 70).[21] Even though not directly related to the revision of the Shareholder Rights Directive, the debate on these other amendments is delaying the advancement of the proposal, which remains, at the time of writing, subject to a trilogue (that is, a three-party

---

[19] At the time of writing, the European Parliament had not taken a final decision on the Commission's proposal. Several amendments had already been agreed to at a plenary session held in July 2015. For more details on the debate at the European Parliament, see Council of the European Union 2015b.

[20] Council of the European Union 2015c provides a comparison of the original version of the Commission's proposed Directive and the versions under discussion at the European Council and at the European Parliament.

[21] Interestingly, some other additions to the Commission's initial proposal have also been discussed. More precisely, reference is made to the JURI Committee's proposed introduction of mechanisms to support long-term shareholding, such as (a) additional voting rights; (b) tax incentives; (c) loyalty dividends; and (d) loyalty shares, and to enhance disclosure on tax payments (see European Parliament 2015: 33 and 53). It is unlikely, however, that these additions will find their way into the final text, because these amendments were not among those adopted by the plenary session of the European Parliament in July 2015.

negotiation) among the European Commission, the European Council and the European Parliament.[22]

Despite the European Parliament's efforts to amend the Commission's proposal, it remains uncertain if the proposal for revision of the Shareholder Rights Directive will ultimately include such amendments. In fact, the impact assessment of the Commission's recent proposal on country-by-country reporting, published in April 2016, clearly stated that it is not the initiative on the revision of the Shareholder Rights Directive, but rather 'specific legislation [that] is the best instrument to achieve the desired goal' (see European Commission 2016: 53 n. 135). Obviously, the impact assessment only reflects the position of the Commission and not that of the European Parliament. However, it seems that the debate on country-by-country reporting is taking a different path from the revision of the Shareholder Rights Directive.

(d)   Risks of making the proposal of the Commission more trivial

Examining the two preliminary documents (the one discussed at the European Council and the other at the European Parliament), both of which are tentative compromises subject to further discussions, it is interesting that many of the original solutions concerning the revision of the Shareholder Rights Directive have been qualified and, in many cases, diluted. The role of the Member States has been significantly enhanced while several parts of the Commission's initial proposal have either been made optional or reformulated to accommodate the needs and specificities of each country. The approach taken by both bodies cannot be faulted for its pragmatism or for accommodating practices that already exist in the Member States; but it will certainly not lead to a uniform, coherent and effective application of European law. More importantly, it is doubtful if it will enhance existing corporate governance practices.

---

[22]   The state of affairs, as of 25 January 2016, was described in a 'Reply' to a 'Question for written answer' that was presented by a Member of the European Parliament (European Parliament 2016). According to the reply, 'the Parliament's proposed amendments with regard to public country-by-country reporting (CBCR) by economic operators were not part of the Commission's proposal and are also outside the scope of [the Shareholder Rights Directive] proposal. Thus, they are not covered by the Commission's impact assessment. The Commission is therefore aiming to present an impact assessment on CBCR in the first quarter of 2016. At the first trilogue, held on 27 October [2015] in Strasbourg, the parties agreed to wait for the results of the Commission's impact assessment on country-by-country disclosure before starting negotiations on this question, while pursuing negotiations on all other parts of the proposal with a view to achieving a positive result as soon as possible'.

The comments are not to say that the revision of the Shareholder Rights Directive – if and to the extent enacted – will have no tangible effects (compare Enriques 2006: 44). It is just far more likely that the ultimate effects of the final version of the adopted text, and the means employed to achieve them, may no longer be consistent with the original proposal. A paradigmatic example of this likely outcome can already be found in the direction the debate on remuneration policies took at the Council: Commissioner Barnier advocated the introduction of a binding shareholder 'say on pay' in order to exercise proper shareholder control over managers, but the Council chose a more cautious approach. Even though some have argued that the Commission's original approach was wrong or quack corporate governance and needed to be modified, it might have been better for the Council or the Parliament to simply reject the Commission's proposal in its entirety, rather than trying to make it palatable by inserting accommodating solutions that are likely to neutralize its effectiveness.

If compared with the original proposal of the Commission, or with the initiatives discussed at the time of the consultation on the corporate governance framework, the measures currently under discussion have a more limited scope and are less invasive. Someone could praise this approach for being able to limit the possible negative consequences that could derive from adopting legislation that is not based on reliable empirical evidence. In the end, a somewhat similar argument was recently advanced to deal with the supposedly quack corporate governance rules concerning the structure of the board of directors of the CRD IV/CRR (Enriques and Zetzsche 2015: specifically 240).

However, that approach, by trying to limit the possible negative consequences of allegedly flawed proposals, could also have implications beyond corporate governance reforms and may further corroborate the broader impression that the relevance of European company law is limited. From this perspective, the likely quackish nature of some of the corporate governance strategies in the texts under discussion before the European Council and the European Parliament could simply result in some practical difficulties, principally deriving from the necessity of getting acquainted with the new rules, and no authentic improvement of the European corporate governance framework.

Perhaps an exception could be made for a few unforeseen additions to the Commission's initial proposal currently under consideration at the European Parliament, though it remains to be seen whether those amendments also rely on empirical evidence, in the unlikely event that they ever find their way into the final text of the Directive (compare supra n. 21, and accompanying text). Yet, the Council's and Parliament's adopted tactic – to accommodate the criticisms of the strategies initially proposed by the Commission – risks further confirming the impression that European company law is, in substance, trivial.

3.5 CONCLUSION

This chapter examined the recent evolution of European legislative initiatives concerning corporate governance. After a review of the legislation recently enacted on this topic, I have examined the measures included in the proposal for a revision of the Shareholder Rights Directive published by the European Commission in 2014. This initiative comes at the end of a long debate on the governance of companies and financial institutions, and proposes an elaborate set of measures to improve the governance of European listed companies.

Examining the first academic reactions to this proposed legislation, I have emphasized how the measures presented by the Commission have been criticized on many grounds, mainly for not being supported by empirical evidence. In spite of these criticisms I have argued that the impact of the proposed measures, if finally adopted, will be modest. They will probably not achieve their intended shareholder empowerment goals, mainly because of the inherent weaknesses of European law in creating a single, coherent legal framework for the governance of European companies. In conclusion, considering the inherent weaknesses of European law, risks are apparent in attempting the proposed corrective legislation that is also not supported by empirical evidence.

REFERENCES

Antunes, J.E. *et al.* (2011), *Report of the Reflection Group on the Future of EU Company Law*, available at http://ssrn.com/abstract=1851654
— (2013), 'Response to the European Commission's Action Plan on Company Law and Corporate Governance' 10 *European Company and Financial Law Review* 304
Böckli, P. *et al.* (2015), 'Shareholder Engagement and Identification', available at http://ssrn.com/abstract=2568741
Council of the European Union (2015a), 'ST 7315 2015 INIT', available at http://data.consilium.europa.eu/doc/document/ST-7315-2015-INIT/en/pdf
— (2015b), 'ST 10626 2015 INIT', available at http://data.consilium.europa.eu/doc/document/ST-10626-2015-INIT/en/pdf
— (2015c) 'ST 11243 2015 INIT', available at http://data.consilium.europa.eu/doc/document/ST-11243-2015-INIT/en/pdf

Davies, P. *et al.* (2011), 'European Company Law Experts' Response to the European Commission's Green Paper "The EU Corporate Governance Framework"', available at http://ssrn.com/abstract=1912548

De Larosière Group (2009), *Report of the High-Level Group on Financial Supervision in the EU Chaired by Jacques de Larosière*, available at http://ec.europa.eu/internal_market/finances/docs/de_larosiere_report_en.pdf

Enriques, L. (2006), 'EC Company Law Directives and Regulations: How Trivial Are They?' 27 *University of Pennsylvania Journal of International Law* 939

— (2015), 'Related Party Transactions: Policy Options and Real-World Challenges (with a Critique of the European Commission Proposal)' 16 *European Business Organization Law Review* 1

Enriques, L. and D. Zetzsche (2015), 'Quack Corporate Governance, Round III? Bank Board Regulation under the New European Capital Requirement Directive' 16 *Theoretical Inquiries in Law* 211

European Commission (2009), *Driving European Recovery*, COM(2009)114 final, available at http://eur-lex.europa.eu/LexUriServ/LexUriServ.do?uri=COM:2009:0114:FIN:EN:PDF

— (2010a), *Report on the Application by Member States of the EU of the Commission 2009/385/EC Recommendation Complementing Recommendations 2004/913/EC and 2005/162/EC as regards the Regime for the Remuneration of Directors of Listed Companies*, COM(2010)285 final, available at http://ec.europa.eu/internal_market/company/docs/directors-remun/com-2010-285-2_en.pdf

— (2010b), *Report on the Application by Member States of the EU of the Commission 2009/384/EC Recommendation on Remuneration Policies in the Financial Services Sector,* COM(2010)286 final, available at http://ec.europa.eu/internal_market/company/docs/directors-remun/com-2010-286-2_en.pdf

— (2010c), *Green Paper, Corporate Governance in Financial Institutions and Remuneration Policies*, COM(2010)284 final, available at http://ec.europa.eu/internal_market/company/docs/modern/com2010_284_en.pdf

— (2010d), *Commission Staff Working Document, Corporate Governance in Financial Institutions: Lessons to be Drawn from the Current Financial Crisis, Best Practices; Accompanying Document to the Green Paper Corporate Governance in Financial Institutions and Remuneration Policies*, SEC(2010)669, available at http://ec.europa.eu/internal_market/company/docs/modern/sec2010_669_en.pdf

— (2010e), 'Feedback Statement: Summary of Responses to Commission Green Paper on Corporate Governance in Financial Institutions', available at http://ec.europa.eu/internal_market/consultations/docs/2010/governance/feedback_statement_en.pdf

— (2011a), *Green Paper, The EU Corporate Governance Framework*, COM(2011)164 final, available at http://ec.europa.eu/internal_market/company/docs/modern/com2011-164_en.pdf

— (2011b), 'Feedback Statement, Summary of Responses to the Commission Green Paper on the EU Corporate Governance Framework', available at http://ec.europa.eu/internal_market/company/docs/modern/20111115-feedback-statement_en.pdf

— (2012), *Action Plan: European Company Law and Corporate Governance – A Modern Legal Framework for More Engaged Shareholders and Sustainable Companies,* COM(2012)740 final, available at http://eur-lex.europa.eu/legal-content/EN/TXT/PDF/?uri=CELEX:52012DC0740&from=EN

— (2013), *Proposal for a Directive of the European Parliament and of the Council amending Council Directives 78/660/EEC and 83/349/EEC as regards Disclosure of Non-financial and Diversity Information by Certain Large Companies and Groups,* COM(2013)207 final, available at http://eur-lex.europa.eu/legal-content/EN/TXT/PDF/?uri=CELEX:52013PC0207&from=EN

— (2014a), *Proposal for a Directive of the European Parliament and of the Council amending Directive 2007/36/EC as regards the Encouragement of Long-term Shareholder Engagement and Directive 2013/34/EU as regards Certain Elements of the Corporate Governance Statement,* COM(2014)213 final, available at http://eur-lex.europa.eu/legal-content/EN/TXT/PDF/?uri=CELEX:52014PC0213&from=EN

— (2014b), *Commission Staff Working Document, Impact Assessment Accompanying the Document Proposal for a Directive of the European Parliament and of the Council amending Directive 2007/36/EC as regards the Encouragement of Long-term Shareholder Engagement and Directive 2013/34/EU as regards Certain Elements of the Corporate Governance Statement and Commission Recommendation on the Quality of Corporate Governance Reporting ('Comply or Explain'),* SWD(2014)127 final, available at http://eur-lex.europa.eu/legal-content/EN/TXT/PDF/?uri=CELEX:52014SC0127&from=ro

— (2014c), *Press Release, European Commission Proposes to Strengthen Shareholder Engagement and Introduce a "Say on Pay" for Europe's Largest Companies,* Press Release Database, http://europa.eu/rapid/press-release_IP-14-396_en.htm?locale=en

— (2016), *Commission Staff Working Document, Impact Assessment Assessing the Potential for Further Transparency on Income Tax Information Accompanying the Document Proposal for a Directive of the European Parliament and of the Council amending Directive 2013/34/EU as regards Disclosure of Income Tax Information by Certain Undertakings and Branches,* SWD(2016)117 final, available at http://eur-lex.europa.eu/legal-content/EN/TXT/PDF/?uri=CELEX:52016SC0117&qid=1465247341661&from=EN

European Parliament (2015), *Report on the Proposal for a Directive of the European Parliament and of the Council amending Directive 2007/36/EC as regards the Encouragement of Long-term Shareholder Engagement and Directive 2013/34/EU as regards Certain Elements of the Corporate Governance Statement (A8-0158/2015),* available at http://europarl.europa.eu/sides/getDoc.do?pubRef=-//EP//NONSGML+REPORT+A8-2015-0158+0+DOC+PDF+V0//EN

— (2016), 'Answer to a Written Question – Negotiation on the Shareholders Rights Directive – E-013384/2015', available at www.europarl.europa.eu/sides/getAllAnswers.do?reference=E-2015-013384&language=EN

Ferran, E. (2012), 'New Regulation of Remuneration in the Financial Sector in the EU' 9 *European Company and Financial Law Review* 1

Ferrarini, G. (2015), 'CRD IV and the Mandatory Structure of Bankers' Pay' European Corporate Governance Institute Law Working Paper No. 289/2015, available at http://ssrn.com/abstract=2593757

Johnston, A. and P. Morrow (2014), 'Commentary on the Shareholder Rights Directive' Nordic and European Company Law Working Paper No. 15–13, available at http://ssrn.com/abstract=2535274

Malberti, C. (2013), 'The Board of Directors after the Crisis: the role of risk management in the recent European perspectives of reform' in L. Nurit-Pontier and S. Rousseau (eds), *Risques, crise financière et gouvernance: Perspectives transatlantiques* (Les Éditions Thémis 2013) 141

Paredes, T.A. (2010), 'Corporate Governance and the New Financial Regulation: Complements or Substitutes?', available at www.ecgi.org/tcgd/2010/documents/paredes_tcgd2010.pdf

Rock, E.B. (2015), 'Institutional Investors in Corporate Governance in Oxford Handbook on Corporate Law and Governance' University of Pennsylvania Institute for Law and Economics Research Paper No. 14–37, available at http://ssrn.com/abstract=2512303

Romano, R. (2004), 'The Sarbanes-Oxley Act and the Making of Quack Corporate Governance' European Corporate Governance Institute Finance Working Paper 52/2004, available at http://ssrn.com/abstract=596101

Strand, T. (2015a), 'Re-Thinking Short-Termism and the Role of Patient Capital in Europe: Perspectives on the New Shareholder Rights Directive', available at http://ssrn.com/abstract=2516844

Strand, S. (2015b), 'Short-Termism in the European Union' 22 *Columbia Journal of European Law* 15

Tröger, T. (2014), 'The Single Supervisory Mechanism: Panacea or Quack Banking Regulation? Preliminary Assessment of the New Regime for the Prudential Supervision of Banks with ECB Involvement' 15 *European Business Organization Law Review* 449

PART II

Capital markets development and the law

4. Revisiting corporate control-enhancing mechanisms

Yu-Hsin Lin

4.1 INTRODUCTION

Since the early twentieth century, there has been controversy over disproportional ownership control through the use of corporate control-enhancing mechanisms. Control-enhancing mechanisms are control structures or contractual arrangements that enable certain shareholders or persons to exercise disproportional control rights in relation to their economic rights in corporations. Concerns over such structures arise from their deviation from the one-share/one-vote principle and their unequal treatment of shareholders. Commentators have argued that such structures facilitate extraction of private benefits of control by controllers at the expense of non-controlling shareholders (Easterbrook and Fischel 1991: 67–70). In contrast, supporters of control-enhancing mechanisms argue that such mechanisms should be allowed because of corporate autonomy and the monitoring benefits brought by ownership concentration (Bernitz 2004).

In the past century, regulators around the globe have not been able to come to a consensus as to whether and how to regulate control-enhancing mechanisms (Ringe 2010: 225). Since the initial public offering (IPO) of US internet giant Google in 2004, the dual-class share structure has become popular among high-tech companies listed in the United States. The popularity of dual-class share structures has extended to recent US-listed Chinese firms. Almost one-third of these companies have adopted a dual-class share structure or other control-enhancing mechanism – the percentage is much higher than that for local US-listed companies. They are mostly Internet companies: Baidu, Shanda Games, Soufun, NetQin, Youku, Renren and Qihoo 360. The most notable case was the IPO of Chinese e-commerce giant Alibaba in 2014. Instead of adopting a dual-class share structure, Alibaba adopted a scheme that is similar to priority shares, which grant their holders specific powers of

95

decision or veto rights in a company irrespective of the proportion of their equity stake. In particular, Alibaba granted a partnership, which consisted of founders and executives, exclusive rights to nominate a simple majority of board members.

Originally, Alibaba sought to list its shares on the Hong Kong Stock Exchange (HKSE). However, due to the one-share/one-vote policy, HKSE rejected its listing request. This was a big loss to the Hong Kong capital market. Since then, market participants in Hong Kong have raised concerns about the competitiveness of HKSE and the impact of a strict one-share/one-vote policy on future listings. In August 2014, HKSE issued a concept paper on 'weighted voting rights' and solicited the opinions of market participants (Hong Kong Stock Exchange 2014). In June 2015, HKSE released its conclusions and suggested allowing dual-class shares in specific industries with certain safeguards (Hong Kong Stock Exchange 2015). Even though HKSE only proposed limited exceptions to the one-share/one-vote principle, the Securities and Futures Commission still refused HKSE's suggestion. While we see regulators in Hong Kong hesitating to allow dual-class shares, scholars in the United States and Canada also warn of corporate governance concerns over dual-class share structures and even call for abandoning such voting regimes in light of the growing use of the dual-class share structure there (see, for example, Bebchuk 2014; Critchley 2015).

The Internet has brought drastic change to human life and new opportunities for business. In the information economy, 'talents' or human resources become a firm's most important capital. This chapter tries to provide explanations for the boom in control-enhancing mechanisms in the information economy from a human resource management perspective. This chapter argues that control-enhancing mechanisms allow a firm to be immune to short-termism. Thus, a firm is able to focus on innovation and long-term value creation. In addition, maintaining key founders' control rights also helps secure a firm's key human capital and sustain the distinct corporate culture which contributes positively to shareholder value. Therefore, control-enhancing mechanisms may well create firm value for shareholders in this respect.

However, control-enhancing mechanisms still suffer from serious agency costs and corporate governance concerns. In light of the come-back of control-enhancing mechanisms in recent IPO markets, it is time to revisit various aspects of control-enhancing mechanisms and reconsider previous regulatory policies. This chapter reviews existing academic and policy debates and proposes to empower minority shareholders of disproportionally-controlled firms to balance the superpower of controllers.

Section 4.2 explains the rise of control-enhancing mechanisms in the information economy from a human capital perspective. Section 4.3 reviews the practice of control-enhancing mechanisms in different countries. Section 4.4 revisits academic and policy debates, and reviews existing empirical studies regarding the effects of these mechanisms on shareholder value. In section 4.5, the chapter proposes a new conceptual and regulatory framework. Section 4.6 is the conclusion.

4.2 CONTROL-ENHANCING MECHANISMS AND HUMAN CAPITAL

4.2.1 Control-Enhancing Mechanisms in the Information Economy

Every company has its own distinctive characteristics, and shareholders should know what is best for their company. That 'one size does not fit all' has been accepted in many corporate governance regulations. The same principle could apply to the regulation of control-enhancing mechanisms. Control-enhancing mechanisms could be beneficial under certain situations and/or for certain companies. Oftentimes, founding families or entrepreneurs are not willing to give up control in exchange for external financing. If, however, control-enhancing mechanisms are not allowed, many start-up companies or family businesses may lose the chance to grow, and that could hamper national economic development.

In terms of industry distribution of disproportional control firms, studies have shown that media firms are more likely to adopt a dual-class share structure in the United States (DeAngelo and DeAngelo 1985; Gompers *et al.* 2010: 1065). In the past decade, the US capital market has seen an increasing number of information technology firms adopting dual-class share structures during IPOs. Facebook, Google, Zynga, LinkedIn and Groupon are among the most notable high-tech firms that have adopted these mechanisms. Some say that the motivation for adopting dual-class shares is that they are a way to fight short-termism, preserve the founder's vision, and pursue long-term shareholder value (Goshen and Hamdani 2016). In recent years, dual-class share structures have also become popular in the Canadian capital market (Hasselback and Shecter 2015). Although control-enhancing mechanisms are not supported by institutional investors and corporate governance institutes, investors seem to accept this extreme governance structure in modern business settings.

This chapter argues that firm-specific human capital has become a major source of competitive advantage in modern firms because of the growth in competition resulting from globalization and emergence of new business models in the information economy era. A resource-based view of the firm regards firm-specific human capital as an isolating mechanism that protects the firm's valuable and rare resources from imitation by rival firms, thus creating a sustained competitive advantage (Wright *et al.* 1994; Mahoney and Pandian 1992). In the information economy, a firm's value creation hinges on innovation and the quality of its human capital. Control-enhancing mechanisms allow a firm to be immune to the threat of takeovers and short-term capricious investors, and thus be able to focus on innovation and long-term value creation. In general, the success of these companies relies heavily on their founding teams, for example, Larry Page and Sergey Brin of Google, Mark Zuckerberg of Facebook, and Jack Ma of Alibaba (Lin and Mehaffy 2016: 460–4). Such an ownership structure can be understood as being a governance design that protects a company's key human capital.

Scholars have argued that without effective incentives and trust-building mechanisms, firms may not be able to accumulate firm-specific human capital and realize the economic rents from it (Cornell and Shapiro 1987: 67–70; Wang *et al.* 2009). Corporate governance mechanisms could serve as a medium to help employees build trust and confidence in firms, which would encourage employees to build firm-specific knowledge and skills. Therefore, it is important to take corporate governance systems into account when ascertaining the effect of human resources on firm performance.

Studies have shown that in highly innovative firms, there is often a high degree of information asymmetry between owners and managers with regard to efficient ways to create value from a firm's resources. Substantial managerial discretion is needed in making decisions about the deployment of innovative knowledge assets. Recent high-tech IPO firms in the United States have mostly been young firms with the founders as the managers. The same applies to Chinese firms recently listed in the US stock exchanges. Among the 34 US-listed Chinese firms that have adopted dual-class shares or other control-enhancing mechanisms, 22 firms are in the Internet industry, with a relatively young history. Traditional human resource literature, which focuses on managers, can apply to the founders of these young Internet or high-tech firms because these founders almost always participate in management. These founder-managers are exactly the firm-specific human capital that creates the competitive advantages of these innovative firms. Dual-class shares or other control-enhancing mechanisms are corporate governance measures that provide incentives to these founder-managers.

Empirical studies show that in highly innovative firms, monitoring-based corporate governance measures are less effective than incentive-based measures. In addition, providing proper incentives to managers can encourage them to accumulate firm-specific human resources, which is vital in contributing to the performance of innovative firms. Reliance on monitoring corporate governance measures, such as independent directors, would negatively impact the performance of highly-innovative firms (He and Wang 2009: 923–4, 932). That means a friendly board would be better for innovative firms than a monitoring board (Adams and Ferreira 2007: 218–19). In this sense, control-enhancing mechanisms that enable founder-managers to elect the majority of the board are beneficial to these innovative firms.

Recent legal scholarship advocates similar views. The prevailing law-and-economics view of concentrated ownership suggests that controlling shareholders retain control in order to extract private benefits of control at the expense of minority shareholders (Zingales 1995). Why would investors allow controllers to extract benefits at their expense? To answer this question, an alternative theory offers an explanation by positing that investors allow controlling shareholders to consume an optimal level of private benefits of control because it is a way of incentivizing controllers to efficiently monitor management. Furthermore, it is a way to compensate controllers for bearing the illiquidity costs of retaining a control block (Gilson 2006).

In contrast with the somewhat cynical view of prevailing law-and-economics accounts, recent legal scholarship tries to explain the prevalence of controlled companies around the world with reference to the benefits that controlling shareholders can bring. Similar to the human resource account, the idiosyncratic vision theory posits that entrepreneurs value corporate control because maintaining control allows them the freedom to pursue their vision for the firm. However, to pursue its vision, the firm has to have external finances to maintain growth. When deciding whether to fund a firm, external investors weigh the potential costs of giving control to the entrepreneurs versus the potential profit-sharing should the entrepreneur successfully pursue the idiosyncratic value (Goshen and Hamdani 2016: 577–9). In the case where investors give excess control to entrepreneurs and allow the use of control-enhancing mechanisms, investors are exposed to a higher chance of expropriation by controller entrepreneurs (Goshen and Hamdani 2016: 588–91). On the other hand, should entrepreneurs successfully pursue their idiosyncratic vision, investors are expected to share the profits. In the modern economy, technology and creativity are the driving forces for growth and profits. With the great advancements in technological development in recent decades, there is greater information asymmetry between entrepreneurs and investors with regard to the future of business enterprises. It seems that an entrepreneur's personal attributes are more important in the technology industry than in traditional industries. Therefore, investors in the technology industry are more willing to give out control and allow control-enhancing mechanisms.

4.2.2   Some Problems with Control-Enhancing Mechanisms

Drawing on existing literature, this chapter provides a new lens through which to evaluate and explain the growing popularity of control-enhancing mechanisms. Recent high-tech IPOs that have adopted dual-class share structures or other similar mechanisms may well find benefit in that these mechanisms help retain firm-specific human capital, which contributes to the competitive advantages of highly-innovative firms. However, the popularity of control-enhancing mechanisms among entrepreneurs and investors does not mean that there is no need to regulate control-enhancing mechanisms. Scholars in the United States and Canada have raised corporate governance concerns over recent IPOs involving mechanisms that create disproportional control. If there is no mechanism to constrain the extraction of private benefits by controllers, the potential benefits from firm-specific human capital may well be sacrificed by increased agency costs.

Recent 'going private', or delisting, of US-listed Chinese firms may be a good example. In the wake of higher valuations of tech stocks in the Chinese stock market, many US-listed Chinese firms plan to de-list in the United States and re-list in China. The 'going private' exercise of these firms typically involves buy-out offers from founders, controllers or private equity investors. Since 2015, 37 US-listed Chinese firms have received buy-out offers totalling US$38.9 billion, even larger than the total US IPO amount of US$30.3 billion in 2015 (Gu 2016). The trend is widespread and has a substantial impact on US capital markets. In a management buy-out 'going private' deal, founders have full control over the process, from offer timing and offer price to funding sources. In a firm that adopts a dual-class share structure, founders typically obtain more than half the voting power through multiple voting shares, which means they have the ability to dominate resolutions at shareholders' meetings.[1] Outside investors are consequently exposed to higher expropriation risks because founders can choose a time when the share price is low to minimize the cost of 'going private'. Even though dissenting shareholders typically receive legal protection for fair-value buyback, the market value of shares around the offer time, which is still in the control of founders, is certainly one of the benchmarks in deciding fair value of the shares for public listed companies.

We will take Qihoo 360, the largest 'going private' of a US-listed Chinese firm, as an example. Qihoo announced the receipt of a buy-out offer from its founders on 17 June 2015. On 18 December 2015, the board, acting upon the recommendation of an independent special committee, approved the proposed buy-out transaction and recommended that shareholders vote for the plan. Qihoo founders owned multiple voting rights shares with five votes per share and controlled more than 61 per cent of the voting power (Qihoo 360 2015). To complete the buy-out transactions, the company needed approval by an affirmative vote of shareholders representing at least two-thirds of the voting power of the shares present and voting. With 61 per cent of the votes at hand, the founders smoothly passed the resolution at the shareholders' meeting, with 69.3 per cent of votes present and 99.8 per cent of those present approving the merger.

As illustrated above, control-enhancing mechanisms help tech firms grow by granting firm-specific human resources, that is, the founders, disproportional control in realizing their idiosyncratic vision. Nevertheless, outside investors are exposed to higher risks of expropriation by controllers. With the growing use of control-enhancing mechanisms by the world's leading firms, it is time to revisit these mechanisms and their impact on investor protection. In the following sections, this chapter will review previous academic and policy debates over control-enhancing mechanisms around the world and propose a new conceptual and regulatory framework for moving forward.

4.3 CONTROL-ENHANCING MECHANISMS AROUND THE WORLD

The conventional governance literature on corporate ownership recognizes two types of ownership: dispersed and controlled. Since Berle and

---

[1] The founders generally have control over the resolution of shareholders' meetings unless the law or the corporate charter requires the majority of the disinterested shareholders' approval.

Means' (1932) piece on separation of ownership and control, most mainstream corporate scholarship has been built on the assumption of dispersed ownership of large public companies and devoted to understanding the agency problems that arise from managerial control (Berle and Means 1932). Perhaps the most well-known and ground-breaking piece is Jensen and Meckling's theorem on agency costs, which detailed the sources of agency costs in a dispersed ownership firm (Jensen and Meckling 1976). In the past two decades, research studies have shown that dispersed ownership is prevalent among US and UK public companies only. Public companies in the rest of the world are actually controlled either by families or the state (La Porta *et al.* 1999).

Control-enhancing mechanisms are voting or control structures that enable shareholders to enjoy voting rights in excess of their cash-flow rights. Commonly seen structures include multiple class shares, pyramids structures, cross-shareholding and voting agreements. Multiple class shares, in their most common form as 'dual class shares', offer voting structures where two share classes are issued, and one class carries a greater number of votes per share or exclusive director election rights. In pyramidal structures, a corporation owns a majority of the stock of another, which in turn holds the majority of the stock of another, and so on. The process can be repeated a number of times. Through pyramid structures, controlling shareholders can control firms through a chain of companies while owning only a minority of the shares. In cross-shareholding, a firm owns shares in another firm that belongs to the same business group. Finally, voting agreements are contracts among certain shareholders to vote in favour of director candidates or other specified corporate decisions proposed by certain shareholders.

The popularity of different control-enhancing mechanisms appears to be quite different across the continents. Faccio and Lang (2002) reported that 44 per cent of Western European firms were family controlled, and 37 per cent were widely held (Faccio and Lang 2002: 366). Public companies in Sweden, Switzerland, Italy and Finland mostly use dual-class shares to secure excess corporate control. Other mechanisms, such as pyramids and cross-shareholding, are less common in Western Europe. On the other hand, corporate control in East Asian countries is typically enhanced by pyramids and cross-shareholding (Claessens *et al.* 2000: 93; La Porta *et al.* 1999: 473). Dual-class shares are not common in East Asian countries because they are banned in some jurisdictions that mandate the one-share/one-vote rule. Pyramids are the most common form of control-enhancing mechanisms among public companies in Indonesia (66.9 per cent), Singapore (55 per cent), Taiwan (49 per cent) and Korea (42.9 per cent). On average, 38.7 per cent of East Asian public companies use pyramids to maintain excess control (Claessens *et al.* 2000: 92–3).

In the United States, the ownership of public companies is mostly dispersed. In 2012, 114 companies in the S&P Composite 1500 Index were controlled firms. In other words, only 7 per cent of S&P Composite 1500 Index companies were controlled firms (IRRC Institute and ISS 2012: 3). Pyramids and cross-shareholding are not common, and most US public companies do not belong to a business group (Kandel *et al.* 2013). The most popular control-enhancing mechanism that US public companies tend to use is dual-class shares. Studies on US public firms reveal that 70 per cent of the controlled firms feature an unequal voting structure. A comprehensive study of US public companies showed that, in total, about 6 per cent had dual or multiple class shares, representing around 8 per cent of the total market capitalization (Gompers *et al.* 2010). Although the number is not large, it has increased in recent years with the growing number of Chinese firms listed on US stock exchanges. As of May 2014, 102 Mainland Chinese companies were listed in the United States and, among them, almost one-third (30 out of 102) had dual-class share structures. This segment with dual-class structures represents 70 per cent of the market capitalization of all US-listed Chinese firms (Hong Kong Stock Exchange 2014).

4.4 THEORETICAL INQUIRIES AND POLICY REVIEW

4.4.1 Theoretical Inquiries

Scholars have raised different theoretical grounds for and against a strict one-share/one-vote rule. The debate has mainly revolved around the issues of economic incentives, agency costs, corporate autonomy, and freedom of contract. This section explores these issues.

(a) Economic incentives and agency cost

Control-enhancing mechanisms can, potentially, lead to greater agency costs and deter the market for corporate control (Easterbrook and Fischel 1991: 70–4). Easterbrook and Fischel argued that shareholders are the only group of corporate stakeholders who have appropriate incentives to make discretionary decisions because they are the residual claimants of corporate assets. They are the ones who bear the risks of bad decisions. As a result, voting is considered an act of risk-bearing (Easterbrook and Fischel 1991: 67–70).

Control-enhancing mechanisms undermine the incentive for managements to be diligent because managers will be entrenched from the
market for corporate control. Shareholders still bear the risks of bad
decisions. However, they do not get to vote in proportion to their
economic benefits (or losses). Those who bear a relatively small proportion of risk get to vote in excess of their economic benefits, usually 10
times more, given that one-share/10-votes is a common feature. Those
who receive excess control do not have the incentive to pursue the
welfare of those who bear the risks. Furthermore, control-enhancing
mechanisms insulate controllers from potential takeovers and entrench
them from being replaced, even if there are inefficiencies (Ringe 2010:
217). Thus, disproportional controllers not only have the incentive but
also the ability to extract private benefits at the expense of risk-bearers
(Bebchuk *et al.* 2000: 301–6). That is, firms with control-enhancing
mechanisms suffer from increased agency costs because of moral hazard
and the mismatch of proper incentives.

(b)   Corporate autonomy and freedom of contract
Counter-arguments for a mandatory one-share/one-vote policy are mostly
based on corporate autonomy and freedom of contract (OECD Steering
Group on Corporate Governance 2007: 6–7; Easterbrook and Fischel
1991: 66–7; Ringe 2010: 219). Shareholders are free to decide a
company's internal affairs because they are the ones who bear the risks in
the end. Companies should enjoy autonomy, and regulators should not
intervene unless a corporate decision causes harm to society as a whole,
assuming that the contracting mechanism works well in the IPO where
shareholders always take into account the governance rules when pricing
the shares. If such adoption would lead to increased agency cost and
lower shareholder value, shareholders can simply place a discount on
share price to reflect the potential expropriation risks arising from the
bad governance design. Therefore, insiders should be free to adopt
control-enhancing mechanisms.

4.4.2   Review on Regulatory Policies

During the past century, there have been fruitful policy debates over how
and whether to regulate control-enhancing mechanisms, both at country
and regional levels. Due to the complexity of the issues involved and the
fact that each jurisdiction operates in very different corporate environments, regulatory responses to control-enhancing mechanisms are drastic-
ally different among jurisdictions.

There are three main ways to regulate dual-class shares. The first is a permissive approach supplemented by substantial disclosure requirements, such as what is done in the United States and Canada. The second approach is outright prohibition of dual-class shares and mandating the one-share/one-vote rule through corporate law, which is the practice in Germany, Spain and Mainland China. The third approach is to allow dual-class shares in unlisted companies, but prohibit listed companies from deviating from the one-share/one-vote rule. Most British Commonwealth jurisdictions, such as the United Kingdom, Hong Kong and Australia, follow this path (Hong Kong Stock Exchange 2014: 10).

The most recent regional policy debate on control-enhancing mechanisms was initiated by European Commission in 2002. According to the Report of the High Level Group of Company Law Experts (Winter Group Report):

> Proportionality between ultimate economic risk and control means that share capital which has an unlimited right to participate in the profits of the company or in the residue on liquidation, and only such share capital, should normally carry control rights. All such capital should carry control rights in proportion to the risk carried. The holders of these rights to the residual profits and assets of the company are best equipped to decide on the affairs of the company as the ultimate effects of their decisions will be borne by them. (European Commission 2002: 21)

Following this report, the European Commission entrusted ISS Europe, the European Corporate Governance Institute, and the law firm Shearman & Sterling to conduct a thorough study on the issue of proportionality of ownership and control. The ISS report was published in 2007 (ISS, Shearman & Sterling and ECGI 2007) and discussed not only at the EU level, but also within various European countries thereafter.

Finally in September 2007, the European Commission (2007: 49–50) declared that:

> [o]ur current information on and understanding of the application of proportionality ... do not provide a basis for mandating proportionality rules across the EU.

Since then, the EU has been regulating control-enhancing mechanisms through strengthened disclosure and transparency rules.

Similarly, the OECD Steering Group on Corporate Governance (2007) conducted an assessment on the issue of proportionality. The report concluded that regulation imposing one-share/one-vote may not be effective because there are many substitutes to voting restrictions. In addition, mandating one-share/one-vote may deter entrepreneurship and thus place substantial costs on society. In the end, the OECD recommended alternatives, such as strengthening the corporate governance framework to reduce the level of private benefits extraction, and targeting specific problems involving proportionality with appropriate regulatory impact assessment.

4.4.3 Impact on Shareholder Value

With opposing theoretical claims and unsettled policy direction, we come to existing empirical evidence for further guidance. The key questions are whether control-enhancing mechanisms affect shareholder value and if so, in what way. One issue to explore is whether these mechanisms create greater agency costs of entrenchment and thus decrease outside shareholders' value (the entrenchment effect). Or does disproportional control actually help controlling shareholders better monitor the firm and maximize firm value (the incentive effect)?

For shareholder value, it should be noted that the value of disproportional control to outside shareholders is different from that of controlling shareholders. For example, in a firm with a dual-class share structure, shares that carry more votes should be worth more than shares that carry only one vote. The extra value the market rewards these multiple-vote shares with is called the 'control premium'. However, multiple-vote shares are usually not tradable in the market. Most prior empirical studies use the market price of shares as a proxy for shareholder value, which in fact only measures the value of shares to outside shareholders (Adams and Ferreira 2008: 62–3). The value of disproportional control to a controlling shareholder is difficult to measure empirically. Typically, it is assessed only in a change-of-control transaction. For the purpose of this chapter, we care more about the impact of control-enhancing mechanisms on the share value of outside shareholders and review empirical studies that address this issue.

Most prior studies use the wedge between the economic rights and control rights of shareholders to measure the level of deviation. These studies examine the impact of such deviation on shareholder value without distinguishing the types of mechanisms that cause the wedge. Using cross-country data, both La Porta *et al.* (2002) and Claessens *et al.* (2002) found that cash-flow rights of controlling shareholders are positively correlated with shareholder value, which is consistent with the incentive effect of cash-flow ownership in agency theory. On the other hand, not all studies find results that support the entrenchment effect hypothesis (Claessens *et al.* 2002: 2256–8, 2268; La Porta *et al.* 2002: 1147–9). Claessens *et al.* (2002) studied firms in eight East Asian economies and found that the wedge correlates with lower firm value. However, they did not find any specific type – pyramids, cross-shareholding or dual-class shares – drove the value discount.

Lins (2003) found similar evidence on the negative impact of the wedge on firm value with 1,433 sample firms from 18 emerging economies (Lins 2003). In contrast, based on a sample of large firms in 27 wealthy economies, La Porta *et al.* (2002) did not find significant correlation between the wedge and firm value, but supported the notion that country-level investor protection increases firm value. Other European country studies do not support the incentive effect and find limited evidence on the entrenchment effect. Cronqvist and Nilsson (2003) analysed a sample of 309 Swedish firms and found that the voting power of controlling shareholders was negatively correlated with firm value. They did not find significant results on cash-flow rights and the wedge, but associated family ownership with negative firm value (Cronqvist and Nilsson 2003). Maury and Pajuste (2005) studied Finnish firms, and used the control-to-ownership ratio to proxy for the entrenchment effect. They found a negative impact of vote concentration on firm value, which supports the entrenchment effect, but they did not find evidence for the incentive effect of cash-flow ownership (Maury and Pajuste 2005).

Apart from large-scale cross-country analysis, studies on US public firms have mainly focused on one mechanism – dual-class shares. Large firms in the United States are freestanding and widely held. Pyramidal ownership is virtually non-existent due to the introduction of the inter-corporate dividend tax in 1935 (Morck and Yeung 2005). A seminal paper by Gompers *et al.* (2010) tried to disentangle the incentive and entrenchment effects by examining US public firms with dual-class share structures. They found that a firm's value increased with an increase of insiders' cash-flow rights and decreased with an increase of insiders' voting rights. They also found a firm's value is negatively correlated with the wedge between cash-flow rights and voting rights. This finding suggests a negative impact of dual-class share structure on shareholder value. Since control-enhancing mechanisms are chosen by a firm, they are inherently endogenous. Hence, these studies are subject to the endogeneity problem and require a cautious interpretation of their results (Adams and Ferreira 2008: 67–8). Gompers *et al.* (2010) attempted to address the endogeneity problem by using seven proxies to instrument ownership concentration (Gompers *et al.* 2010: 1071–2).[2] However,

---

[2] A good instrument would be one that induces changes in the endogenous ownership variable but has no independent effect on firm value, which is the

scholars contest the quality of the instruments and more research is needed to address the endogeneity issue (Bennedsen and Nielsen 2010: 2223–4; Adams and Ferreira 2008: 64–5). In summary, there is empirical evidence to support the correlation between control-enhancing mechanisms and lower firm value, but a causal link between the two has yet to be established (Adams and Ferreira 2008: 64–5). If our policy goal is to protect outside shareholders, it is then justified to implement policies that align the proportionality between control and ownership.

Most papers have focused on the degree of deviation from proportionality; very few discuss whether the mechanisms used also matter. Bennedsen and Nielsen (2010) addressed this issue by studying a large sample of European firms. Consistent with prior studies, they found large and significant value discounts in firms with disproportional control. In particular, the value discount in firms with dual-class shares was more than twice as large as the discounts in firms with a pyramidal structure, while cross-shareholding and other mechanisms did not have a significant impact on firm value. When comparing firms with different mechanisms, they found that the larger value discount in dual-class share firms may be attributed to inferior operating performance, lower dividend pay-outs, and lower growth in assets relative to pyramidal firms. Since family firms are over-represented among firms with disproportional ownership structures, it is not clear whether the lower value discount is driven by the over-representation of family firms among dual-class firms.

Villalonga and Amit (2009) studied whether different forms of mechanisms matter in US firms by examining the individual effects of dual-class shares, voting agreements, pyramids and disproportional board representation (Villalonga and Amit 2009). They found that dual-class shares and disproportional board representation had a negative impact, while pyramids and voting agreements had a positive impact on the market value of firms. Based on the research so far, the difference in value discount between dual-class firms and pyramidal firms, which is both economically and statistically significant, implies that future policymakers and researchers need to pay more attention to the impact of different forms of control-enhancing mechanisms (Bennedsen and Nielsen 2010: 2227). However, we still need to note that, similar to other ownership studies, these studies also faced the problem that firms do not

---

dependent variable. Gompers *et al.* 2010 tested several instruments, including the percentage of all firms located in the same metropolitan or micropolitan statistical area (MSA) and percentage of all sales by firms located in the same MSA.

randomly choose their ownership structure, and it is very hard to dissect the pure effect of adopting control-enhancing mechanisms.

With regard to the channels through which the wedge leads to lower shareholder value, empirical studies have shown that the operating performance of disproportional control firms is not significantly different from regular firms, yet the market value of disproportional firms is significantly lower than regular firms. The result indicates that controlling shareholders efficiently monitor firm operations but extract a disproportional surplus after the operations have been carried out (Bennedsen and Nielsen 2010: 2213, 2227). Masulis *et al.* (2009) found evidence that supports the notion that managers in US dual-class firms extract private benefits at the expense of outside shareholders (Masulis *et al.* 2009). They also found that as the wedge between voting rights and cash-flow rights widens, cash reserves are worth less to outside shareholders, CEOs receive higher compensation, managers make shareholder value-destroying acquisitions that benefit themselves more often, and capital expenditures contribute less to shareholder value.

Despite the fact that there are certain variations in the empirical results, most of the research we surveyed suggests that disproportional ownership correlates with lower firm value. That is, there is a value discount on firms with disproportional ownership. There is limited evidence showing that the value discount may not come from the inefficient monitoring of controllers. Rather, it comes from the extraction of private benefits of control by controllers. For an outside shareholder, the cost of extraction is higher than the benefits of efficient monitoring. Furthermore, the mechanism that is used to create disproportional control matters. Dual-class share structures seem to receive a higher discount than pyramidal structures. Yet we do not know much about the reasons contributing to such difference.

4.5 RETHINKING THE CURRENT REGULATORY FRAMEWORK

4.5.1 Re-conceptualizing Control-Enhancing Mechanisms

Conceptually, there are two types of control-enhancing mechanisms: participative and non-participative. 'Participative mechanisms' are based on contractual arrangements among shareholders. They can be altered through amendments of corporate charters. The most common participative mechanisms are multiple classes of shares, exclusive rights to appoint directors and ceilings on voting rights. Dual-class share structures are the most widely used participative mechanism in the United States. In contrast, ceilings on voting rights are the most widely adopted participative mechanism among European countries.

'Non-participative mechanisms' are control structures that are adopted by founding shareholders, usually families or the state, before IPO, to achieve stable control with minimal monetary investment. The term 'non-participative' is coined to refer to structures that are not subject to change by non-controlling shareholders. Pyramids, cross-shareholdings and shareholder voting agreements are among the most popular non-participative mechanisms. Non-participative mechanisms, except for voting agreements, are almost absent in the United States due to tax disadvantages (Kandel *et al.* 2013: 16–21). Conversely, non-participative mechanisms are more popular than participative mechanisms in European countries. A 2007 survey found that non-participative mechanisms were legally available in all EU jurisdictions (ISS, Shearman & Sterling and ECGI 2007). Among them, pyramid structures were used in 75 per cent of the surveyed EU jurisdictions and shareholder agreements were used in 69 per cent of them (European Commission 2007: 16).

4.5.2 Justifications for Regulatory Intervention

The purpose of regulating control-enhancing mechanisms is to check the level of private benefits controllers can extract from corporations. In a perfect market, non-controlling shareholders will apply discounts to the share price if the costs of private benefit extraction outweigh the benefits the controllers can bring to the firm. Presumably, if the non-controlling shareholders expect a high level of extraction by the controller, they will apply a large reduction to the share price, and vice versa. In this situation, there is no need for regulators to step in because an optimal price will be reached under efficient market conditions. Empirical studies show that shareholders apply discounts to shares of inferior voting rights (Adams and Ferreira 2008: 85; Gompers *et al.* 2010: 1084) .

Some argue that regulators need not intervene because the controllers bear the costs of control-enhancing mechanisms during IPO (Gilson 1987: 808–9). However, in practice, an efficient market never exists – contract may be incomplete, information may not flow efficiently, and externalities may exist. The Winter Group Report (European Commission 2002: 26) observed, 'Currently, however, such efficient markets do not exist across Europe'.

The effect of disproportional ownership may go beyond its impact on shareholder value and spill over to impact on social welfare (Adams and

Ferreira 2008: 81). Regulation is justified if market failure occurs and social welfare suffers (Cooter and Ulen 2012: 41–2). The categorization of participative and non-participative mechanisms has important regulatory implications. In the case of participative mechanisms, since these mechanisms are stipulated in corporate charters, outside shareholders can amend the charters and block inefficient control-enhancing mechanisms through shareholder voting. In other words, if the control block created by control-enhancing mechanisms does not exceed the threshold required for amending the charter, there will be no need for further regulation because outside shareholders can always change the inefficient mechanisms through charter amendment.

However, regulatory intervention is justified if the control block created by control-enhancing mechanisms exceeds the threshold for charter amendment or the threshold for amendment is so high that there is no chance of passing an amendment (for example, requiring a 95 per cent supermajority vote for amending a control-enhancing mechanism). Such efforts call for the law to cure the imbalance in voting power by allowing outside shareholders to exercise voting that is commensurate with their economic rights, post-IPO or upon the occurrence of specific events. Empowering non-controlling shareholders through regulatory intervention would strike a balance between controllers and non-controllers. Such voting could be both regular and event-based. Regular voting requirements would subject disproportional structures to non-controlling shareholder approval every three years after IPO. Such *ex post* shareholder approval resembles the binding shareholder vote on directors' pay policy under the UK Enterprise and Regulatory Reform Act 2013, s. 79.

Event-based voting requirements would entail non-controlling shareholder approval in case there is change-of-control event. The takeover protective provisions, such as the 'coat-tails' in Canada, can be an example. Section 624 of the Toronto Stock Exchange Company Manual specifies that if a takeover offer has been made to the super-voting class, shareholders of the inferior voting class will be given the opportunity to participate in the offer through a right of conversion into the super-voting common shares (Robinson *et al.* 2002: 427).[3] In Nordic countries, which

---

3   Each company has to design its own 'coat-tail' provision in the articles of association. See s. 624(l) of the Toronto Stock Exchange Listed Company Manual ('If there is a published market for the Common Securities, the coattails must provide that if there is an offer to purchase Common Securities that must, by reason of applicable securities legislation or the requirements of a stock exchange on which the Common Securities are listed, be made to all or

allow dual-class shares, the law requires majority votes based on equity ownership for sensitive actions such as directed issuances of shares (Gilson 2014: 102).

In the case of non-participative mechanisms, there is no prospect for non-controlling shareholders to change the structure because the mechanism is solely decided by controllers. Therefore, whether prohibition of non-participative mechanisms is justified would depend on the existence of complementary investor protection regimes. In jurisdictions with sound investor protection regimes, the amount of private benefits of control that can be extracted by controlling shareholders is low. Thus, the agency costs of entrenchment to outside investors are lower. With a complementary investor protection regime, there is no need to prohibit non-participative mechanisms. However, in jurisdictions with weak investor protection regimes, the agency costs of entrenchment is high. Therefore, regulation that prohibits pyramids or cross-shareholding may well be justified. For instance, in South Korea, the economy is dominated by large Chaebols, which are family-controlled conglomerates. Pyramids and cross-shareholding are frequently used to enhance control by Chaebol family groups. To improve corporate governance of Chaebols, the government of South Korea passed a rule that bans any new cross-shareholding investment among the affiliates of conglomerates. Under South Korea's Monopoly Regulation and Fair Trade Act, affiliates of large conglomerates with assets of five-trillion won (US$4.8 billion) or more are banned from making new investments in one another (Kyu-wook 2014).

4.6   CONCLUSION

The growing popularity of control-enhancing mechanisms in recent years reopens the debate over the issue of ownership-control proportionality. The way business operates in the digital economy is different from the past. Talent and human capital constitute the core competitive advantages of modern business enterprises. Control-enhancing mechanisms are viewed as a tool to retain a firm's core human capital and, in turn, contribute positively to firm value. Nevertheless, excess control by insiders exposes outside investors to high expropriation risks and raises corporate governance concerns. This chapter proposes a new taxonomy to

---

substantially all holders of Common Securities who are in a province of Canada to which the requirement applies, the holders of Restricted Securities will be given the opportunity to participate in the offer through a right of conversion').

re-conceptualize control-enhancing mechanisms and identifies situations where further regulation is needed to protect outside shareholders.

REFERENCES

Adams, R. and D. Ferreira (2007), 'A Theory of Friendly Boards' 62 *Journal of Finance* 217

— (2008), 'One Share-One Vote: The Empirical Evidence' 12 *Review of Finance* 51

Bebchuk, L. (2014), 'Alibaba's governance leaves investors at a disadvantage', *New York Times*, 16 September

Bebchuk, L., R. Kraakman and G. Triantis (2000), 'Stock pyramids, cross-ownership, and dual class equity: the mechanisms and agency costs of separating control from cash-flow rights' in *Concentrated Corporate Ownership* (University of Chicago Press) 295

Bennedsen, M. and K.M. Nielsen (2010), 'Incentive and Entrenchment Effects in European Ownership' 34 *Journal of Banking and Finance* 2212

Berle, A.A. and G.C. Means (1932), *The Modern Corporation and Private Property* (Macmillan)

Bernitz, U. (2004), 'The Attack on the Nordic Multiple Voting Rights Model: The Legal Limits under EU law' 15 *European Business Law Review* 1423

Claessens, S., S. Djankov, J.P. Fan and L.H. Lang (2002), 'Disentangling the Incentive and Entrenchment Effects of Large Shareholdings' 57 *Journal of Finance* 2741

Claessens, S., S. Djankov and L.H. Lang (2000), 'The Separation of Ownership and Control in East Asian Corporations' 58 *Journal of Financial Economics* 81

Cooter, R. and T. Ulen (2012), *Law and Economics* (6th edn, Prentice Hall)

Cornell, B. and A.C. Shapiro (1987), 'Corporate Stakeholders and Corporate Finance' 16 *Financial Management* 5

Critchley, B. (2015), 'Time for regulators to take major look at dual class shares', *Financial Post*, 14 May

Cronqvist, H. and M. Nilsson (2003), 'Agency Costs of Controlling Minority Shareholders' 38 *Journal of Financial and Quantitative Analysis* 695

DeAngelo, H. and L. DeAngelo (1985), 'Managerial Ownership of Voting Rights: A Study of Public Corporations with Dual Classes of Common Stock' 14 *Journal of Financial Economics* 33

Easterbrook, F.H. and D.R. Fischel (1991), *The Economic Structure of Corporate Law* (Harvard University Press)

European Commission (2002), *Report of the High Level Group of Company Law Experts on Issues Related to Takeover Bids in the European Union* (Winter Group Report), available at http://ec.europa.eu/internal_market/company/docs/takeoverbids/2002-01-hlg-report_en.pdf

— (2007), *Impact Assessment on the Proportionality Between Capital and Control in Listed Companies*, available at http://ec.europa.eu/smart-regulation/impact/ia_carried_out/docs/ia_2007/sec_2007_1705_en.pdf

Faccio, M. and L.H. Lang (2002), 'The Ultimate Ownership of Western European Corporations' 65 *Journal of Financial Economics* 365

Gilson, R.J. (1987), 'Evaluating Dual Class Common Stock: The Relevance of Substitutes' 73 *Virginia Law Review* 807

— (2006), 'Controlling Shareholders and Corporate Governance: Complicating the Comparative Taxonomy' 119 *Harvard Law Review* 1641

— (2014), 'The Nordic Model in an international perspective: the role of ownership' in Per Lekvall (ed), *The Nordic Corporate Governance Model* (SNS Förlag)

Gompers, P.A., J. Ishii and A. Metrick (2010), 'Extreme Governance: An Analysis of Dual-Class Firms in the United States' 23 *Review of Financial Studies* 1051

Goshen, Z. and A. Hamdani (2016), 'Corporate Control and Idiosyncratic Vision' 125 *Yale Law Journal* 560

Gu, W. (2016), 'Scrutiny greets overseas-listed Chinese companies returning home to relist', *Wall Street Journal*, 6 May 2016, available at www.wsj.com/articles/china-scrutinizes-deals-for-foreign-listed-companies-to-relist-at-home-1462537821

Hasselback, D. and B. Shecter (2015), 'From Cara Operations Ltd to Shopify Inc: why dual class shares are suddenly cool again', *Financial Post*, 5 May

He, J. and H.C. Wang (2009), 'Innovative Knowledge Assets and Economic Performance: The Asymmetric Roles of Incentives and Monitoring' 52 *Academy of Management Journal* 919

Hong Kong Stock Exchange (2014), *Weighted Voting Rights Concept Paper*, available at www.hkex.com.hk/eng/newsconsul/mktconsul/Documents/cp2014082.pdf

— (2015), 'Consultation Conclusions: To Concept Paper on Weighted Voting Rights', available at www.hkex.com.hk/eng/newsconsul/mktconsul/Documents/cp2014082cc.pdf

IRRC Institute and ISS (2012), *Controlled Companies in the Standard & Poor's 1500: A Ten Year Performance and Risk Review*, available at http://irrcinstitute.org/wp-content/uploads/2015/09/FINAL-Controlled-Company-ISS-Report1.pdf

ISS, Shearman & Sterling and ECGI (2007), *Report on the Proportionality Principle in the European Union*, available at http://ec.europa.eu/internal_market/company/docs/shareholders/study/final_report_en.pdf

Jensen, M.C. and W.H. Meckling (1976), 'Theory of the Firm: Managerial Behavior, Agency Costs and Ownership Structure' 3 *Journal of Financial Economics* 305

Kandel, E. *et al.* (2013), *The Great Pyramids of America: A Revised History of US Business Groups, Corporate Ownership and Regulation, 1930–1950*, available at www.nber.org/papers/w19691

Kyu-wook, O. (2014), 'New cross-shareholding ban takes effect: conglomerates pressured to improve governance', *Korea Herald*, 25 July 2014, available at www.koreaherald.com/view.php?ud=20140725000716

La Porta, R., F. Lopez-de-Silanes and A. Shleifer (1999), 'Corporate Ownership Around the World' 54 *Journal of Finance* 471

La Porta, R. *et al.* (2002), 'Investor Protection and Corporate Valuation' 57 *Journal of Finance* 1147

Lin, Y.-H. and T. Mehaffy (2016), 'Open Sesame: The Myth of Alibaba's Extreme Corporate Governance and Control' 10 *Brooklyn Journal of Corporate, Financial and Commercial Law* 437

Lins, K.V. (2003), 'Equity Ownership and Firm Value in Emerging Markets' 38 *Journal of Financial and Quantitative Analysis* 159

Mahoney, J.T. and J.R. Pandian (1992), 'The Resource-Based View Within the Conversation of Strategic Management' 13 *Strategic Management Journal* 363

Masulis, R.W., C. Wang and F. Xie (2009), 'Agency Problems at Dual-Class Companies' 64 *Journal of Finance* 1697

Maury, B. and A. Pajuste (2005), 'Multiple Large Shareholders and Firm Value' 29 *Journal of Banking and Finance* 1813

Morck, R. and B. Yeung (2005), 'Dividend Taxation and Corporate Governance' 19 *Journal of Economic Perspectives* 163

OECD Steering Group on Corporate Governance (2007), *Lack of Proportionality Between Ownership and Control: Overview and Issues for Discussion*, available at www.oecd.org/daf/ca/corporategovernanceprinciples/40038351.pdf

Qihoo 360 (2015), *Press Release, Qihoo 360 Enters into Definitive Agreement for Going Private Transaction* (18 December), available at http://ir.360.cn/phoenix.zhtml?c=243376&p=irol-newsArticle&ID=2123936

— (2016), *Press Release, Qihoo 360 Announces Shareholder Approval of Merger Agreement* (30 March), available at http://ir.360.cn/phoenix.zhtml?c=243376&p=irol-newsArticle&ID=2151620

Renaissance Capital IPO Center (2016), 'IPO Proceeds Raised', available at www.renaissancecapital.com/ipohome/press/ipovolume.aspx

Ringe, W.-G. (2010), 'Deviations from ownership-control proportionality-economic protectionism revisited' in U. Bernitz and W.-G. Ringe (eds), *Company Law and Economic Protectionism: New Challenges to European Integration* (Oxford University Press)

Robinson, C., J. Rumsey and A. White (2002), *The Value of a Vote in the Market for Corporate Control: Canadian Evidence* (Oxford University Press)

Toronto Stock Exchange (2016), *TSX Company Manual*, available at http://tmx.complinet.com/en/tsx_manual.html

Villalonga, B. and R. Amit (2009), 'How are U.S. Family Firms Controlled?' 22 *Review of Financial Studies* 3047

Wang, H.C., J. He and J.T. Mahoney (2009), 'Firm-Specific Knowledge Resources and Competitive Advantage: The Roles of Economic-and Relationship-based Employee Governance Mechanisms' 30 *Strategic Management Journal* 1265

Wright, P.M., G. McMahan and A. McWilliams (1994), 'Human Resources and Sustained Competitive Advantage: A Resource-based Perspective' 5 *International Journal of Human Resource Management* 301

Zingales, L. (1995) 'Insider Ownership and the Decision to Go Public' 62 *Review of Economic Studies* 425

5. Law and finance: from 'transplantation' to 'better' corporate governance in China

Heida Donegan

5.1 INTRODUCTION

Almost four decades ago in 1978, China started adopting an open-door and market-oriented policy. There have been, from time to time, attempts by the Chinese government to recentralize and maintain control (Tam 2000). Yet the Chinese economy has been growing from strength to strength and has gradually become more open and compatible with its Western counterparts. In 2014, the International Monetary Fund (IMF) reported that China had surpassed the United States to become the largest economy in the world, based on GDP adjusted for purchasing power parity (PPP), putting the United States in the second place for the first time in 142 years (Bird 2014; Duncan and Martosko 2014). At mid-July 2016, China's GDP based on PPP was US$19.4 trillion and the United States' GDP was US$17.95 trillion, meaning that China holds onto its number one spot in these terms. However, with a US$10.98 trillion economy in terms of nominal GDP, China is still behind the United States with its US$17.95 trillion economy in the same terms. China thus holds second place (Bajpai 2016).

With China's accession to the World Trade Organization (WTO) at the turn of this century, the development of its corporate governance law has attracted increasing attention in academic, business and policy discussions. A question is raised as to whether corporate governance is important to China. It almost appears to be stating the obvious that there is a certain conundrum when looking at what China has been able to achieve, in terms of economic growth, within such a short time span, with its earlier negligible and recently 'improved' corporate governance law. Is the idea that having an effective or efficient corporate governance system is essential for economic growth still valid?

This chapter will demonstrate that the answer should be in the affirmative. The development of corporate governance law is closely related to China's ongoing economic reforms, especially those of the state-owned enterprises (SOEs), the development of financial and securities systems for the country's capital markets and the ability to withstand financial crises. China was not one of the Asian countries severely hit by the Asian Financial Crisis in the late 1990s. This was largely due to foreign exchange controls that were in place (Tam 2000) and the fact that the renminbi (RMB) was/is not fully convertible (Nolan 2005). However, insolvency and resulting collapses and comprehensive restructurings of some high-profile finance and investment institutions in the late 1990s, such as Guangdong International Trust and Investment Company (GITIC), China's then second largest non-bank financial institution, and Guangdong Enterprises (GDE), which included five listed 'red chip' companies, did expose the vulnerability of China's burgeoning financial and securities systems and its stock market (Nolan 2005).

After the Asian Financial Crisis in the late 1990s, the Chinese government launched a massive attempt to 'clean up' its financial institutions, and this revealed significant evidence of the lack of good governance in the corporate and finance sectors. As a matter of fact, the Chinese government did not automatically introduce reforms in the wake of the Asian Financial Crisis. Revelations of serious weaknesses in its corporate and financial markets made the development of a modern and appropriate corporate system the focus of economic reform and mandated the establishment of corporate governance structures as being the crucial means of achieving this goal, as early as 1993 (CCP Decision 1993).[1] That was a significant year because China's first Company Law[2] was enacted in that year to take effect in 1994. Five years later in 1998, China's Securities Law was promulgated to become effective in 1999. The Company Law and Securities Law were revised in 2005 (respectively the Company Law 2005 and Securities Law 2005)[3] to give new attention, and hopefully better roles, to various aspects of corporate

---

[1] Decisions on Some Issues in Establishing the Socialist Market Economic System, adopted by the Third Plenary Session of the Fourteenth Congress of the Chinese Communist Party (November 1993).

[2] Company Law of the People's Republic of China (adopted 1993 (Company Law 1993), first amendment 1999, second amendment 2004, revised 2005 (Company Law 2005), and third amendment 2013 (Company Law 2013).

[3] Securities Law of the People's Republic of China (1998, took effect 1999) (revised 2005 (Securities Law 2005), amended 2013 and 2014).

governance imported from the West. They included the rights of share-holders, protection of their rights and equitable treatment of all share-holders, corporate boards and directors, fiduciary duties of directors and officers, balance between directors' responsibilities and the reasonable protection of directors, and corporate disclosure and transparency. The Company Law 2005 was amended in 2013 to take effect in 2014. The Securities Law 2005 is in the process of being amended as part of China's attempt to implement its stock issuance registration system reform (NPC Decision 2015;[4] Howson 2015). China's corporate govern-ance law reform is likely to be an ongoing process.

5.2 HISTORICAL BACKGROUND

Since China became a socialist state in 1949, the State assumed the ownership of most of the land and the properties therein and thereon. Industrial and commercial activities were conducted largely by enter-prises and units owned and controlled by the State. By the end of the 1970s, China remained a static and underdeveloped economy. Having undergone a gradual and evolutionary process of economic reforms since then, China has transformed its SOE system from a completely state-controlled model where the State holds all property ownership and managerial rights to a contract-based model where enterprises are responsible for their own profits/losses, and further to a model where numerous large SOEs are listed on local and overseas stock exchanges, in just over three and half decades. The evolution of China's SOE govern-ance models may be categorized as follows: (i) traditional model (1949–84); (ii) transitional model (1984–93); and (iii) modern corporate model (1993 till now) (Cheung *et al.* 2010; Schipani and Liu 2002). Salient characteristics of the three models are set out below.

5.2.1 Traditional Model (1949–84)

Traditionally, most of the production and provision of goods and services in China was conducted by SOEs, which were referred to as 'factories' (*gong chang*). From the 1950s to 1984, this was the only legal form available to protect and manage State property. Concepts such as

---

⁴ Decision of the Standing Committee of the National People's Congress on Authorizing the State Council to Adjust the Relevant Applicable Provisions of the Securities Law of the People's Republic of China in the Implementation of Stock Issuance Registration System Reform (27 December 2015).

'corporation', 'company', or 'legal person' were non-existent in this traditional 'state-controlled' or 'central-planning' model (Schipani and Liu 2002).

Accordingly, governance structures in SOEs mirrored the government. Executives or managers of SOEs were appointed and removed by the government authorities in charge of the relevant industry sectors and enjoyed the same political and economic status and benefits as government officials of similar rankings.[5] These managers were responsible and accountable to their respective supervising government authorities. Their performance was not assessed based on the SOEs' financial performance, but by their compliance with the plans stipulated by the supervising authorities. This model bound the State, SOEs and their employees together in that the state organized SOEs' economic resources and activities, with SOEs serving as the production and social security units for the State and 'work units' (*gong zuo dan wei*) or 'iron rice bowls' (*tie fan wan*) for their employees (Schipani and Liu 2002: 8). Consequently, China was weighed down by a static and uncompetitive economy with a high proportion of under-/non-performing SOEs and a workforce with little incentive to perform.

5.2.2 Transitional Model (1984–93)

The transitional SOE governance model is also known as the contracting model. Long-term contracts were established between SOEs and their supervising authorities with a view to improve SOEs' financial performance under the contract management system (*cheng bao zhi*). This was adopted, nationwide, in 1988 under the Provisional Regulations on the Contract Management System in State-Owned Enterprises (SOEs Contract Management Regulations).[6] The new system was also meant to turn SOEs into enterprises responsible for their own profits/losses and was a part of the nationwide reform of the economic system (CCP Decision 1984).[7] The significance of this reform is that the Chinese government allowed productive enterprises, including SOEs, which were traditionally

---

[5] This practice continued until the issuance of the Decision on the Implementation of the State-owned Enterprises Reform in 1999 in which the Chinese government declared that official rankings would no longer be bestowed on enterprises' leaders.

[6] Provisional Regulations on the Contract Management System in State-Owned Enterprises (1988).

[7] Decision of the Central Committee of the Chinese Communist Party on Several Issues Concerning the Reform of the Economic System.

not considered legal persons, to become enterprise legal persons (*qi ye fa ren*). In this manner, the substance of what constitutes corporate govern-ance in the West gained a foothold in China even though the concept of corporate governance was little known then (Tam 2002).

To facilitate economic reform, the Law on Industrial Enterprises Owned by the Whole People (SOEs Law) was promulgated in 1988 to formally convert the traditional SOEs into industrial enterprises with the status of legal persons. They would be headed by factory directors (managers) (*chang zhang (jing li)*) whose appointment and removal had to be approved by the State (SOEs Law, arts 7, 44, 45).

The contracting model did not, however, make much headway largely due to problems arising from the basic principle of requiring SOEs to lock in a minimum amount of profits to pay the State and remain liable to pay the fixed amounts to the State even if they did not make sufficient profits (SOE Contract Management Regulations, art. 5). Weaknesses in the contracting system included failure to check arbitrary and short-term performance-oriented behaviours, whereby contractors benefited while the enterprises were profitable but had no individual liabilities when losses were incurred. It also failed to find a satisfactory solution to the challenge of separating the State from the enterprises.

In 1992, the Regulation on the Transformation of Operational Mech-anisms of Industrial Enterprises Owned by the Whole People was introduced. It conferred 14 independent operational powers on SOEs, to accelerate the pace at which SOEs advanced from a planned economy to a market economy (CSRC 2010). The contracting system was eventually phased out in the mid-to-late 1990s, following the issuance of directions by the government in 1994 not to renew the contracts of SOEs (Yang 1998). Given these problems, Chinese policy-makers started to look to modern corporate models in the West for viable solutions (Schipani and Liu 2002).

Amid transition from a centrally planned economy to a market economy where the legal system was not well defined, China also established its own stock market. Regulatory institutions and relevant laws and regulations were gradually put in place after two stock exchanges began operation in 1990, one in Shanghai and the other in Shenzhen. The China Securities Regulatory Commission (CSRC) was established in 1992 to monitor and regulate China's stock market. This presents a classic example of China's modus operandi in installing a greenfield for growth first, then introducing law reform as a 'facilitator' or legal 'transplant' to forge further market growth and plug loopholes. In other words, law reforms were employed as a secondary instrument to achieve the agenda of economic development.

5.2.3 Modern Corporate Model (1993 Onward)

In response to the call for the introduction of a market economy in 1992 by Deng Xiaoping, China's architect of modernization and economic reforms, the third stage of SOE reform began in 1993. The Communist Party endorsed the installation of a modern corporate system (Cheung *et al.* 2010). This reform policy accelerated the promulgation of corporate legislation, which was perceived as an essential instrument for corporatizing SOEs (Schipani and Liu 2002).

5.3 KEY LEGAL SOURCES OF CHINA'S CORPORATE GOVERNANCE

The key legal sources of the corporate governance framework in China are (a) Company Law; (b) Securities Law; (c) Code of Corporate Governance for Listed Companies in China (Corporate Governance Code) issued by CSRC and the State Economic and Trade Commission (SETC) in 2001; and (d) Guidelines for the Installation of Independent Directors to the Board of Directors of Listed Companies issued by CSRC in 2001 (Independent Directors Guidelines) (Shan and Round 2012).

5.3.1 Company Law

(a) An overview
The Company Law 1993 was the starting point in the development of the country's corporate governance systems. It was the first attempt since 1949 to create limited liability companies without regard to the nature of ownership as part of a modern economic system (Feinerman 2007). It was amended in 1999, and again in 2004, to resolve some technical issues. In 2005, the Company Law 1993 was in essence rewritten, leaving only 24 articles unchanged from the original version. Hence, the 2005 enactment is customarily referred to as the 'new Company Law' or simply 'Company Law 2005' as new legislation (Wang 2014). This revision was primarily driven by the need to provide equal treatment to the state-owned economy and the private economy, and strengthen corporate governance for the protection of creditors, minority shareholders and employees. The Company Law was amended again in 2013 to further streamline company registration formalities, relax the incorporation threshold and simplify incorporation procedures to encourage and promote investment, entrepreneurship, innovation, commercial freedom and business development (Wei 2014).

The Company Law recognizes two types of companies: companies with limited liability and companies limited by shares (Company Law 2013, art. 2; Rajagopalan and Zhang 2008). A company with limited liability does not issue shares to shareholders. Its registered capital is the amount of capital invested, in cash or kind, by the persons registered with the company registration authority under the State Administration for Industry and Commerce (SAIC) (Company Law 2013, arts 23–35). There are different rules in the Company Law for (1) companies with limited liability that are wholly owned by the State (commonly known as corporatized, but not privatized, SOEs where the State retains ownership despite the changes in their corporate structure) (arts 64–70); and (2) companies that have foreign investor(s). The second category, commonly known as foreign-invested enterprises, can be a Chinese-foreign equity joint venture, a Chinese-foreign contractual joint venture or a wholly foreign-invested enterprise.

A company limited by shares may be incorporated through promotion, which entails the subscription of all the issued shares by the promoters, or share offer, in which the promoters take up a portion of the issued shares and the remainder is offered to the public or specific groups (Company Law 2013, arts 76–97). Special rules in the Company Law enable companies limited by shares to list on stock exchange(s) (arts 120–24).

(b) Company Law and SOEs
Under the Company Law, traditional SOEs were restructured to become corporatized SOEs with limited liability, or corporatized SOEs limited by shares. Both classes were given better defined governance structures to enhance shareholders' rights, corporate efficiency and accountability. It would be fair to say that the Company Law provides a solid start for transforming SOEs into business corporations. The crucial features facilitating this reform are permitting diversified forms of ownership and introducing a modern corporate governance framework for SOEs. The ownership reform of SOEs is twofold under the Company Law. First, SOEs were transformed into limited liability companies (Company Law 1993, art. 64).[8] This theoretically enables the separation of government and business functions and the creation of incentives structures for the managers to act in the interests of the corporate shareholders or owners.

---

[8]   There are two types of SOEs under Company Law 1993: first, SOEs that were corporatized into limited liability companies and second, SOEs that were reorganized to become companies limited by shares and were listed on the stock market.

Second, SOEs were given a new fundraising avenue through listing on stock exchanges (arts 75 and 151). Since then, there have been ongoing corporate governance reform initiatives and continuing enactments of numerous laws, rules, regulations and guidelines to deal with loopholes and enhance the performance of listed companies (Cheung *et al.* 2010).

(c) Governance structure

The Company Law requires both companies with limited liability and companies limited by shares to form three governing bodies: (i) shareholders, acting as a body at the general meeting or assembly (Company Law 2013, arts 36–43 for companies with limited liability, and arts 98–107 for companies limited by shares); (ii) boards of directors (BOD) (arts 44–48, 50, 67 and 69 for companies with limited liability, and arts 108–12 and 114 for companies limited by shares); and (iii) boards of supervisors (BOS) (arts 51–56 and 70 for companies with limited liability, and arts 117–19 for companies limited by shares).

The Company Law introduces two corporate positions: (i) chairman of BOD; and (ii) manager (*jing li*), which is a concept akin to CEO in the Anglo-American model. Managers of companies with limited liability are accountable to the BOD and attend BOD meetings as non-voting attendants (art. 49). This implies that the BOD chair in a company with limited liability may not also be its manager. However, a smaller company with limited liability may have an executive director instead of a BOD, and the executive director may concurrently serve as the manager (art. 50).

The BOD of a company limited by shares may appoint one of its members as the manager. This means the BOD chair in a company limited by shares may concurrently serve as its manager. The BOD chair, executive director or manager (as applicable) must serve as the legal representative of the company and must be registered with the SAIC (art. 13). In both types of companies – those with limited liability and those limited by shares – shareholders have the right to appoint and remove directors and supervisors and decide on their remuneration. Boards of directors and boards of supervisors function on an equal level and are independent of each other.

(d) Overseas influence

In terms of the types of companies and some rules on corporate governance, the drafters of the Company Law have, understandably, looked both to the American and continental models, and have transplanted a few features for China's use. For instance, the two-tier board system is considered to be explicitly modelled on, and is often compared to, the German system (Clarke 2006a). German corporations are, similarly, governed by a board of directors and a supervisory board (German Stock Corporation Act 1965 (Aktiengesetz), s. 84; Bradley *et al.* 1999).

There are, however, differences between the German and Chinese systems. One significant example is the absence of any hierarchical relationship between the Chinese BOD and BOS. Both directors and supervisors are appointed and dismissed by shareholders (Company Law 2013, art. 37 for companies with limited liability, and art. 105 for companies limited by shares). In contrast, the German supervisory board monitors the management board and the members of the management board are appointed and removed by the supervisory board (German Stock Corporation Act 1965, s. 84; Andre Jr 1995; Charny 1998).

The approach in China appears to be consistent with some scholars' findings that emerging economies have attempted to transplant legal frameworks of developed economies, either as a result of internally driven reforms (for instance, China and Russia) or as a response to international demands (for example, Thailand and South Korea) (Young *et al.* 2008). However, although the corporate governance structures in emerging economies often adopt or transplant the appearance of corporate governance mechanisms from developed economies, these mechanisms rarely function like their counterparts in the developed economies. In other words, their governance structures resemble those of the developed economies in form but not necessarily in substance (Peng 2004).

5.3.2 Securities Law

The Chinese Securities Law was enacted in 1998 and entered into force in 1999. It aims to protect investors' lawful and public interests, maintain social and economic order and promote the development of a market economy (Securities Law, art. 1; CSRC 2012). The Securities Law regulates the issuance and trading of stocks, corporate bonds and other securities, government bonds and securities, investment fund units and related matters. Under the Securities Law, the State audit authority exercises audit supervision over stock exchanges, securities firms, securities depository and clearing houses and securities regulators (art. 9). The law also prohibits insider trading, market manipulation and other fraudulent activities (arts 73–84).

Ironically, not long after the Securities Law came into force, corporate scandals emerged in 2001 prompting CSRC officials and other regulatory authorities to further improve the governance of listed Chinese companies (Rajagopalan and Zhang 2008). In 2001, just as the United States was experiencing a spate of flagship corporation collapses from Enron to WorldCom to Global Crossing due to corporate governance failures, media exposure of an Enron-type, RMB745 million fraud committed by Ying Guang Xia, a 'blue chip' company listed on the Mainland, became the largest economic scandal in China's history (Rajagopalan and Zhang 2008). Several other scandals, of similar nature but perhaps slightly smaller in scale, highlighted the importance of the effective implementation of good corporate governance in China (Feinerman 2007).

The companies involved in the scandals were leading businesses and their share prices had performed well before they collapsed. CSRC's investigations revealed the dire predicaments of the companies – in general, fabricated sales receipts, inflated profits figures, concocted production facilities and/or manipulated share prices. BOD chairmen and senior managers and executives were sent to prison. The list included the chairman and six executives of Guangdong Kelon Electrical Holdings (for overstating revenues and profits by over RMB2 billion), and Zhou Zhengyi of Nongkai Development Group, then one of China's richest men (for manipulating share prices and falsifying registered capital). The corporate collapses also provided insights into the vulnerability of China's financial institutions and its stock market. The failures of GITIC and GDE, mentioned earlier, epitomized the malfunctioning of corporate governance systems even in major financial institutions.

In early 2002, it was revealed that five officials of one of the Big 4 state-owned banks in a branch in Guangdong swindled the equivalent of nearly US$500 million. The problems penetrated to the apex of the country's banking system. Earlier in 1999, one of the former premier's right-hand men, Zhu Xiaohua, a former deputy governor of the People's Bank of China (the equivalent of the reserve bank in a developed country) was arrested and jailed for 15 years (Nolan 2005).

In view of the scandals and the problems encountered, the Securities Law was subsequently revised in 2005, along with the Company Law, to take effect in January 2006. The amendments aimed to strengthen the supervisory powers of the government, implicitly the CSRC, and investor protection mechanisms (Jia *et al.* 2009). It is anticipated that ongoing reforms will be imperative for the improvement of the functioning of China's stock market (NPC Decision 2015; Howson 2015).

5.3.3 Corporate Governance Code

Even before some of the failures discussed above, the Corporate Governance Code had been developed and came into force in 2002. The corporate scandals in 2001 outlined above catalysed policy-makers, regulators at the CSRC, SETC and other relevant authorities to make corporate governance a priority issue on their agenda. Additionally, and importantly, with China's accession to the WTO in December 2001, and according to the terms of the WTO agreement, China had to commit to capital market liberalization and corporate reforms. A workable and viable corporate governance system must conform to international standards, as China was preparing its first step forward to gain a foothold on the international stage.

The Corporate Governance Code follows the US model (Rajagopalan and Zhang 2008) and the Principles of Corporate Governance (2004) of the Organisation for Economic Co-operation and Development (OECD 2004). Since their endorsement by the OECD Ministers in 1999, the OECD Principles have been regarded as an international benchmark by policy-makers, investors, corporations and other stakeholders across the world. They have also provided guidance for developing good corporate governance systems in numerous countries, both for OECD members and non-OECD countries.

The OECD Principles (2004) comprise six themes: (i) promoting transparent and efficient markets; (ii) protecting and facilitating the exercise of shareholders' rights; (iii) ensuring equitable treatment of *all* shareholders; (iv) recognizing the legal rights of stakeholders; (v) ensuring timely and accurate disclosure of all material corporate matters; and (vi) ensuring effective monitoring of management by boards of directors, with boards being accountable to the company and the shareholders. Each of these principles has relevance for China and its reforms.

The Chinese Corporate Governance Code (2001) is applicable to and mandatory for all companies listed on the two stock exchanges in China (Shanghai and Shenzhen). It is intended to be the major standard for assessing whether a listed company has a good corporate governance practice. All listed companies are required to act in the spirit of the Corporate Governance Code in their efforts to improve corporate governance (Corporate Governance Code, Preface). It stipulates the rights and responsibilities of shareholders (arts 1–11 and 15–21), directors and BOD (arts 28–58 and 71–72), supervisors and BOS (arts 59–68), stakeholders (arts 81–86) and, generally, management (arts 69–70 and 73–80).

Disclosures (for instance, about controlling shareholders (arts 22 and 27) and related-party transactions (arts 12–14)) are crucial and remain an ongoing responsibility of all listed companies. Further, all shareholders have equal rights to receive accurate, complete, truthful and timely information (art. 87). Every listed company should ensure timely disclosure of its controlling shareholders' interests (arts 92–94). The Corporate Governance Code also introduces a system of independent directors (arts 49–51) and tightens the supervision of management (art. 91).

The Corporate Governance Code strengthens shareholder rights, mandating that minority shareholders should possess equal status with other shareholders (art. 2) and empowers shareholders to protect their interests by civil litigation and other legal actions (art. 4). At the same time, the Code gives controlling shareholders more weight in the decision-making process (for instance, in nominating directors and supervisors (art. 20)) and strengthens BOD (arts 49–50) and BOS (arts 52–58).

In 2015, OECD and G20 (the grouping of 20 major international economies) jointly published a new set of Principles of Corporate Governance (OECD 2015). They were developed from the 2004 OECD Principles, following global consultations and a review process conducted by the OECD Corporate Governance Committee in 2014–15 with all G20 countries being invited to participate. The exercise was a strategic response to the various corporate governance challenges resulting from the Global Financial Crisis of 2008–09. The perceived challenges included the increased complexity of the investment chain, the changing role of stock markets with the arrival of new investors, investment strategies and business practices (OECD 2015).

Like the 2004 OECD Principles, the 2015 OECD Principles also comprise six themes but with different emphases. To illustrate, the 2015 OECD Principles highlight the symbiosis between stock markets and corporate governance, the quality of listing rules and criteria, and the importance of independent supervision, especially because stock markets are increasingly operated by companies that are themselves listed. Significant additions are the inclusion of extensive and stricter rules on related-party transactions and say-on-pay (requiring shareholder approval for equity-based remuneration schemes and material changes for board members and key executives) (OECD 2015). Needless to say, the G20/OECD rules, which represent a broader spectrum of countries, stand a better chance of adoption in various jurisdictions. They build on lessons drawn from the issues that contributed to the massive corporate collapses in the United States/Europe during the Global Financial Crisis of 2008–09.

As a G20 member country, China is expected to direct its policymakers and regulators to the 2015 G20/OECD Principles for adaptation and guidance when they prepare to revise the Corporate Governance

Code in the future (CSRC 2016).[9] The issue became more urgent in August 2015 with the plunge of China's stock market by the biggest margin since its largest one-day loss in February 2007 (Dong and Yu 2015), which occurred around the same time as the adoption of the 2015 Principles by the OECD Council in July 2015 and their endorsement by the G20 countries in September 2015.

The question is whether adaptations, transplants or borrowings from other jurisdictions will be carried out in form but not in substance, as has often been the case in the past. Not surprisingly, China may find its own way of employing the same tools for promoting its political and/or economic agendas. For instance, reform aligned to international standards will likely be introduced in a form that will win public support and maintain the sustainability and stability of its stock market, and in turn the one-party rule.

5.3.4 Independent Directors Guidelines

Since the rise of takeover activities in the 1980s, policy-makers in the West have turned to independent directors as an important element of legal and policy reform in corporate governance (Clarke 2006b). In the United States, although the New York Stock Exchange (NYSE) has only required a majority of independent directors on the boards of listed companies since 2004, insider-dominated boards have been rare for years (Bhagat and Black 1999). As at 2001, around 75 per cent of NYSE-listed companies had already attained such majorities (Clarke 2006b).

In the wake of Enron and other corporate scandals, listed companies were mandated under the Sarbanes-Oxley Act of 2002[10] to establish audit committees comprised of independent directors, of which at least one member had to be a financial expert (Armour and McCahery 2006). Similarly, corporate scandals in the United Kingdom led to efforts to step up the role of outside/non-executive directors under the Combined Code on Corporate Governance 2003 (Armour and McCahery 2006; Clarke 2006b). The Code embraced insights from earlier reports and studies on the subject through the 1990s and early 2000s.

---

[9] CSRC and the China Association for Public Companies jointly hosted an international corporate governance conference 31 August–1 September 2016 to discuss the revision of the Corporate Governance Code with experts from around the globe.

[10] Sarbanes-Oxley Act 2002, Pub. L107–204, 116 Stat. 745.

The scandal-driven moves in the United States/Europe to strengthen outside/independent directors did not go unnoticed by Chinese policy-makers. As a matter of fact, the Chinese were half a step ahead, having the Independent Directors Guidelines promulgated in 2001, possibly because China was also plagued by similar corporate scandals. The Independent Directors Guidelines aimed to eliminate the dominant powers of boards in listed Chinese companies and required at least one-third of the boards of listed companies to be independent by 30 June 2003. Not only did the Independent Directors Guidelines represent a decisive measure by CSRC to regulate internal corporate governance, the guidelines were also portrayed as a borrowing or a legal transplant from US law and practice (Clarke 2006b). However, if China did borrow or transplant the concept of independent directors from the United States, it is no more than in name only (in form but not in substance), because independent directors appear to be as new an institution in the United States as they are in China (Clarke 2006a).

5.4 CHINA'S STOCK MARKET: SOME FEATURES

5.4.1 Origin and Growth

China's stock market became operative in the 1990s. There are two stock exchanges: the Shanghai Stock Exchange (SHSE) and the Shenzhen Stock Exchange (SZSE), both established in 1990. Like the NYSE, China's two stock exchanges are, to a certain extent, self-regulatory organizations. The CSRC was established in October 1992, with authority to regulate and supervise the stock market in China. Headquartered in Beijing, CSRC comprises 21 functional departments and four specialized units. It also has 38 regional offices across the country and supervises 19 affiliated institutions (CSRC 2014).

In terms of market growth, in 2000 there were 1,088 listed companies in China with a total market capitalization of over RMB4.8 trillion (CSRC 2012). This was a huge increase from 14 listed companies in 1991 (Tam 2002). By 2014, the number of listed companies in China had risen to 2,613 and market capitalization had soared to around RMB37.25 trillion, ranking second globally behind the United States (CSRC 2014).

Despite rapid growth, the Chinese market has a number of unique institutional features that make it different to its counterparts in the West. This can be construed as another example of institutional transplants being in form rather than substance (Young *et al.* 2008). These issues are explored below.

5.4.2 Tradable and Non-Tradable Shares

In order to preserve socialist structure in the Chinese economy, SOEs issued a significant portion of their shares to the State when they went public. The shares held by the government and/or government agencies were respectively called State and legal person shares. Before 2005, neither of these two types of shares were tradable in the stock market. Thus, the shares of listed companies in China started off being divided into two categories, namely, tradable and non-tradable shares, because the State intended to maintain control of most of the listed companies (Cheung *et al.* 2010).

5.4.3 Tradable Shares

Tradable shares are divided into several categories: A-shares, B-shares, H-shares and N-shares. A-shares are traded in RMB on both the Shanghai and Shenzhen Exchanges and were only available to domestic investors until May 2003. Subsequently, A-shares were made available to Qualified Foreign Institutional Investors (QFIIs), to enhance the presence of institutional investors in the market and to honour China's commitments under the WTO agreement. Thereafter, UBS and Nomura Securities became the first two QFIIs to trade in China's A-share market (Yang, Chi and Young 2011).

B-shares are traded in US dollars on the Shanghai Exchange and in Hong Kong (HK) dollars on the Shenzhen Exchange. Prior to February 2001, B-shares were only available to non-residents or investors from outside mainland China. Since then, domestic investors have been allowed to invest in B-shares (Yang, Chi and Young 2011). H-shares refer to the shares of mainland Chinese companies listed on the Hong Kong Stock Exchange (HKSE). N-shares are the shares of mainland Chinese companies listed on the US stock market in the form of American Depository Receipts (ADRs) (Cheung *et al.* 2010). Cross-listed shares are known as S-shares (if listed in Singapore) and L-shares (when listed in London).

Prior to the non-tradable share reform in 2005, State shares could only be transferred privately to other government agencies, legal entities or foreign investing firms, always subject to State approval. In reality, non-tradable shares were often transferred through private negotiations and sales (generally without proper and professional valuation). Large or controlling shareholders holding non-tradable shares were able to divert funds and wealth from the listed companies.

The trends, outlined above, worked to the detriment of the stock market because it created a split in the market and led to discrepancies in the pricing mechanism. This, in turn, adversely affected the market's price discovery process and restricted mergers-and-acquisitions activities. In order to curb these problems and protect the stock market, the government began the non-tradable share reform in 2005. CSRC introduced a compensation scheme to substantially slow down the transfer of non-tradable shares and restrict the number of such shares being transferred at 12- to 24-month intervals (Yang, Chi and Young 2011).

As non-tradable shares gradually become tradable, it was anticipated that this would result in improved corporate governance of listed companies and greater capital liquidity. This would, in turn, bring positive returns for the stock market in the long run. Non-tradable shares have been called 'restricted shares' since 2005 in anticipation of eventually becoming tradable shares. By the end of 2007, it was reported that more than half of the listed SOEs had put in place a set plan and timetable to gradually convert all non-tradable shares to tradable shares. By 2012, the majority of shares were tradable in more than half of those listed firms (Jiang and Kim 2015). It is therefore imperative for China to continue with law reforms and promote an orderly stock market by introducing and improving mechanisms that hold listed companies' controllers and managers accountable.

5.5 MAJOR ISSUES SURROUNDING CHINA'S CORPORATE GOVERNANCE

An overview of the development of China's corporate governance system, viewed through the prism of its legal framework and stock market, demonstrates that China has taken a top-down legalistic approach to corporate governance out of necessity. It was adopted to facilitate economic reforms through piecemeal transplants of basic structures from Western models (Tam 2000).

The trajectory of economic development in China appears to suggest growth first, followed by law reforms to plug loopholes that are impeding growth, and then more growth. In sum, China's reform style is one of 'gradualism' or 'trial and error'. China appears to have adopted a relatively prudent approach (Nolan and Ash 1995) in transforming a centrally-planned economy into a market economy, which is an un-precedented project. The course of its development has been 'growth–reform–law–further growth–further reform–further law'.

Chinese policy-makers and regulators also appear to be eager to learn from, and introduce, proven foreign experience. They are, however, unsure which system(s) would suit them best. Hence, the development of a corporate governance model suitable to the Chinese situation requires further refinement (Shan and Round 2012). Major issues adversely affecting China's corporate governance and stock market include a concentrated ownership structure, shareholders' issues, undesirable related-party transactions, weak BOD independence, and ineffective BOS.

5.5.1 Concentrated Ownership Structure

China has experienced great difficulties in separating government from enterprise (Nolan 2002). Despite the ongoing reforms, the State continues to control the majority of listed companies, directly or indirectly, meaning that problems such as insider control still dominate and majority power remains extremely concentrated (Feinerman 2007).

To add to the woes, CSRC as the major regulator and enforcement agency for the State Council is susceptible to political influence, local protectionism and other forms of pressure. As the major or controlling shareholder of most listed companies, the government is reluctant to enforce the law or impose penalties lest such measures adversely impact on companies' performance (Tsui 2010). There is thus a serious misalign-ment and conflict of interests between the State as the major shareholder, on one hand, and minority shareholders, on the other. The former's interest lies in maintaining social stability and State assets as well as other self-interests, while the latter are concerned about their economic welfare (Trifiro 2007).

Jurisdictions in the West recognize a duty of fair dealing by majority shareholders in relation to minority shareholders. In fact, it is one of the six themes of good corporate governance principles stipulated by the OECD (OECD 2004). Fiduciary duties of controlling shareholders are nowhere to be seen in the relevant Chinese law, and their liability for losses suffered by minority shareholders are not obvious (Feinerman 2007). A duty of diligence (*qin mian*) owed to the company was added to art. 147 of the Company Law; however, there is no mention of whether and how this can be enforced. Also, no duty of care can be found in the legislation (Clarke 2006a).

5.5.2 Shareholders' Issues

The Company Law provides that shareholders may exercise the following powers at the shareholders assembly: (1) decide on company's operational policies and investment plans; (2) elect or replace directors and supervisors, and determine their remuneration; (3) examine and approve the BOD reports; (4) examine and approve the BOS reports; (5) examine and approve company's annual financial budget plan and final accounts plan; (6) examine and approve plans for profit distribution and for making up losses; (7) adopt resolutions on the increase or reduction of registered capital; (8) adopt resolutions on corporate bonds issuance; (9) adopt resolutions on merger, division, dissolution, liquidation or transformation; (10) amend company's articles of association (arts 37 and 99).

In the United States, some of these powers, for instance, the power to approve the company's profit distribution plans and the power to decide on the directors' remuneration, are reserved for BOD rather than shareholders (Schipani and Liu 2002). The rationale behind this institutional arrangement in China is that shareholders are considered the ultimate source of authority. This means the powers enjoyed by BOD and BOS are derived from shareholders rather than from the legislature. This corporate governance philosophy resembles the political governance philosophy expressed in China's Constitution. The National People's Congress (NPC), China's highest ruling body, is an example. The NPC is the supreme power centre in the Chinese political arena and all other state bodies derive their powers from the NPC under the Constitution (art 57). Given the similarities between the governance structures in the political state and in business enterprises, it was understandable for the Chinese legislature to extend the political model into corporate governance, hence the comparison between shareholders' assemblies and the NPC (Schipani and Liu 2002).

Another weakness in the shareholder protection regime is the fact that the Supreme People's Court allows people's courts to hear only very limited types of securities-related claims as class actions (Xu 2005).[11] The Company Law provides minority shareholders with the right to bring lawsuits to people's courts to curb the continuation of unlawful conduct by directors, supervisors or senior management personnel (arts 151 and

---

[11]   According to Xu (2005), the Supreme People's Court promulgated a set of guidelines in 1993 on class actions which restrict local courts to only accepting cases regarding fabricated statements, which virtually rules out investors' chances of taking listed companies to court for other misdemeanours.

152). However, there do not appear to be any relevant regulations or implementation rules to spell out the liabilities or penalties should the shareholders choose to invoke such a right and pursue the parties concerned. The Securities Law is not specific as to whether and when investors or shareholders may take civil action against directors and officers for false or negligent disclosures which give rise to losses being suffered by the companies they serve (Feinerman 2007). Hence, such a remedy is simply a 'lame duck' and unable to render the minority shareholders much assistance. This is mainly because supporting regulations are yet to be promulgated to specify the relevant penalties or liabilities under the Company Law. Such lapses have been common in China.

The dilemma in Chinese company law, as in corporate law across the world, is that majority shareholders have the power to control companies. Corporate law has long recognized the need to counter this right so that majority shareholders may not exercise their control to gain disproportionate benefits at the expense of companies or non-controlling shareholders (Cox, Hazen and O'Neal 1997). By the same token, opportunistic behaviour by minority shareholders may have to be contained or monitored as well. It then boils down to the need for corporate law to strike a sensible balance between the control rights of majority shareholders and the protection of minority shareholders from abuse (Black and Kraakman 1996).

The Company Law has made some good progress in this direction; however, it still falls short of protecting minority shareholders in crucial respects, as discussed above. More importantly, the managers, directors and controlling shareholders remain sheltered by the power of the State, as in most cases these companies are corporatized and/or partially privatized SOEs (Feinerman 2007). These features will have to change if reformers want corporate governance law to have some 'teeth' to sort things out and produce a transformational effect in China.

5.5.3   Undesirable Related-Party Transactions

Majority shareholders are typically powerful in a Chinese listed company while minority shareholders are terribly weak. In this setting, related-party transactions between controlling shareholders and listed companies usually work to the detriment of minority shareholders (Cha 2001; Mei 2005; Schipani and Liu 2002; Tam 2002).

There is evidence that an increasing number of Chinese listed companies have been defrauded by their controlling shareholders directly or

indirectly as a result of shoddy related-party transactions and expropriations, affecting the interests of minority shareholders. The absence of
strong regulations mandating disclosure of related-party transactions has
given many listed companies and their controlling shareholders incentives
to engage in potentially damaging practices, for example, tunnelling, loan
guarantees and/or earnings management (Mei 2005; Shan and Taylor
2008).

The Corporate Governance Code has three requirements for related-
party transactions. First, written agreements must be entered into for
transactions between a listed company and its connected parties. Such
agreements must observe the principles of equality, voluntariness and
provision of fair value of compensation (art. 12). Second, efficient
measures must be adopted by listed companies to prevent connected
parties from interfering with corporate operations and/or damaging
companies' interests by way of monopolizing the sale and purchase
channels. Companies must fully disclose the basis for pricing in related-
party transactions (art. 13). Third, companies must adopt effective
measures to prevent shareholders and their affiliates from misappropriat-
ing or transferring the capital, assets or other resources of companies
through various means (art. 14).

That said, the Corporate Governance Code is merely a guideline for
good governance practice. There is no provision under the Code which
sets out the consequences for breach of any of the provisions therein. The
requirements are not sufficiently strict to achieve the high levels of
disclosure that some of China's Western counterparts may have achieved.

5.5.4 Weak BOD Independence

China's corporate governance is affected by weak independent BOD in
listed companies. The major problems of independence lie with the
directors and managers of listed companies. Chinese directors are normally insulated from responsibility for their companies' economic
performance. Their remuneration is not linked to company performance,
and they cannot be dismissed prior to the expiry of their terms of office
without 'cause', albeit what constitutes 'cause' in this context is not
defined. The Company Law and other laws and regulations do not define
nor explicitly set out directors' duties of care and good faith, and general
fiduciary duties, nor do they create any enforcement mechanisms (Feinerman 2007). Some scholars opine that 'fiduciary duties' are not norms
that exist in China. There is no dynamic equivalent in Chinese for this
concept, which is largely an Anglo-American idea practised in the

common law jurisdictions. Hence, it was not borrowed when Chinese law-makers drafted the Company Law (Clarke 2006a).

Compared with other markets, Chinese BOD have less decision-making power within the current legal framework, whereas government ministries have ample decision-making power. As mentioned above, the range of decisions which must be made by the shareholder assemblies is exceptionally huge in comparison with the position in Anglo-American corporate law. Consequently, Chinese BOD are overshadowed by share-holder assemblies. The discretion left to BOD is substantially diminished (Feinerman 2007; Schipani and Liu 2002).

As discussed above, CSRC stipulated the Independent Directors Guidelines to require one-third of the BOD directors to be independent. Following the enactment of the Independent Directors Guidelines, CSRC promulgated a series of provisions to confer independent directors with special powers to convene shareholder assemblies, invite independent auditors, recruit or dismiss accounting firms, offer independent financial reports, and review proposed related-party transactions before submission to the BOD for discussion. All these measures are designed to strengthen independent directors in performing their duties and discharging their responsibilities in a more effective manner and to promote greater accountability, transparency and fairness for companies (Shan and Round 2012).

Despite CSRC's efforts, the reality is that most listed companies only fulfil the minimum regulatory requirements and most of them have no or inadequate systems for the installation of board committees. In fact, board committees do not appear to be on anyone's priority list (Feiner-man 2007). Hence, it is difficult to expect that the Independent Directors Guidelines will have any significant impact on the ways that Chinese listed companies are run (Clarke 2006b) or give rise to any other significant effect on China's corporate governance system in the near future.

5.5.5 Ineffective BOS

Under the Company Law, BOS are officially conferred with powers that are supervisory and independent. A Chinese BOS is, however, often described as having a 'symbolic rather than practical function' (Young 2009). Unlike their German counterpart, which has powers to appoint and dismiss members of the management board (German Stock Corporation Act 1965, s. 84; Charny 1998), Chinese BOS play no effective govern-ance role. Their effectiveness is undermined by their composition. Chinese BOS are small in size and usually consist of members from labour unions, local party members (possibly government political officials), non-functional trade union members or leaders, friends of BOD members elected by the shareholders and the like.

Chinese BOS have investigative powers and may request correction or rectification from the directors should they find any errors. But the Company Law does not provide BOS with powers to impose sanctions or penalties against BOD members or managers if serious problems are detected in companies' operations or if any BOD members or managers refuse to cooperate or rectify a wrongful act (Tsui 2010).

The key problems in Chinese BOS can be summarized as follows: first, managements not only appoint supervisors, but also determine their remuneration. Thus, BOS have no independence from management. Second, supervisors are not involved in the selection or election of directors or managers, and have no means to discipline them. Third, given the dominant roles that BOD and senior managers play in companies, BOS members are normally treated as 'rubber stamps' or 'censored watchdogs' who should only sing praises of managements installed by controlling shareholders or other government agencies, depending on the company's ownership structure. Fourth, BOS usually have limited access to corporate information. Hence, it is virtually impossible for them to make informed decisions or proposals. Fifth, most of the supervisors are insiders as opposed to outsiders because they either work directly for, or have close connections with, companies, directors, managers or shareholders (Shan and Round 2012). Consequently, it is hardly surprising to find that there is a fundamental lack of independence. In sum, it would be fair to say that Chinese BOS will likely make no impact, despite being designed, supposedly, to improve corporate governance in China.

5.6 PROPOSED IMPROVEMENTS FOR GOVERNANCE ISSUES

As noted above, the current corporate governance system in China has been put together by way of transplanting and/or borrowing institutions in form, rather than substance, from developed and mature economies in the West. Such transplants or borrowings have not proven to be very effective as China has its own unique conditions and realities to deal with. This section proposes some improvements that may help resolve some of the observed corporate governance issues in China.

5.6.1   Restructuring the Role of Government

As discussed above, the Chinese government has the dual role of being a 'market player' and 'regulator' in the development of its economy and stock market and in the implementation of various economic reforms. The State is the ultimate shareholder in most of the listed companies. This undermines the various measures introduced to promote effective corporate governance in China. The State and/or its agencies are always in the way when measures aiming to improve the system are introduced. It is probably time for the Chinese government to restructure or reshuffle its roles in the development of the country's economy. It should focus on fostering a fair and competitive environment for the corporatized and partially privatized SOEs, to further develop them into truly mature companies. This would enable the companies to compete on their own on the international stage. The State can step back and be a fair judge, facilitator and regulator for all types of companies in China, whether domestic or foreign.

5.6.2   Restraining Controlling Shareholders

The most common complaint regarding China's corporate governance system is probably about the heavy hands of controlling shareholders in listed companies. These shareholders are considered to be economic 'superpowers', beyond the reach of corporate governance values and mechanisms. As discussed above, the largest controlling shareholder in China is ultimately the State itself. The way forward is for this shareholder to eventually abdicate the driver's seat and sit back to enjoy the scenery along the road. Through gradually reducing state ownership in listed companies, diversifying its highly concentrated ownership and introducing effective measures to protect strategic industries, China should be able to develop a better economic environment for people in all walks of life.

5.6.3   Improving and Strengthening the Existing Legal System

Various laws, including the Company Law, the Securities Law, the Corporate Governance Code, the Independent Directors Guidelines, and other relevant and incidental rules and regulations, can be further improved and revised to become a more cohesive system. The 'transplanted' measures relating to BOD, BOS and independent directors that have been introduced in China are sound measures *per se*. But China will need to make adjustments to give them more teeth by introducing proper, effective enforcement measures so they work as well together in China as they have done in their home countries in the West. This is proposed because most of the laws have been introduced to plug certain loopholes or resolve issues along the road of economic development. Many of the measures have not been well thought through, and have either conflicted with each other or been ineffective or unworkable for want of the means to implement and enforce them.

In order for various parties' rights to be protected in the market, the judiciary has to step up to perform the functions of supporting the legislation and enforcing it. It is quite obvious from the above discussion that the judiciary has not been given the chance to do its job properly so far (Feinerman 2007), largely because the State has one foot on the accelerator and the other on the brake as far as the judicial enforcement arena is concerned.

5.7 CONCLUSION

Effective corporate governance is absolutely essential to China's economic development. It canvases many facets and issues, and has profound implications. China's current dual board system of corporate governance has not worked very well in improving corporate performance and the accountability of listed companies. As suggested above, a more robust top-down and bottom-up approach must be taken to mould the existing system into one with better and more effective practices.

In this transition process, China has at least taken the first steps to embrace the OECD Principles (2004) and other Western concepts for its corporate governance, stock market and economic development. There will be a lot more to do, and more adjustments to be made, in order to graduate to a better system. Further in-depth studies on other corporate governance systems across the world will be needed so that China may follow new developments and improve its existing practices, having due regard to its own social and economic situations, and achieve its ultimate goals and success.

REFERENCES

Andre, T.J. Jr (1995), 'Some Reflections on German Corporate Governance: A Glimpse at German Supervisory Boards' 70 *Tulane Law Review* 1819
Armour, J. and J.A. McCahery (2006), 'Introduction' in J. Armour and J.A. McCahery (eds), *After Enron: Improving Corporate Law and Modernising Securities Regulation in Europe and the US* (Hart Publishing)

Arslanalp, S., T. Helbling J. Lee and K. Mathai (2016), 'Who Wins and Who Loses as China Rebalances', *iMFdirect* (12 May), available at https://blog-imfdirect.imf.org/2016/05/12/who-wins-and-who-loses-as-china-rebalances/

Bajpai, P. (2016), 'The World's Top 19 Economies', *Investopedia* (18 July), available at www.investopedia.com/articles/investing/022415/worlds-top-10-economies.asp

Backman, M. (1999), *Asian Eclipse: Exposing the Dark Side of Business in Asia* (J Wiley Singapore)

Bhagat, S. and B. Black (1999), 'The Uncertain Relationship Between Board Composition and Firm Performance' 54 *Business Lawyer* 921

Bird, M. (2014), 'China Overtook the US as the World's Largest Economy', *Business Insider Australia* (9 October), available at www.businessinsider.com.au/china-overtakes-us-as-worlds-largest-economy-2014-10

Black, B. and R. Kraakman (1996), 'A Self-Enforcing Model of Corporate Law' 109 *Harvard Law Review* 1911

Bradley, M., C.A. Schipani, A.K. Sundaram and J.P. Walsh (1999), 'The Purposes and Accountability of the Corporation in Contemporary Society: Corporate Governance at a Crossroads' 62 *Law and Contemporary Problems* 9

Cha, L. (2001) 'The Future of China's Capital Markets and the Role of Corporate Governance', The speech delivered at the China Business Summit, 18 April, available at www.csrc.gov.cn/pub/csrc_en/newsfacts/release/200708/t200708 10_69189.html

Charny, D. (1998), 'The German Corporate Governance System' *Columbia Business Law Review* 145

Cheung, Y., P. Jian, L. Piman and T. Lu (2010), 'Corporate Governance in China: A Step Forward' 16 *European Financial Management* 94

China Securities Regulatory Commission (CSRC) (2010), *China Listed Company Corporate Governance Report: OECD-China: Corporate Governance Joint Assessment Programme Self-Assessment* (China Finance Publishing)

— (2012), *Annual Report 2012*, available at www.csrc.gov.cn/pub/csrc_en/about/annual/201307/P020130716403852654782.pdf

— (2014), *Annual Report 2014*, available at www.csrc.gov.cn/pub/csrc_en/about/annual/201506/P020150612564204379767.pdf

— (2016), 'CSRC Hosts Corporate Governance Seminar 01-09-2016', available at www.csrc.gov.cn/pub/csrc_en/newsfacts/PressConference/201609/t20160901 _302902.html

Clarke, D.C. (2006a), *Lost in Translation? Corporate Legal Transplants in China*, George Washington University Law School Public Law Research Paper, available at https://papers.ssrn.com/sol3/papers.cfm?abstract_id=913784

— (2006b), 'The Independent Director in Chinese Corporate Governance' 31 *Delaware Journal of Corporate Law* 125

Cox, J., T. Hazen and F.H. O'Neal (1997), *Corporations* (Aspen Law and Business)

Dong, T. and B. Yu (2015), 'China's stock market suffers biggest one-day fall since 2007', *New Zealand Herald*, 24 August 2015

Duncan, H. and D. Martosko (2014), 'America usurped: China becomes the world's largest economy – putting USA in second place for the first time in

142 years', *Mail* Online, 9 October 2014, available at www.dailymail.co.uk/news/article-2785905

Feinerman, J.V. (2007), 'New Hope for Corporate Governance in China?' 191 *China Quarterly* 590

Ho, D., A. Lau and A. Young (2012), 'Enterprise Ownership and Control in China: Governance with a Chinese Twist' 55 *Business Horizons* 575

Howson, N.C. (2015), 'Amending China's Insider Trading Prohibition: An Immodest Proposal', paper presented at 21st Century Commercial Law Forum, 15th Annual International Conference, Commercial Law Research Centre, Tsinghua University, 31 October–1 November

Investopedia (2015), 'How Chinese Stock Market Heavily Affects the US', *Investopedia* (13 August), available at www.investopedia.com/articles/investing/081315/how-chinese-stock-market-heavily-affects-us.asp

Jia, C., S. Ding, Y. Li and Z. Wu (2009), 'Fraud, Enforcement Action, and the Role of Corporate Governance: Evidence from China' 90 *Journal of Business Ethics* 561

Jiang, F. and K.A. Kim (2015), 'Corporate Governance in China: A Modern Perspective' 32 *Journal of Corporate Finance* 190

Lu, X. and J. Chen (2014), 'Capitalism with Chinese Characteristics? The Case of the Developing Securities Law in China' 22 *Asia Pacific Law Review* 93

Mei, S. (2005), 'The corporate governance of listed companies in China: some problems and solutions' in R. Tomasic (ed), *Corporate Governance: Challenges for China* (Law Press China)

Nolan, P.H. (2002), 'China and the Global Business Revolution' 26 *Cambridge Journal of Economics* 119

— (2005), 'China at the Crossroads' 3 *Journal of Chinese Economic and Business Studies* 1

Nolan, P.H. and R.F. Ash (1995), 'China's Economy on the Eve of Reform' 144 *China Quarterly* 980

OECD (2004), 'OECD Principles of Corporate Governance', available at www.oecd.org/corporate/ca/corporategovernanceprinciples/31557724.pdf

— (2015), 'G20/OECD Principles of Corporate Governance', available at www.oecd.org/daf/ca/Corporate-Governance-Principles-ENG.pdf

OECD Asia Roundtable on Corporate Governance (2011), 'Corporate Governance in Asia', available at www.oecd.org/daf/ca/48806174.pdf

Peng, M.W. (2004), 'Outside Directors and Firm Performance during Institutional Transitions' 25 *Strategic Management Journal* 453

Rajagopalan, N. and Y. Zhang (2008), 'Corporate Governance Reforms in China and India: Challenges and Opportunities' 51 *Business Horizons* 55

Schipani, C. and J. Liu (2002), 'Corporate Governance in China: Then and Now' *Columbia Business Law Review* 1

Shan, Y.G. and D.K. Round (2012), 'China's Corporate Governance: Emerging Issues and Problems' 46 *Modern Asian Studies* 1316

Shan, Y.G. and D.W. Taylor (2008), 'Related-Party Disclosures in the Two-Tier Board System in China: Influences of Ownership Structure and Board Composition' 4 *Corporate Board: Role, Duties and Composition* 37

Tam, O.K. (2000), 'Models of Corporate Governance for Chinese Companies' 8 *Corporate Governance: An International Review* 52

— (2002), 'Ethical Issues in the Evolution of Corporate Governance in China' 37 *Journal of Business Ethics* 303

Trifiro, N. (2007), 'China's Financial Reporting Standards: Will Corporate Governance Induce Compliance in Listed Companies' 16 *Tulane Journal of International and Comparative Law* 271

Tsui, M. (2010), 'Corporate Governance in China', *Bond University Corporate Governance eJournal*, available at http://epublications.bond.edu.au/cgi/viewcontent.cgi?article=1019&context=cgej

Wang, J.Y. (2014), *Company Law in China: Regulation of Business Organizations in a Socialist Market Economy* (Edward Elgar)

Wei, G. and M. Geng (2008), 'Ownership Structure and Corporate Governance in China: Some Current Issues' 34 *Managerial Finance* 934

Wei, S. (2014), 'Fading Registered Capital Rules under the Amended Chinese Company Law: Sweeping Changes in Uncertain Contexts' 8 *International Company and Commercial Law Review* 270

Xu, B. (2005), 'Securities legislation protects investors', *China Daily*, 28 February 2005, available at www.chinadaily.com.cn/english/doc/2005-02/28/content_419958.htm

Yang, J., J. Chi and M. Young (2011), 'A Review of Corporate Governance in China' 25 *Asian-Pacific Economic Literature* 15

Yang, P. (1998), 'Re-examination of the Contract Management System', *China Economic Reference Daily* (24 November)

Young, A. (2009), 'Conceptualising a Chinese Corporate Governance Framework: Tensions Between Tradition, Ideologies and Modernity' 20 *International Company and Commercial Law Review* 235

Young, M.N., M.W. Peng, D. Ahlstrom *et al.* (2008), 'Corporate Governance in Emerging Economies: A Review of the Principal–Principal Perspective' 45 *Journal of Management Studies* 196

PART III

Crowdfunding

6. The two-sided effect of crowdfunding: the visible effect on capital markets regulation and the unperceived effect on company law

Teresa Rodríguez de las Heras Ballell

6.1 'ACCESS TO FINANCE' CHALLENGES AND THE SEARCH FOR ALTERNATIVE SOURCES

Credit availability and access to finance with reasonable conditions are declared to be the most pressing factors in the launching and the development of business projects.[1] Particularly, entrepreneurs and small-and-medium sized enterprises (SMEs) in their start-up stage face financing problems. The financial crisis visibly aggravated the situation, bringing with it a serious funds shortage, higher credit costs (direct costs such as interest rates as well as indirect costs such as greater demands for additional suretyships and security interests), and a general reluctance to support innovative, creative or emerging projects with higher levels of risk.

Financing strategies can be shaped by internal funding sources or external ones and are essentially based on equity or debt. Start-ups and entrepreneurs tend to rely on external financing (Ipsos MORI 2013). Limited retained earnings in the start-up period and a lack of personal financial availability usually force them to look for external funds sources in multiple forms: bank loans, credit lines, public grants, borrowing funds from family and friends, or investments from business angels or venture capitalists (European Commission 2016a). All these types of external financing present benefits and risks, advantages and

---

[1] According to the European Commission (2015a) survey, only 41 per cent of EU SMEs declare not to encounter difficulties in accessing credit. The Ipsos MORI (2013) survey also came to a similar conclusion.

drawbacks. Likewise, not every external funding model is suitable for all business projects. The economic sector in which a business operates, the growth potential, and the development phase are determinant factors in assessing the most suitable (or simply the available) external funding method for each business project.

Another recent trend is a progressive shift of venture capital and bank finance towards subsequent phases of the business finance curve. Venture capitalist and banks are continuously displacing their targets to projects of bigger size, higher financial needs and, as a consequence, lower risk. Below such quantitative thresholds, the finance gap is becoming broader and broader accordingly. The resultant effect of that tendency is an appreciable abandonment of start-up initiatives, innovative projects and emerging business.

The perverse combination of the contraction of traditional financing sources and the increasing finance gap proves to be devastating for the market of start-up business finance. Hence, entrepreneurs and start-ups are pressed to explore and find alternative financing sources beyond the traditional framework of equity- and debt-based funding options. Diversification of financing sources, along with the needed recovery of the credit market, has become a crucial strategy in economic stimulus policies. In such a context, crowdfunding has burst into our economies and stands to fill the gap (European Commission 2016b; see also Collins and Pierrakis 2012).

Certainly, crowdfunding is not a new phenomenon. The possibility of funding a project by raising small (albeit, continuously increasing) contributions from a large number of sources (investors, lenders, donors, users), instead of relying on a few investors to put in the whole amount, has launched many projects and made them feasible throughout history. However, the extraordinary vigour, exponential growth and increasing popularity of crowdfunding at the present time mark a clear inflexion point. More than a simple emulation in digital form of public funds collection, crowdfunding has today gained a unique profile (Rodríguez de las Heras Ballell 2014a) and has become a genuine alternative model for the financing market. Recent studies provide data endorsing the revolutionary potential of crowdfunding for the future of the business finance market.[2]

---

[2] InfoDev/World Bank (2013) estimated the total market potential for crowdfunding by 2025 would be up to US$90–96 billion per year, i.e. 1.8 times today's global venture capital industry.

Three concurrent factors explain its emergence and increasing popularity (see Rodríguez de las Heras Ballell 2013; Rodríguez de las Heras Ballell 2014c). Although the above-described retraction in traditional financing sources and the narrowing of available credit are the trigger for the need to search for alternative funding sources, a social factor and a technological enabler have been decisive in forming the current shape of crowdfunding.

On the one hand, a social movement towards the empowering of communities has encouraged the design of bottom-up processes and decentralized structures. Crowdfunding takes advantage of crowd-based decision-making, collective creation and innovation, and virality of digital activities, and applies them to the funding of projects or businesses (Infodev/World Bank 2013). As a matter of fact, crowdfunding seems to be inspired by and, at the same time, share to a great extent, the philosophy of the growing 'Sharing Economy'. The so-called 'Sharing Economy' describes an economic model that is fuelled by trust, is built of communities and evolves through interaction, collaboration and co-participation relationships (Rodríguez de las Heras Ballell 2014b).

On the other hand, the advent of electronic platforms has created the ideal structural conditions for realizing an authentic crowd-based financing alternative. Digital technology has been a powerful enabler for the creation of multilateral environments based on centralized management, peer-to-peer interaction schemes and contract-based operations (Rodríguez de las Heras Ballell 2006).

6.2 CROWDFUNDING: CONCEPT, VARIATIONS AND REGULATIONS

According to the description formulated by the World Bank, 'crowdfunding is an Internet-enabled way for businesses or other organizations to raise money in the form of either donations or investments from multiple individuals' (InfoDev/World Bank 2013). Certainly, in its infancy, crowdfunding appeared on the market simply as a 'crowd-based funding' method. Nonetheless, it promptly evolved into a more comprehensive model assisting entrepreneurs and SMEs, especially in developing their business strategy. Today, crowdfunding provides more than just funding.[3]

---

[3] 'In addition to providing an alternative source of financing directly, crowdfunding can offer other benefits to firms: it can give proof of concept and idea validation to the project seeker; help attract other sources of funding, such as venture capital and business angels; give access to a large number of people

Crowdfunding permeates the whole business model and helps project promoters to launch marketing campaigns, test markets, interact with clients, validate products and process feedback. At present, crowdfunding is a more complex phenomenon with varied implications.

It is commonplace to classify crowdfunding models into several variations according to the nature of the relationship entered into between contributors and promoters (De Buysere *et al.* 2012). Beyond mere classification purposes, the interest in identifying the diverse categories and their differences is multi-fold. First, through the spectrum of crowd-funding variations one can trace and discover the evolutionary line of crowdfunding. Second, it is easier to visualize and more clearly under-stand the scope and application of the regulatory rules that have been enacted or are in the process of being adopted. Here, a comparison of different crowdfunding models reveals how a variety of interest-protection mechanisms is available but that they are different in each case. Third, as the market moves towards financial crowdfunding models, namely, equity-based and debt-based crowdfunding, the impact on cor-porate governance requirements and on business strategy needs appreci-ably intensifies.

Within the context outlined above, the following variations are already quite familiar in European jurisdictions. In donation-based crowdfunding, donors contribute to projects without expecting any monetary or financial compensation. Reward-based crowdfunding has several variations. In pure reward models, funders receive a token gift of appreciation in return for the contribution. Under pre-sale models, however, the amount contrib-uted by funders represents advance payment of the price for the provision of future services or delivery of goods. Unlike pure rewards, where the value of the gift is symbolic, in pre-sale crowdfunding the contribution may equal the price.

Invoice trading is a form of asset-based financing whereby promoters sell unpaid invoices or receivables, individually or in a bundle, to a pool of investors through the crowdfunding platform. Should the crowdfund-ing model be based on debt, funders contribute an amount of money that will be deemed a loan. Accordingly, they will receive in return a debt instrument entitling them to interest and return of principal on the stipulated date. In social lending models, however, no interest is expected. More sophisticated models are equity-based ones. Two varia-tions may operate here (Association for UK Interactive Entertainment

---

providing the entrepreneur with insights and information; and be a marketing tool if a campaign is successful' (European Commission 2016b: 3).

2012). The securities model implies that investors receive equity instruments in return for their investment and become partners/shareholders of the funded company. Contrarily, the collective investment scheme (CIS) model does not deem funders' contributions to be equity. Funders can only participate in profits under profit-sharing arrangements without exercising ownership or partners' rights. Therefore, the second category may be more accurately defined as investment-based crowdfunding.

All the above-mentioned crowdfunding variations co-exist in the market, but with different levels of popularity, intensity of presence and potential for growth depending on the sector.[4] Nonetheless, an invisible line of evolution can be traced – from non-financial models (donation and reward) to financial models, namely, lending and equity, in recent times. The trend towards financial models has contributed to crowdfunding emerging as a real alternative to traditional financing techniques.

Furthermore, that progressive shift has immediately attracted regulators' attention and increasingly aroused legal concerns. Considering existing regulations, regulatory and supervisory focus has undoubtedly been placed on financial models, namely, equity-based crowdfunding and lending crowdfunding repayable with interest. Funders in donation-based and reward-based crowdfunding models would arguably be protected by general contract rules and consumer protection legislation, but lending and equity-based variations invade the realm of the financial regulations, interweaving multiple public and private interests. Although specific risks have been identified and denounced in non-financial crowdfunding, greater concern arises from financial models of crowdfunding. The legislative milestones reached up until now and the path of regulation reveal the focus of the approach.

Concurrently, the progressive intensification of institutional involvement in crowdfunding is reported (Cambridge Centre for Alternative Finance and Nesta 2016).[5] Venture capital, angel investors and even bank

---

[4] A large percentage of platforms were involved in reward-based crowdfunding (30 per cent), followed by platforms involved in equity crowdfunding (23 per cent) and loan-based crowdfunding (21 per cent) (European Commission 2016b).

[5] Revealingly, in 2015 the European Investment Bank approved a pilot project to provide financing to small and medium-sized enterprises (SMEs) in the United Kingdom through a crowdlending platform, for an amount of approximately £100 million (European Investment Bank 2015). Likewise, as per the market survey conducted within the EU, 45 per cent of platforms in the United Kingdom reported institutional involvement.

entities increasingly co-invest, along with or in parallel to 'crowd investors' through crowdfunding platforms. This trend would confirm the thesis that crowdfunding is permeating the financial markets beyond the limits of the 'finance-gap' area and is shaping an entire financing model. The growing involvement of both institutional and professional investors, and the consequent increase in the average amount of contributions, is also enabling a continuous expansion of sectors and industries. Thus, crowdfunding activity is increasing in renewable energy and real estate.

From the perspective of corporate governance and business strategy, crowdfunding affects various layers. Donation-based crowdfunding and, above all, reward crowdfunding in the pre-sale model exert a visible influence on product design and the deployment of business strategy. It illustrates the contrast with traditional financing contexts where entrepreneurs first seek funds in order to subsequently run the project and attract clients. In contrast, crowdfunding encourages entrepreneurs to restructure the stages of the business strategy process. Hence, promoters first publish their project, test the market, attract clients/users and, subsequently, with a critical mass of clients and a tested idea, address prospective investors for fund-raising. Donation and reward crowdfunding infuses business models with the opportunity to exploit different priorities and competitive advantages.

Lending and, primarily, equity-based crowdfunding are the types that more directly influence promoters' corporate governance requirements and corporate structure. Certainly, as further discussed below, the crowd of investors/lenders calls for a corporate structure that is suitable for managing scattered and numerous financial partners. Likewise, the funding campaign requires more sophisticated and complex disclosures similar to standards that underpin the transparency paradigm in financial markets. However, crowdfunded projects lack a genuine trading market providing liquidity. As a consequence, promoters have to deal with entry and exit requests from existing and prospective investors using available company law tools. This inside effect has nevertheless mostly been disregarded in recent regulations on crowdfunding. Specific solutions provided by funding platforms, creative responses formulated by promoters or the general rules of company laws are the main boundary markers for exploring issues and proposing possible solutions.

6.3 REGULATORY MODEL FOR FUNDING PLATFORMS: 'OUTSIDE EFFECT'

The number of crowdfunding platforms and funded projects has skyrocketed in recent years and the average amount of funds raised has significantly increased (European Commission 2015b; Massolutions 2012). Interestingly, an expansion of crowdfunding beyond micro-credits and micro-investments is more and more visible. Some expansion trends clearly reveal the ambitious enlargement of the scope of crowdfunding. First, as indicated above, the participation of accredited investors or the running of funding platforms where solely accredited investors are eligible entails an increase in investments, funds raised and projects. Second, business angels and venture capitalists are more and more acknowledging the great added value that funding platforms contribute to the financing process (reduction of transaction costs, transparency, centralization of resources, economies of scale, rating services, provision of searchers, comparators or aggregators). Accordingly, these professional and institutional investors are willing to participate as users (prospective investors) in crowdfunding platforms. Wisely, funding platforms are not only filling the gap left by the shift of banks and investors towards later stages of the finance curve, but they are also serving as enablers and intermediaries at the very core of professional investment. Third, as an example of how project budget is increasing and how the focus on start-up projects is being displaced to other economic sectors further from genuinely innovative fields, real estate crowdfunding platforms are making their debut.

Whereas some crowdfunding models, such as donation-based or reward-based ones, have peacefully settled in sectors (such as music, arts, scientific research) that eagerly claimed the diversification of financing sources, the purely financial version, namely, equity crowdfunding and debt crowdfunding, soon aroused legal concerns and attracted regulators' attention, insofar as it invades the natural field of regulated markets. Notwithstanding the complexity added by the cross-border, or delocalized, factor in crowdfunding financing transactions, general contract rules and consumer laws apply to donation-based and reward-based crowdfunding. Therefore, general protection mechanisms for consumer transactions would be activated in the pre-sales, reward-based or, to a certain extent, donation-based model. Nonetheless, such crowdfunding schemes are not totally free of legal concerns. It might be well worth noting, for instance, that the mere conceptualization of crowdfunding financing transactions as being consumer transactions in all cases is indeed questioned. In pre-sales models where the promoter carries out the activity on a regular basis, the application of consumer rules is more easily justified. However, in many peer-to-peer (P2P) transactions (activities that are undertaken sporadically, such as micro-credit for personal/family purposes, donations for non-professional projects, social lending, non-habitual activities) the imbalance between parties is less and this undermines claims for weak-party protection.

In contrast, lending and equity-based crowdfunding encroach upon highly regulated sectors. Attempts to subsume these transactions within the general legal framework for lending contracts and corporate finance might not be enough. Supervision and schemes to regulate intermediaries, market conditions and client protection rules require more complex consideration than just devising legal machinery for financial crowdfunding. Reports, consultation papers and legislative initiatives have successively been elaborated on and adopted in jurisdictions such as France, Spain, Italy and the United States, as explained a little later.

In general terms, two regulatory approaches can be perceived. On the one hand, there is an approach that attempts to subsume debt- and equity-based crowdfunding into existing legal categories. In that regard, some EU Directives tackle crowdfunding-related issues, although they did not originally envision regulating the new phenomenon as such.[6] This approach achieves stability and provides a common playing field for all market players, both traditional and newcomers. Besides, since the rules are adopted at European level, albeit in the form of a Directive, the

---

[6] Directive 2003/71/EC of 4 November 2003, on the prospectus to be published when securities are offered to the public or admitted to trading, as amended by Directive 2010/73/EU of 24 November 2010 [2010] OJ L327/1 (Prospectus Directive) regulates fund-raising by companies. Directive 2009/65/EC of 13 July 2009 on the coordination of laws, regulations and administrative provisions relating to undertakings for collective investment in transferable securities [2009] OJ L302/32 deals with fund-raising by investment companies. Directive 2006/48/EC of 14 June 2006 relating to the taking up and pursuit of the business of credit institutions [2006] OJ L177/1 (Capital Requirements Directive) and Directive 2009/110/EC of 16 September 2009 on the taking up, pursuit and prudential supervision of the business of electronic money institutions [2009] OJ L267/7 (E-Money Directive) governs crowdfunding platforms, and Directive 2011/61/EU of 8 June 2011 on Alternative Investment Fund Managers [2011] OJ L174/1 (Alternative Investment Fund Manager Directive) regulates their dealings with investment companies. Directive 2004/39/EC of 21 April 2004 on markets in financial instruments [2004] OJ L145/1 (Market in Financial Instrument Directive, MiFID) can also impact on the regulation of crowdfunding platforms.

harmonizing potential is higher. But it may fail to detect particularities of crowdfunding and, as a consequence, asphyxiate the emergence of the new sector with unsuitable requirements.

On the other hand, some national jurisdictions have enacted or are planning to adopt specific legislation for crowdfunding; more precisely, in most cases, for lending and equity crowdfunding. The EU is also working on a harmonization solution for crowdfunding. To that end, an Expert Group called the 'European Crowdfunding Stakeholders Forum' (ECSF) was set up in June 2014 to assist the European Commission in exploring the potential and risks of this growing form of finance, as well as the national legal frameworks applicable to it, in order to identify whether there would be added value in European-level policy action in this field. Compared to the non-specific approach, this is more likely to produce a more consistent solution embracing all of the legal issues related to crowdfunding. Nonetheless, the risk of different treatment of market players providing competing financial services (traditional financial intermediaries and funding platforms) has to be carefully managed and attenuated.

The European Commission (2016b: 31) recently concluded that:

> to promote the growth of crowdfunding and appropriately protect investors, EU Member States have put in place a range of measures to regulate crowdfunding – either using the EU legislative framework where appropriate or via national regimes.

It is argued that given the predominantly local nature of crowdfunding and the limited cross-border activity, there is no strong case for EU-level policy intervention at present. National frameworks that have been developed so far are considered by the Commission to be broadly consistent in terms of the objectives and outcomes, even if they are tailored to local markets and domestic regulatory approaches. Therefore, EU monitoring of the sector can be expected to test the adequacy of national approaches and their progressive degree of convergence, to facilitate the consideration of a more intense response at EU level.

All the regulatory initiatives stem from observing that funding platforms have entered the capital market scene and joined the ecosystem of financial intermediaries. A number of regulatory and supervisory issues immediately derive from that development. This is the most visible effect of crowdfunding – the outside effect – which regulators have perceived and skilfully tackled. Tellingly, many of the rules adopted so far deal with issues such as risk management goals, protecting investors' interests, preventing systemic effects, ensuring smooth functioning of the market and enhancing transparency (Baritot 2012; Burkett 2011; Fink 2012; Weinstein 2013).

Schematically, regulations adopted at all levels provide for rules relating to three actors engaged in crowdfunding financing, namely, funding platforms, project promoters and investors/lenders ('the crowd'). These three pillars of regulation are discussed below.

6.3.1 Crowdfunding Platforms

With regard to crowdfunding platforms, although legal models differ in their specific requirements, the regulatory schemes are essentially under-pinned by several or all the following elements: registration, licence/approval and prudential requirements (minimum capital, insurance, organizational form). Under such a regulatory policy, two main approaches seem to be feasible.

On the one hand, countries may opt to subject crowdfunding platform operators to the general rules of financial intermediaries provided that the operators effectively provide regulated services (for example, under the US CROWDFUND Act).[7] A funding platform must hold a broker licence and comply with broker-dealer regulations. On the other hand, legislators may decide to devise a new (bespoke) legal framework for crowdfunding platforms. Newly adopted regulatory requirements may arguably result in a trade-off between (1) the need to protect involved interests and prevent unfair competition with incumbent players; and (2) the inadvisability of imposing an excessive regulatory burden on crowdfunding platforms, which is likely to asphyxiate the emerging sector. So, in France, platform operators must obtain a newly created licence as an 'investment-crowdfunding adviser' (*conseillers en investessements participatifs*) (Ordonnance No. 2014-559, art. 1).[8] As well, in Spain, under the Business Finance Promotion Act 2015 (LFFE 2015),[9] platforms have to be registered, obtain a licence and be named, on an exclusive basis, as a

---

[7] Capital Raising Online While Deterring Fraud and Unethical Non-Disclosure (CROWDFUND) Act of 2012, Pub. L112–106, Title III, 126 Stat. 318.

[8] Ordonnance no. 2014-559 du 30 mai 2014 relative au financement participatif, JORF no. 0125 du 31 mai 2014, 9075, texte No. 14, available at www.legifrance.gouv.fr/eli/ordonnance/2014/5/30/FCPX1406454R/jo/texte.

[9] Business Finance Promotion Act, No. 5 of 2015, Ley 5/2015 de Fomento de la Financiación Empresarial, as published in the Official Bulletin (BOE) 101, 28 April 2015.

'participative financing platform' (*Plataforma de Financiación Participativa* (PFP)). Italy provides an alternative hybrid model, as platforms must be attached to a financial institution.

Under the EU approach, four broad models of authorization for crowdfunding platforms adopted by EU Members in accordance with national legislation can be identified. First, authorization under EC Directive 2004/39/EC[10] and related Directives grants a passport to carry out regulated services and activities throughout the EU (Austria, Germany and France, for transferable securities). This Directive (also known as MiFID, short for Markets in Financial Instruments Directive) enables crowdfunding platforms to provide specified investment services listed in the Directives in relation to listed financial instruments, in particular transferable securities (such as shares and bonds) or units of collective investment undertakings.

Second, there is the national authorization model developed under the exemption provided in MiFID.[11] In this approach, employed in Italy, authorized platforms can carry on crowdfunding-related services and activities at national level also in relation to MiFID financial instruments, but they are not allowed to passport their activities across the EU without getting a full MiFID authorization. In the third national model, authorization for crowdfunding platforms enables them to carry out non-MiFID activities and/or activities not related to instruments covered by MiFID (such as stakes in private companies insofar as they are not deemed negotiable instruments). Spain and Portugal have adopted this model. The fourth national authorization model is outside the MiFID framework and is tailored for crowdfunding platforms.

In sum, all the regulatory requirements create barriers to entry, limit the number of players in the market and impose costs on the platforms accordingly. On the other hand, regulatory requirements are expected to prevent fraud, enhance market stability, enable supervision and minimize risks. Compliance entails costs and, insofar as domestic regulations differ, forum shopping risk increases.

---

[10] European Council Directive 2004/39/EC (MiFID).

[11] Under MiFID, art. 3, Member States may choose not to apply the Directive to any person for whom they are the home Member State who: are not allowed to hold clients' funds or securities; are not allowed to provide any investment service except the reception and transmission of orders and the provision of investment advice; in the course of providing that service, are allowed to transmit orders only to authorized entities; provided that the activities of those persons are regulated at national level.

6.3.2   Investor Protection

To protect investors' interests and minimize systemic risks, investing is limited or capped by statute. Legislation may opt to require prospective investors to be previously accredited/certified in accordance with a set of criteria or establish limits on investments/credits by maximum amount (per project, per investor, in a period of time), frequency or percentages. These limitations adopt different forms and range from fixed maximum ceilings to variable shares of personal income, wealth or financial assets. Diverse forms of cap on investment aim to cushion the risk of loss. Notwithstanding this protection purpose, it has been debated whether the thresholds are too low or likely to hamper crowdfunding potential.

In general terms, quantitative caps are effective, easy to apply and free of interpretation difficulties. Nevertheless, protection purposes can be achieved or enhanced by the implementation of more sophisticated mechanisms. The provision of a set of obligations to inform helps potential investors to make an informed decision, assess risks and protect themselves. These mechanisms operate on a qualitative basis and alleviate the rigidities arising from the application of simple quantitative thresholds. Legislation does indeed combine both approaches.

Spanish legislation (LFFE 2015), for example, relies on a combination of limits on investment. First, investors are divided into two categories: accredited and not accredited, according to a set of criteria (incomes, revenues, patrimony) (LFFE 2015, art. 81). Second, funding platforms are required to monitor non-accredited investors' investment decisions and prevent them from investing either more than 3,000 Euros in the same project as published in one platform or a higher total amount of 10,000 in all projects published in the same platform within a period of 12 months (LFFE 2015, art. 82.1).

Quantitative thresholds are intended to lessen the financial risk taken on by non-accredited investors. Certainly, setting a cap on investment per specific project reduces risk exposure in case of failure and forces diversification. Under Austrian[12] and Portuguese[13] laws, limits on

---

[12]   Austria, Alternative Financing Act (Federal Act on alternative means of financing, Federal Law Gazette Vol. I No. 114/2015, Alternativfinanzierungsgesetz, AltFG), Obligations for issuing bodies as well as operators of Internet platforms ('crowdfunding') regarding the financing of terrorism (s. 4 para. 5 and s. 5 para. 1(2).

[13]   Portugal, Lei no. 102/2015 de 24 de agosto, Regime jurídico do financiamento colaborativo, Diário da República, 1.a série, No. 164, 24 de agosto de 2015.

investable amounts per year (and per individual and/or per project) established by statute are not applicable to legal persons and professional investors. German[14] rules fix different limits on investable amount according to a double test of available assets and monthly income.

It might be worth pointing out here some of the trust-generating formulas implemented in national legislation aiming to provide retail investors with additional factors to assess the risks and potential benefits of each project. The participation of professional investors or own funding platforms in crowdfunding campaigns is supposed to infuse credibility indicia into decision-making and valuation. In that regard, Italian regulation (Regolamento),[15] for example, requires that 5 per cent of the subscription of shares (equity crowdfunding) is to be made by professional investors. Professional investors are here playing the role of trusted third parties. A critical point to further investigate would be potential liability arising from wrong valuation by professional investors.

Theoretically, crowdfunding platforms could perform the role of trusted third parties as well. However, more legal concerns are aroused by the participation of funding platforms, because a trade-off between the prescription effect (trust generation) and the risk of conflict of interest should be carefully managed. On the one hand, when funding platforms are required to invest in every project they agree to publish, a serious valuation and precautionary risk analysis of the project can be expected to be undertaken by other investors. On the other hand, conflicts of interests are more likely to arise, insofar as the funding platform is no longer a neutral venue and is more inclined to favour projects in which it holds an interest or otherwise participates.

Spanish rules on crowdfunding illustrate how a compromise can be managed. First, funding platforms must formulate and publish a policy to prevent conflicts of interest and internal rules guiding the participation of the platform in projects. Second, funding platforms are entitled (but not obliged) to participate in any project that they publish within a limit. The platform's participation can neither be higher than 10 per cent of the financing goal nor entitle it to control the company (LFFE 2015, art. 63). Moreover, in such cases, investors have to be readily informed about the participation (LFFE 2015, arts 63.1.b and 63.2.b). Specific rules on the

---

[14] Germany, Small Investor Protection Act (Kleinanlegerschutzgesetz, Budesgesetzbakatt Teil I, 2015, No. 28 of 9 July 2015).

[15] Italy, Regolamento sulla raccolta di capitali di rischio da parte di start-up innovative tramite portali on-line, art. 24.2. Delibera no. 18592, and the attached Regulation of 26 June 2013, as modified by Delibera no. 19520, 24 February 2016.

management of conflicts of interest, the obligation to adopt reasonable steps to avoid and prevent conflicts, and disclosure duties are similarly provided for under Italian (Title III Regolamento),[16] Portuguese[17] and UK[18] regulations.

Nevertheless, it has long been discussed whether the simple fixing of investment limits, as well as accreditation requirements, are wise decisions, particularly given that non-accredited investors cannot request to be deemed accredited investors unless they can prove that they meet the accreditation criteria. As a matter of fact, some successful funding platforms operating before the enactment of the currently in-force legislation in Spain were intended to offer a platform for business angels (www.thecrowdangel.com). Average investing funds were far from micro-investments, for instance, with a minimum of 3,000 Euros per contribution. Clearly under the newly enacted rules only accredited investors are eligible investors (LFFE 2015, art. 81). The rationale behind that crowdfunding business model is to exploit crowd-based benefits at a later stage of the business finance cycle. Searching, monitoring and transaction costs also impact on the investment process of business angels, venture capitalists and other private equity investors. Funding platforms provide them with a centralized venue to access available projects, compare variables, make selections in accordance with predetermined factors, exchange information, request further data and then decide about investing.

Notwithstanding that the legal technique based on static limits is not particularly sophisticated, in practice, the accreditation criteria set out in Spanish legislation are reasonably attainable. For natural persons, annual incomes must be higher than 50,000 Euros or financial patrimony (investment in the form of financial instruments) must be at least 100,000 Euros (LFFE 2015, art. 81.2.c). Companies must have assets valued at more than 1 million Euros, revenues of at least 2 million Euros, and own resources at least 300,000 Euros (LFFE 2015, art. 81.2.b).

Additionally, SMEs are entitled to be deemed accredited investors on request, provided that the funding platform evaluates the requestor's

---

[16]   Italy, mainly Titolo III, Regole di Condotta, Regolamento sulla raccolta di capitali di rischio da parte di start-up innovative tramite portali on-line, as cited previously.

[17]   Portugal, Lei 2015, in particular arts 11 and 21.

[18]   United Kingdom, Financial Conduct Authoriy, Policy statement 14/4 (March 2014) (UK FCA PS 14/4); see also Financial Conduct Authority, *Review of the Regulatory Regime for Crowdfunding and the Promotion of Non-Readily Realisable Securities by Other Media* (April 2015).

experience and knowledge and ensures the investor can take informed investing decisions and understand the risks involved (LFFE 2015, art. 81.2.d). The reasonableness of limits is only to be assessed in relation to non-accredited investors. These points of reference can be compared to other jurisdictions.

US regulators elected to limit the amount and frequency of investments. Individuals can annually invest up to a threshold. If the investor's net worth plus income is less than US$40,000, he/she can only invest up to US$2,000. If his/her net worth and income combined are less than US$100,000, investment is limited to 5 per cent of his/her income. When income or net worth is greater than US$100,000, the investment limit is raised to 10 per cent of his/her income (US CROWDFUND Act, s. 302).

6.3.3 Regulating Projects and Crowdfunding Campaigns

Projects and crowdfunding campaigns are also regulated. Limits can be either qualitative or quantitative. The Italian case is most revealing in demarcating the personal scope of crowdfunding on grounds of the nature of the project promoter. Thus, regulations initially[19] permit equity crowdfunding for innovative start-ups only. To qualify as innovative, a start-up may not be older than 48 months, and must have a yearly turnover value not exceeding 5 million Euros. It must aim to develop, produce and market innovative products and services of high technological value, and invest a minimum level in research and development. Additionally, innovative start-ups can only raise up to 5 million Euros in a 12-month period. Interestingly, Italy combines the limitation of the personal scope with a cap on the offering amount. In that way, Italian regulations align with other jurisdictions that regulate crowdfunding.

US regulations (CROWDFUNDING Act, s. 302a), as well as rules in France (Décret no. 2014-1053, art. 2),[20] limit the maximum offering

---

[19] Italy, Legge 212/2012, 17 December 2012, di conversione in legge, con modificazioni, del decreto-legge 18 ottobre 2012, no. 179, recante ulteriori misure urgenti per la crescita del Paese, published in *Gazzetta Ufficiale* no. 245, 19 October 2012 – supplemento ordinario – converted, with modifications, into Law of 17 December 2012 no. 221 (12G0244), in force since 13 January 2014, arts 25–31.

[20] Décret no. 2014-1053 du 16 septembre 2014 relatif au financement participatif JORF no. 0215 du 17 septembre 2014, 15228, texte No. 11, available at www.legifrance.gouv.fr/eli/decret/2014/9/16/FCPT1415064D/jo/texte.

amount to 1 million Euros every 12 months. UK regulations[21] also limit the amount raised to £5 million in a 12-month period to avoid having to comply with the prospectus requirement. Likewise, under Spanish legislation on crowdfunding, each campaign cannot exceed the limit of 2 million Euros per year and per platform, unless the project is exclusively addressed to accredited investors, in which case the limit is increased to 5 million Euros (LFFE 2015, art. 68.2).

6.4 CROWDFUNDED BUSINESSES AND GOVERNANCE: THE INSIDE EFFECT

Notwithstanding the regulation of crowdfunding discussed, a second effect has been largely unperceived: the inside effect. This is about the effect crowdfunding has on the inside of the company raising capital from the crowd. In effect, a crowdfunding-based financing strategy challenges traditional company law rules. Rules governing non-public companies are, overall, neither well designed nor effectively operational for managing multiple dispersed partners, atomized capital and go-public-like demands. Since recent rules on crowdfunding are mainly inspired by capital-market regulatory concerns, the dysfunctions are amplified.

Non-public companies embarking on crowdfunding campaigns must suddenly struggle through an unfamiliar field of challenges. These include corporate governance requirements, disclosure duties, complex decision-making, exit strategies when facing illiquidity, finding pure investing partners, public exposure and reputational strategies. Is company law flexible enough to internalize all these required adaptations? Can solutions be implemented in bylaws? Or is legal reform needed? Moving forward, these are important questions for law and public policy. The challenges thrown up by crowdfunding are several. They include the issue of separation of ownership and control, liquidity problems for investors, and disclosure duties for crowdfunded businesses.

6.4.1 Separation of Ownership and Control

First, there is an issue concerning crowdfunded companies prioritizing investors' interests over management's motivations and shareholding

---

[21] As clarified in para. 4.20 (UK FCA PS 14/4), some exemptions to publish a prospectus are available for securities issues meeting certain requirements under Financial Services and Markets Act 2000 (FSMA), ss. 85 and 86.

patterns in closely-held corporations.[22] Under the traditional distinction between public and private (or more precisely, closely held) companies, the latter are commonly characterized by the singular involvement of shareholders[23] in company matters. Since the personal features of shareholders in closed corporations matter, they are not usually deemed to be simple investors but are supposed to be interested in decision-making, management and business development generally. With crowdfunding, a closely held corporation can become more and more open, in which case the presence of investors or purely financial shareholders is more and more likely.

In sum, starting from the hypothesis that many, albeit not all, companies launching crowdfunding campaigns are in the start-up stages of the evolutionary line, they will have to deal with different types of shareholders. Along with the founders and subsequent shareholders willing to engage in company issues, most other participants will be simply motivated by financial aims. Furthermore, a number of micro/small investors will co-exist with founding shareholders. Such a scattered, fragmented and extensive ownership base has to be managed.

Decision-making criteria, director appointment process and voting majorities should be devised accordingly. When a scattered and fragmented base of investing shareholders strengthens, on the one hand, control is concentred in a reduced number of shareholders. But on the other hand, if control is very extensive or broad-based, it may also dilute

---

[22] The general statement may certainly require precision and its accuracy depends on the crowdfunding model, kind of project, sector and other circumstances. In fact, the survey *Crowdfunding from an Investor Perspective* (Financial Services Users Group 2015) revealed that investors in P2P lending cared more about returns, while interest and excitement are more important drivers of investment in equity crowdfunding. Poor returns or losses are the most important risk factors. The survey is cited by the European Commission (2016b: 15).

[23] The term 'shareholders' is used, for convenience and simplification purposes, to refer to those 'members' of the company holding shares or parts or units of the company. In some jurisdictions, members of private companies, with separate legal personality and limited liability for members, would not be shareholders because capital stock is not divided into shares. The contributors of their capital are usually described as members in general. See, for instance, the Spanish Company Act (Real Decreto Legislativo 1/2010, 2 July, por el que se aprueba el texto refundido de la Ley de Sociedades de Capital, published in the Official Bulletin 161, 3 July 2010), which makes a distinction between stock corporations (*Sociedad Anónima*), which include both listed and unlisted companies that issue shares, and private companies (*Sociedad Limitada*).

the decision-making process due to absenteeism, passivity and investors being motivated solely by financial interests in the form of higher dividends.

6.4.2 Liquidity for Investments: Some Possibilities

Second, equity investment in non-public companies is highly illiquid due to the absence of a secondary market. Therefore, exit options have to be carefully considered in bylaws. Illiquidity certainly is the weakest operational feature of crowdfunding as an alternative finance model compared to exchange markets or other functionally equivalent competing schemes. Crowdfunding emulates exchange markets' operation in the fundraising stage insofar as it facilitates the entry and escalates the benefits of collecting funds from the public. Yet today it is still unable to provide liquidity at the exit phase.

Along with business risks, crowd-investors have to face and manage exit risks. Crowdfunding investments lack the uniformity and standardization that can enable negotiability in a liquid market. Investors are exposed to the risk of becoming prisoners of projects. Illiquidity is not a problem created or aggravated by crowdfunding. Certainly, investors and business angels also face such exit difficulties when investing in start-ups and emerging businesses. Nevertheless, illiquidity does hamper the ability of crowdfunding to effectively compete with traditional financial markets. It would be reasonable to foresee that in response to illiquidity investors would tend to maintain their contributions at limited amounts. Accordingly, it would be very difficult for crowdfunding to take off.

It is therefore vital that crowdfunding platforms evolve and develop secondary market functionalities. Within the same crowdfunding platform, as an added-value service, or through another platform entirely specializing in enabling negotiability/liquidity, a secondary market to trade interests (shares, stakes, units) in crowdfunding projects can operate. Thus, funding platforms can be fuelled by higher liquidity. Although this service is not provided systematically, there are already some examples of different models and forms providing such secondary marketplaces (European Commission 2016a).

One model entails the direct involvement of the crowdfunding platform, enabling the connecting and interaction among investors who intend to sell and potential acquirers of such investments. In practice, such liquidity-providing platforms acting as emerging exchanges will likely compete with traditional markets. It might be predicted that the regulatory response would be similar to the approach initially followed in dealing with Alternative Trading Systems, or Multilateral Trading Facilities, as labelled under EU MiFID) (see generally Maynard 1992; De Bel 1993; Nyquist 1995; Lee 1998: 117–39). In another model, crowdfunding platforms may opt to collaborate with existing trading platforms for unlisted companies and thus enable investors to buy and sell securities that have been offered through crowdfunding platforms.

In enabling liquidity, any restriction on the transfer of shares, securities or other interests held by investors in crowdfunded companies as laid down in regulations (such as a minimum holding period or transfer solely under limited circumstances) should be taken into consideration to assess the scope and the feasibility of proposed secondary-market facilities. Likewise, provisions in shareholders'/partners' agreements will be relevant to assess the marketability of shares, securities or other interests.

6.4.3 Disclosure Duties for Crowdfunded Companies

Third, whereas publicly traded companies are familiar with multifarious disclosure duties, these duties can represent a huge burden for unlisted companies, particularly for small private enterprises.[24] Regulations on crowdfunding have essentially opted for disclosure duties as the most effective instrument to enhance transparency, market efficiency and investor protection. As in stock markets, project promoters have to disclose relevant information and provide the platform, prospective investors and investors with increasingly varied data.[25]

The ultimate aim is to prevent insider trading and ensure informed investing decisions. Benefits of large access to finance would arguably compensate publicly traded companies for the high cost of complying with disclosure duties. For start-ups and SMEs, however, the increasing information requirements might exhaust the expected benefits of collecting funds. Along with other legal concerns related to confidentiality issues and idea protection, disclosure and reporting duties in crowdfunding should ideally find an equilibrium between, on the one hand, the need to protect investors and promote market efficiency and, on the other, the costs for project promoters and the reasonableness of such duties, taking

---

[24] Some commentators stress the enormous potential benefits of crowdfunding as being a genuine revolution for corporate finance (see, e.g., Privé 2012). But there have also been criticisms about the complexity of investments, difficulties in standardizing the investment process and the high cost of regulation compliance (Isenberg 2012).

[25] See, e.g., Spain (LFFE 2015, arts 70, 72, 73, 75, 76, or 78); Portugal (Lei No. 102/2015, arts 14, 17 or 19).

into consideration the size, early evolutionary stage and organizational base of enterprises.

In France and Portugal, the required information has to be provided in a certain document or format.[26] In the United Kingdom, there is a general obligation to provide sufficient information in a clear, fair and not misleading manner.[27] More interestingly, domestic laws differ in the solution adopted about the allocation of such disclosure of information duties and liability. Whereas under some legislation all obligations regarding information are imposed on the promoter, other legal models also entrust platform operators with some duties regarding the provision of sufficient information.[28] Although responsibility for the information should be ultimately taken on by the promoter, the latter model would be expected to encourage platforms to implement procedures and rules to ensure that the required information is provided in a timely manner and is sufficient for investor decision-making.[29]

Certainly, if the specific aim of regulation reform is to provide regulatory relief to emerging growth companies to encourage initial public offerings, that should entail exemptions or phasing-in of certain requirements. But, if duties and requirements are not properly gauged, the process may become expensive and time-consuming.

---

[26] Under French regulations, key information has to be provided in a predefined template (Annex 1 to the Autorité des Marches Financiers (AMF) instruction DOC-2014-12). The format in which to provide the required information, as well as the key data to include, are considered in the public consultation launched by the Portuguese Securities Market Commission (CMVM) (Portuguese Financial Markets Authority 2015).

[27] United Kingdom (Financial Conduct Authority Review (UK) 2015); Spain (LFFE 2015, art. 70.1).

[28] A comparative table included in the European Commission Staff Working Document (2016b: 43) illustrates the different national approaches. See also n. 29 below.

[29] Spanish legislation provides an illustrative example in that regard. LFFE 2015, art. 71 sets out that the platform shall ensure that the information supplied by the promoter is complete and provided in accordance with the legal provisions, and shall publish any information pertaining to the project and/or the promoter in its possession; LFFE 2015, art. 73 states that the promoters will be accountable to investors for all the information provided to the platform for publication.

6.5 CORPORATE GOVERNANCE STRUCTURES FOR CROWDFUNDED COMPANIES

It is important that crowdfunded (non-public) companies adopt appropriate structures for their governance. Certainly, crowdfunding provides an extraordinary opportunity for start-ups and SMEs, along with individuals and unincorporated businesses, to access finance. In return, project promoters opting for crowdfunding must accept market scrutiny. Likewise, should funding campaigns result in a wide and fragmented investing mass/crowd, promoters would suddenly face the complications, needs and challenges that openness entails and which a small/closely-held corporation is not usually familiar with. The concluding section discusses some options for the governance of crowdfunded companies and the use of digital technologies in the effort.

6.5.1 Shareholder Participation and Digital Technologies

First, the crowdfunded company should protect and facilitate the exercise of shareholders' rights. Given the potentially high number of investors, the supposedly reduced participation in the company, the possible cross-border element, and the investing/financial profile of investors, crowdfunded companies will have to design and adopt corporate schemes to facilitate the decision-making process. In that regard, Spanish legislation requires that bylaws should include the right to participate and attend shareholders' meetings through electronic means and the right to use a proxy to be represented at meetings by any person (LFFE 2015, art. 80.1.a). Provisions regulating both rights necessarily have to be included in promoters' bylaws, and any provision in the bylaws that is likely to infringe the said legal provisions shall be null and void (LFFE 2015, art. 80.2). The use of digital technology in company operations can hugely minimize the corporate governance challenges for crowdfunded companies. The availability of digital functionalities for corporate purposes can remove obstacles to the free and widespread exercise of shareholders' rights.

Effective use of digital technology and implementation of interactive applications can facilitate the management of a company, irrespective of the size and the number of members, with due protection of different rights and interests. Nonetheless, an effective electronic exercise of rights has to be based on state-of-the-art electronic procedures and interactive environments. Cost and accessibility to technology are other important factors. Crowdfunding platforms can find here an appealing business opportunity. These platforms can decide to offer, as an added value to their users (promoters and investors), technological infrastructure to enable digital meetings, live interaction and other functionalities to assist promoters in the management of crowdfunded companies.

6.5.2 Dealing with Large Shareholder Bases

From a different perspective, the problem of a massive number of shareholders (especially minority shareholders) in start-ups or small-sized companies can be managed by the implementation of structural solutions aimed at 'isolating' crowdfunded corporations from their 'crowds'. According to applicable legislation, available options may differ.

(a) Minimum shareholding requirements for voting

The rationale of effective shareholder participation would be behind the need to consider fixing by bylaws the minimum number of shares to be held for attending and/or voting at company meetings. Otherwise, it might happen that shareholders' meetings become massive, that a quorum is in practice difficult to attain, or that the exercise of the right to be informed about company issues overloads company managers with information requests.

(b) Use of non-equity models

Investment can be in convertible bonds that will be subsequently converted or be susceptible of conversion into equity within a specific period or at a specific date at a predetermined conversion rate – transitioning from debt-based crowdfunding to equity-based crowdfunding. Alternatively, investment can be articulated as a profit-sharing/revenue-sharing model. In such models, investors do not hold ownership interests in the company. Their contribution to and the participation in the project operate through contractual instruments (for example, silent partnerships, *cuentas en participación*), aimed at regulating distribution of revenues and, if agreed, losses.

(c) Use of nominee accounts

When possible under applicable legislation, investors may invest in the equity of a crowdfunded company through a nominee account, whereby a third party holds the legal title to the equity on behalf of the investors who would be beneficial owners of the securities. Crowdfunding platforms can also offer, require or simply permit the use of organizational vehicles to gather investors, unify and channel investors' decisions and participate as a sole shareholder in the crowdfunded company. In this structure, crowdfunded companies would benefit from having a more limited numbér of shareholders to deal with. There would be less complexity in managing a highly-atomized ownership base, and the structure could also contribute to controlling transaction costs in enabling the effective exercise of shareholder rights, and streamlining company decision-making processes and structures.

(d) Intermediary vehicles
In the intermediary organizational model, investors do not invest directly in crowdfunded companies; instead they join and participate in an organizational vehicle acting as an intermediary. The role of that vehicle is merely and solely instrumental, as it aims to merge dispersed and varied shareholders into a single layer and direct their participation on a unified basis towards the target company. At a second layer, the intermediary vehicle becomes a shareholder of the crowdfunded company. Investors only participate indirectly in the target company.

The intermediary vehicle, as a separate and distinct legal entity, may in principle adopt any legal form available under applicable legislation (partnership, closed corporation, limited liability company, stock corporation, collective investment scheme). It would be advisable to choose a legal form that is not too costly to create and sufficiently simple and flexible to manage. Should the intermediary vehicle be likely to generate costs, a decision to distribute and allocate such costs should be discussed.

If the prospective investors are expected to be minority partners, given the envisaged amount of their contributions, the allocation of costs associated with the intermediary-based structure to backers would seem inadequate and will very likely be a clear disincentive for small investors. Alternatively, either the platform or the promoter may consider taking responsibility for the structure. So, on the one hand, it might be offered as an added-value service provided by the platform, or, on the other hand, it might be assumed to be an inherent cost of the fund-raising process by the promoter. Besides, it should be remembered that any actions likely to delay the immediacy presumed in online transactions, to hinder the advantages of a non-intermediated financial environment or to complicate or prolong investment decisions may exert destructive effects on the competitiveness of crowdfunding models compared to other funding options. Consequently, the option for implementing any of the described structural schemes as a business strategy should be carefully considered.

Another critical issue is to ensure that the distribution of power according to investors' contributions in the vehicle is not distorted in the second stage and a reasonable level of representativeness is achieved. As the intermediary vehicle is the only genuine shareholder in the crowd-funded company, decision-making processes and management rules within the intermediary vehicle have to be carefully devised. Decisions are first adopted within the intermediary vehicle and, subsequently, its designated representative or agent will participate in deliberations and vote to adopt decisions in the target company's meetings. If the intermediary company internally applies measures aimed at limiting voting rights by fixing caps or imposing the holding of a minimum number of units/shares in order to attend meetings and/or to vote, the participation expectations of investors in the target company could be frustrated.

In fact, having voting majorities (minimum number of votes representing capital and/or number of members to validly adopt decisions) and quorum rules (minimum number of members holding or duly representing capital attending the meeting to deem it constituted) are also decisive issues. As an example, should the threshold for adopting decisions (voting majority) be too low, minority members in the intermediary vehicle will see their (indirect) representation significantly diluted in the target company.

The complexity of the implementation of an intermediate organizational level could dissuade from creating an intermediary legal entity. Hence, other solutions should be considered. An associative or simply consensual formula might provide effective solutions without the costs and drawbacks of an intermediary legal entity. To the extent that the applicable legislation permits, the following solutions can be considered.

(e) Co-ownership agreements

Investors can hold as co-owners the stakes (whole or part) of the target company offered in crowdfunding. Each investor would hold a portion or quota of the total. An agreement signed among the co-investors would provide the rules on the distribution of dividends and profits, representation scheme and decision-making. Structurally and operationally, the 'crowd' forms a community that acts in unity through its designated representative in the running of the target company. As a result, the crowdfunded company is not headed towards the complex situation of managing a high number of small and dispersed shareholders.

(f) Syndicates and voting agreements

Voting agreements, syndication or functionally equivalent formulae may provide a solution to the management of decision-making processes involving numerous shareholders. Under a voting agreement, the legal title would remain with individual shareholders. Therefore, the solution is partial. It only ensures united action in the exercise of the right to vote by the delegation of the right, on a revocable basis, to a representative under the voting agreement. But the company still has to manage multiplicity and dispersion in the compliance of its information duties, distribution of dividends and in other situations. Even more, in many cases, the voting agreement would not involve the designation of a representative. Parties to voting agreements can agree to vote separately and individually, although in the same agreed direction. In some jurisdictions, voting trusts are available as an alternative device.

Any agreement (voting syndication, shareholders' agreement) affecting voting rights in a company to any extent may impact upon the merchantability of the company's shares/stakes due to any conditions or limitations that are imposed. These should be disclosed and immediately communicated to all members of the company. Such a rule is provided for in Spanish legislation, which extends a typically financial-market-oriented mechanism to unlisted companies (LFFE 2015, art. 80.1.c). The same rule is stated in Italian regulations (Regolamento, art. 24.1.b).

Efforts to consider and carefully manage the new corporate governance challenges for crowdfunded companies will make the inside effect of crowdfunding more perceptible. A first step would be to assess the degree of adaptability of company law schemes to emerging needs. As access to financial markets has shaped the legal regime for publicly-held companies, crowdfunding-based finance options also impact on company issues. The success of a crowdfunding campaign, especially the continuity of the financed project, depends upon the adequacy of the organizational model and the suitability of the corporate decisions made in the strategic configuration of the organization running the project.

Crowdfunding rules adopted in several domestic jurisdictions do not tackle organizational issues, or they do so only tangentially. The outside effect requires more prompt and effective attention due to the potential systemic risks and interests at stake. The inside effect should now be considered to contribute to the development of crowdfunding as an alternative finance option and the consolidation of crowdfunded projects. The organizational and governance dimensions of crowdfunded projects are critical enablers that should be strategically designed and effectively implemented in the market given the specific features and particular implications of crowdfunding campaigns.

REFERENCES

Association for UK Interactive Entertainment (2012), *UKIE Crowd Funding Report: A Proposal to Facilitate Crowd Funding in the UK*, available at

http://ukie.org.uk/sites/default/files/UKIE%20Crowd%20Funding%20Report%
20-%20A%20Proposal%20to%20Facilitate%20Crowd%20Funding%20in%20
the%20UK%20-%20%20February%202012.pdf

Baritot, J.F. (2012), 'Increasing Protection for Crowdfunding Investors Under the
Jobs Act' 13 *UC Davis Business Law Journal* 259

Burkett, E. (2011), 'A Crowdfunding Exemption? Online Investment Crowdfunding and U.S. Securities Regulation' 13 *Transactions: Tennessee Journal of
Business Law* 63

Cambridge Centre for Alternative Finance and Nesta (2016), *Pushing Bound-
aries: The 2015 UK Alternative Finance Industry Report* (February)

Collins, L. and Y. Pierrakis (2012), 'The Venture Crowd: Crowdfunding Equity –
Investment into Business' (Nesta, July), available at www.nesta.org.uk/sites/
default/files/the_venture_crowd.pdf

De Bel, J. (1993), 'Automated Trading Systems and the Concept of an
"Exchange" in an International Context. Proprietary Systems: A Regulatory
Headache!' 14 *University of Pennsylvania Journal of International Business
Law* 169

De Buysere, K., O. Gajda, R. Kleverlaan and D. Marom (2012), *A Framework
for European Crowdfunding*, available at http://eurocrowd.winball2.de/wp-
content/blogs.dir/sites/85/2013/06/FRAMEWORK_EU_CROWDFUNDING.pdf

European Commission (2015a), *Survey on the Access to Finance of Enterprises
(SAFE): Analytical Report* (December), available at http://ec.europa.eu/
DocsRoom/documents/14321/attachments/1/translations/en/renditions/native

— (2015b), *Crowdfunding: Mapping EU Markets and Events Study* (30 September), available at http://ec.europa.eu/finance/general-policy/docs/crowdfunding/
20150930-crowdfunding-study_en.pdf

— (2015c), *Action Plan on Building a Capital Markets Union*, Communication
to the European Parliament, the Council, the European Economic and Social
Committee and the Committee of the Regions 468/2

— (2016a), *Commission Staff Working Document, Capital Markets Union: First
Status Report* (25 April), available at http://ec.europa.eu/finance/capital-
markets-union/docs/cmu-first-status-report_en.pdf

— (2016b), *Commission Staff Working Document, Crowdfunding in the EU
Capital Markets Union* (3 May), available at http://ec.europa.eu/finance/
general-policy/docs/crowdfunding/160428-crowdfunding-study_en.pdf

European Investment Bank (2015), *Innovative SME Financing: P2P Pilot
Facility* (28 September), available at www.eib.org/projects/pipeline/2014/
20140307.htm

Financial Conduct Authority (UK) (2014), 'The FCA's regulatory approach to
crowdfunding over the Internet, and the promotion of non-readily realisable
securities by other media' (Policy Statement 14/4, March), available at
www.fca.org.uk/static/documents/policy-statements/ps14-04.pdf

— (2015) *Review of the Regulatory Regime for Crowdfunding and the Promotion
of Non-Readily Realisable Securities by Other Media*, available at www.
fca.org.uk/static/documents/crowdfunding-review.pdf

Financial Services Users Group (2015), *Crowdfunding from an Investor Perspective* (September), available at http://ec.europa.eu/finance/finservices-retail/
docs/fsug/papers/160503-fsug-position-crowdfunding_en.pdf

Fink, A.C. (2012), 'Protecting the Crowd and Raising Capital through the Crowdfund Act' 90 *University of Detroit Mercy Law Review* 1

InfoDev/World Bank (2013), *Crowdfunding's Potential for the Developing World*, available at www.infodev.org/infodev-files/infodev_crowdfunding_study_0.pdf

Ipsos MORI (2013), *2013 SMEs' Access to Finance Survey: Analytical Report* (European Commission, 14 December), available at http://ec.europa.eu/DocsRoom/documents/7864/attachments/1/translations/en/renditions/native

Isenberg, D. (2012), 'The Road to Crowdfunding Hell' *Harvard Business Review*, 23 April, available at https://hbr.org/2012/04/the-road-to-crowdfunding-hell

Lee, R. (1998), *What is an Exchange? The Automation, Management, and Regulation of Financial Markets* (Oxford University Press)

Massolutions (2012), *Crowdfunding Industry Report: Market Trends, Composition and Crowdfunding Platforms* (May), available at www.ncfacanada.org/wp-content/uploads/2012/10/Massolution-Full-Industry-Report.pdf

Maynard, T.H. (1992), 'What is an "Exchange"? Proprietary Electronic Securities Trading Systems and the Statutory Definition of an Exchange' 49 *Washington and Lee Law Review* 833

Nyquist, P. (1995), 'Failure to Engage: The Regulation of Proprietary Trading Systems' 13 *Yale Law and Policy Review* 281

Portuguese Financial Markets Authority (2015), 'Public Consultation 7/2015', available at www.cmvm.pt/pt/Legislacao/ConsultasPublicas/CMVM/Documents/Financiamento%20Colaborativo%20%20Documento%20de%20consulta%20p%C3%BAblica%20da%20CMVM_04.12.2015.pdf

Privé, T. (2012), 'Top 10 benefits of crowdfunding', *Forbes*, 10 December, available at www.forbes.com/sites/tanyaprive/2012/10/12/top-10-benefits-of-crowdfunding-2/#3b95a1fb371a

Rodríguez De Las Heras Ballell, T.R. (2006), *Régimen Jurídico de los Mercados Electrónicos Cerrados (e-Marketplaces)* (Marcial Pons, Madrid)

— (2013), 'Modelos jurídicos para el Crowdfunding : Nuevas formas de financiación colectiva de proyectos' *La Ley Argentina* 1

— (2014a), 'Las plataformas de financiación participativa (crowdfunding) en el Proyecto de Ley de Fomento de la Financiación Empresarial: Concepto y funciones' 15 *Revista de Derecho del Mercado de Valores* 8

— (2014b), 'Refusal to Deal, Abuse of Rights and Competition Law in Electronic Markets and Digital Communities' 22 *European Review of Private Law* 685

— (2014c), 'El Crowdfunding como mecanismo alternativo de financiación de proyectos' 1 *Revista de Derecho Empresarial* 121

The Crowd Angel (2016), 'The Crowd Angel: business angeling made easy', available at www.thecrowdangel.com

Weinstein, R. (2013), 'Crowdfunding in the U.S. and Abroad: What to Expect When You're Expecting' 46 *Cornell International Law Journal* 428

7. Regulating equity crowdfunding in India: walking a tightrope

Arjya B. Majumdar and Umakanth Varottil

7.1 INTRODUCTION

Start-up companies are hamstrung when it comes to raising finances, as they rarely have access to venture capital, angel investment or more conventional forms of financing. This is particularly so with new ventures in pioneering fields that carry a high risk of failure. Such a financing shortage was exacerbated by the Global Financial Crisis in 2008. It was around this time that crowdfunding made its appearance as an attractive alternative capital-raising mechanism for start-ups, harnessing technology (primarily the Internet) to access funding from the 'crowd'. Since then, while crowdfunding has grown exponentially, it has also encountered regulatory constraints in the form of securities laws in various countries that could stand in the way of unleashing its full potential.

Crowdfunding has been defined as the means by which an entrepreneur or business raises financing by way of small contributions from a large number of individuals using mass communication through the Internet (Bradford 2012: 10; Mollick 2014: 2; Schwienbacher and Larralde 2010: 4). The funds are usually raised through an online crowdfunding platform.

7.1.1 Types of Crowdfunding

Although there are various types of crowdfunding, they can be divided into two broad categories. In one, a business idea can be funded by individuals either without the expectation of financial gain (donation crowdfunding) or in return for specified units of the product or service, the development of which is being funded (reward crowdfunding). In the other category, an entrepreneur or business may obtain funding either in the form of a loan against interest (peer-to-peer lending) or for an equity stake in the business (equity crowdfunding). The second category of crowdfunding attracts greater regulation as the funders bear a financial exposure to the business that they have funded.

Among the last two sub-categories, peer-to-peer lending is proximate to banking from a regulatory perspective, while equity crowdfunding involves an investment in a company and therefore falls within the realm of securities regulation. While the different types of crowdfunding may attract varied sets of legal issues, this chapter is primarily concerned with equity crowdfunding.

Equity crowdfunding is advantageous to start-ups as it enables them to cast a wide net in raising funds and, given the power of the Internet, from investors anywhere in the world. It helps them overcome the limitations of pre-existing forms of financing. It is also beneficial to investors (referred to as the 'crowd') as it democratizes investment activity by making opportunities available to all investors, and not necessarily only the wealthy or the sophisticated (Schwartz 2015: 619–20). All of these can help increase economic growth and the development of the market for innovation and entrepreneurship (Vitins 2013: 116).

7.1.2   Factors Shaping the Regulatory Approach

At the same time, crowdfunding activity involves significant risks for the crowd. As most businesses engaged in crowdfunding are in new-age business activities, the profitability of which is unknown, the chances of failure are magnified. Moreover, the rather anonymous nature of online activity accentuates the risk of fraud, principally due to information asymmetry between businesses and investors. This leads us to the core question: how should one regulate equity crowdfunding in a manner that both enhances its appeal to engender the development of small and new-age businesses through accessible funding opportunities and, at the same time, protects the investors against undue risks, such as fraud, which arise from the activity?

Regulators are faced with two rather opposing considerations: on the one hand, to promote fundraising by small businesses in an economical and friendly manner and, on the other hand, to fulfil the investor protection function in the equity markets. Is it possible for regulators to locate the sweet spot for regulating crowdfunding by balancing the various considerations? Given the novelty of crowdfunding, regulators in several countries are grappling with these tensions with a view to designing an appropriate regulatory regime.

In this chapter, we explore these core questions and the regulatory conundrum by examining the legal regime for crowdfunding in India. The country presents itself as an ideal laboratory for crowdfunding. It has a burgeoning but vibrant start-up culture that has spawned the growth of innovation and start-ups, which have constant funding needs. The government too has played its part by introducing measures such as the 'Start Up India' initiative in January 2016 to create jobs and boost economic productivity through new businesses using modern technology (Ministry of Commerce and Industry 2016). On the supply side, the enormity of India's crowd presents unparalleled crowdfunding opportunities: a population of over 1.3 billion people with approximately 24.5 million households that actively invest in securities markets, either through mutual funds or directly through secondary markets (SEBI 2011: xiv).

Despite the existence of a combination of factors that ought to facilitate equity crowdfunding, the idea is yet to take off in India. While donation and reward crowdfunding have witnessed a gradual expansion, equity crowdfunding has been a non-starter. This can be attributed to the existence of stringent regulation that prohibits businesses from raising finances from the crowd unless they comply with the stringent, expensive and time-driven norms relating to the public offerings of companies, which are entirely incommensurate with the needs and abilities of small businesses.

As we discuss in this chapter, the rules in India relating to fundraising by companies have been considerably tightened under the Companies Act, 2013. Unless fundraising offers are made to a very limited number of participants, they will be treated as public offers that require businesses to follow a plethora of disclosures and compliances. Such a strict regime was the result of several scandals that involved corporate groups raising millions of dollars in investments from tens of thousands of investors in the garb of private placements without complying with the necessary regulatory requirements. Similarly, there have been several cases whereby businesses have raised money from gullible investors in the form of illegal collective investment schemes, which have incurred the wrath of the securities regulator, the Securities and Exchange Board of India (SEBI).

These developments led to regulatory reforms culminating in the Companies Act, 2013 with stringent requirements for fundraising from a larger body of investors. SEBI too has been given additional powers to crack down on illegal collective investment schemes. Given the prevailing regulatory sentiment towards fund-raising by Indian businesses, which has effectively attenuated the options available for receiving investments from non-accredited investors, equity crowdfunding has received a death-knell even before it has been introduced in the country. However, SEBI has expressed some interest in creating a market for crowdfunding in India by issuing a consultation paper (SEBI 2014), which proposes a framework for ushering in equity crowdfunding in India by providing capital market access to small businesses.

7.1.3 Favouring a Cautious Approach?

SEBI's proposals contain significant limitations and onerous conditions that would have the effect of stifling rather than promoting the growth of crowdfunding in India. Moreover, since its consultative effort in 2014, SEBI has not provided any indication as to whether a specific regulatory regime will in fact be introduced, let alone its timing (Khan 2016).

In analysing equity crowdfunding regulation in India, we find that the regulators have engaged in a tightrope-walking exercise by signalling their interest in promoting a market for crowdfunding to enable small businesses, but at the same time introducing significant measures to protect the crowd. In our view, the unduly onerous conditions imposed by SEBI, including limiting crowdfunding to accredited investors and retail investors, who must meet high thresholds of eligibility, will have the effect of 'taking the crowd out of crowdfunding' (Garside 2014), thereby rendering it hollow and unable to provide the intended benefits to small businesses. On the other hand, due to the prevailing perception in India about mass fund-raising efforts and large-scale frauds that often accompany them, we do not believe that the Indian markets are equipped to handle a more liberal regime towards fund-raising.

More so, it would be imprudent to expect the regulators to make an about-turn in their regulatory efforts towards fund-raising. Either way, we are not sanguine that regulatory efforts will promote or facilitate equity crowdfunding in the Indian markets. Hence, start-ups may have to confine themselves to venture capital, angel investment and other traditional forms of financing. Crowdfunding in India is likely to be confined to types that do not involve a financial return.

Following this introduction, section 2 outlines the promises and challenges of equity crowdfunding, and considers how regulation can play a balancing role. Section 3 examines various strategies for regulating equity crowdfunding by comparing the regimes in various countries. Section 4 is the core of this chapter. It analyses crowdfunding regulation in India, its philosophy, policy and proposals, and critiques the same. Section 5 concludes the chapter. Although crowdfunding regulation encompasses several aspects of securities markets, here we focus on issues pertaining to primary markets. Constraints of space do not permit us to discuss matters pertaining to secondary markets or the regulation of crowdfunding platforms, although they are an integral part of regulating crowdfunding in the overall sense.

7.2 PROMISES AND CHALLENGES OF EQUITY CROWDFUNDING: A REGULATORY BALANCING ACT

When regulating crowdfunding, it is necessary to consider both its promises and perils, and then arrive at an appropriate balance. Crowdfunding is beneficial to start-ups as well as potential investors, who may wish to partake in the financial successes of such firms. It has emerged as a viable alternative to existing forms of start-up financing. On the other hand, equity crowdfunding carries significant risks, particularly for investors. In this section, we highlight the key benefits and risks of equity crowdfunding, as prefatory to understanding the goals of regulation.

7.2.1 Benefits of Equity Crowdfunding

Using crowdfunding, start-ups and their founders are able to raise financing by accessing investors who are beyond their personal networks and connections (Hu 2015: 56–7). Using the Internet, they are able to obtain funds from a wider range of investors, from varied geographies. Due to the lower cost of such capital, crowdfunding offers an affordable and attractive fund-raising option to start-ups (Kirby and Worner 2013: 4). Crowdfunding also enables start-ups to test their ideas with the market by inviting potential customers to participate in the financial future of such ideas. The collective 'wisdom of the crowd' can provide a good indication as to the acceptability of the product or service being offered by the start-up (Hu 2015: 58). All of these features are expected to engender a vibrant environment for entrepreneurship that ultimately promotes economic growth.

Apart from start-ups, crowdfunding is beneficial for the crowd too. Until recently, only wealthy and sophisticated investors had access to investing in start-ups. By extending access to investments beyond such investors, referred to in securities regulations as 'accredited investors', crowdfunding allows a wider community of investors to participate in the success of start-ups. Such a diversity of investors enables due diligence by the crowd, by which investors are able to piggyback on the efforts of some to ascertain information regarding the start-up in which they are investing. It also allows for wider decision-making and monitoring by the crowd (Schwartz 2015: 627–8).

In all, by providing a viable alternative means of funding start-ups, equity crowdfunding is immensely beneficial both to entrepreneurs as well as the investors who form part of the crowd.

7.2.2 Risks of Equity Crowdfunding

The benefits of equity crowdfunding must be balanced against a number of risks that the activity poses. The first of these includes the risk of investing in an early-stage company. Start-up companies carry an inherent risk of failure. Failure statistics universally show that over 50 per cent of newly founded firms will fail during their first five years (Kirby and Worner 2013: 24). Consider the case of Bubble and Balm, a Fair Trade soap company. In 2011 it raised £75,000 through an equity crowdfunding platform, Crowdcube, based in the United Kingdom. In return, it issued 15 per cent of the company's equity. In July 2013 the business closed abruptly, leaving contributors in the lurch. The contributors ended up losing their entire investment (Kirby and Worner 2013: 25).

The second risk relates to illiquidity of the investment. Crowdfunded securities are not traded on any stock exchange or crowdfunding portal. Hence, investors are unable to sell their securities on a market to recoup their investments. Given that investments in start-ups are unlikely to yield dividends for a long period of time, investors are likely to be stuck with their investments without realizing any return on them (Hu 2015: 60).

The third is the risk of outright fraud, which arises due to information asymmetry, lack of transparency and the relative inexperience of investors in crowdfunding. Start-ups and their founders will be privy to substantial information regarding the status of their business that is not available to the investors. Further, while investing in a crowdfunded project, investors tend to rely solely upon the representations of fund-raisers and generally do not undertake due diligence on the business they are investing in (Agrawal *et al.* 2013: 19).

The lack of a detailed review of the fund-raising start-up's affairs opens up the possibility of the company concealing information relevant to its future, whether actively or passively (Fink 2012: 31–2). Studies have shown that detailed disclosures about risks can promote the success of the fund-raising efforts (Ahlers *et al.* 2015: 957), although factors such as friendships and social networks cannot be discounted (Lin *et al.* 2013: 17).

Apart from fraud, information asymmetry also leads to adverse selection resulting in the 'market for lemons'. Under this theory, since issuers have more information than investors, the investors are unable to distinguish between good investments and bad ones. The crowdfunding market is clearly susceptible to the market for lemons (Schwartz 2015: 631–2), which is likely to suffer an oversupply of 'dumb money' (Ibrahim 2015: 591–2).

Finally, due to the dispersed and diverse nature of the crowd, the investors are likely to suffer from collective action problems. Their inability to coordinate can prevent them from effectively monitoring the founders and managers of start-ups who raise funds from them. In any event, given that the crowd consists of unsophisticated and inexperienced investors, it would be too much to expect any kind of monitoring from them. Hence, the crowdfunding investors can suffer from agency problems between managers and shareholders that strike at the heart of corporate governance (Schwartz 2015: 633–6).

As we have seen, crowdfunding carries with it risks that are above and beyond traditional forms of finance. Hence, any regulatory response needs to address these concerns directly.

7.2.3   A Regulatory Conundrum

To begin with, crowdfunding involves raising capital from a wide variety of investors. Hence, in most jurisdictions, it falls within the purview of a public offer of securities requiring fully-fledged compliance with a prospectus and other requirements. This makes it immensely costly for start-ups, which therefore cannot utilise that fund-raising method. In order to facilitate crowdfunding, it may be necessary to carve out a separate regime under securities regulations in order to enable a wider range of investors, including non-accredited investors, to invest in these start-ups. In designing the appropriate regulatory regime for crowdfunding, regard must be had to the twin (somewhat competing) considerations of promoting economically beneficial start-up activity and at the same time ensuring investor protection. This would result in a 'win-win' situation where the benefits of crowdfunding are harnessed while the risks are mitigated.

Heminway and Hoffman (2011: 937–8) set out the foundational principles for the appropriate regulation of crowdfunding. The objectives are to:

> Limit investor risk; Optimize fraud protection; Enhance informational transparency; Foster standardization of disclosures and enforcement; Constrain regulatory costs; and Minimize costs to issuers and investors.

They also argue that, in arriving at a regulatory balance, it is important not to impose excessive costs on issuers or regulators such that they operate as disincentives, thereby rendering crowdfunding unattractive. However, it is generally the case that regulators tend to tilt their efforts in favour of investor protection at the cost of promoting a vibrant start-up market (Bradford 2012: 98–9).

Although there could be several methods of regulating crowdfunding, it is clear that steps must be taken to address the problem of information asymmetry. Given that the problem is severe in the case of small businesses and start-ups, any regulatory strategy must lay emphasis on meaningful disclosures (Hazen 2012: 1737). Disclosure rules could operate as a useful regulatory tool to balance between the growth of small businesses and investor protection. However, there is no consensus yet on whether disclosure norms ought to be introduced on a mandatory basis or whether alternative market-based mechanisms would be more effective (Black 1998: 92; Choi 1998: 30).

After analysing how regulation ought to balance the benefits and risks of crowdfunding so as to meaningfully unleash its potential, we move on to various regulatory strategies that have been adopted in several jurisdictions, before dealing with the situation in India.

7.3 COMPARATIVE PERSPECTIVES ON REGULATING EQUITY CROWDFUNDING

The regulatory treatment of equity crowdfunding in various jurisdictions around the world can be placed into three broad categories (Kirby and Worner 2013: 30). In the first category, the regulatory regime prohibits equity crowdfunding in its entirety while reiterating the existing law on fund-raising by companies. The second category involves countries that have begun to accept this novel method of raising capital and treat it within the realm of public offers of securities, albeit by building in appropriate exemptions. In the third, some countries have adopted tailor-made regulations that seek to encourage this form of financing without, at least apparently, compromising investor protection.

7.3.1 Prohibiting Crowdfunding

Hong Kong is a prime example of a jurisdiction that reiterates its existing law on prohibiting fund-raising in relation to methods such as equity crowdfunding. The Securities and Futures Ordinance, 2002 (SFO) provides for the regulation of activities connected with financial products, the securities and futures market and the securities and futures industry, as well as the protection of investors in Hong Kong. It prohibits the issue of an advertisement, invitation or document that contains an invitation to the public to purchase securities, unless it is authorized by Hong Kong's Securities and Futures Commission (SFC) (SFO 2002, s. 103(1)). However, offers of securities made to professional investors such as banks, insurance companies, investment schemes and other financial intermediaries are exempt from this rule (SFO 2002, s. 103(3)(k), Sch. 1, Pt 1). While equity crowdfunding aimed solely at professional investors is arguably possible, there are no specific rules on equity crowdfunding in Hong Kong. Moreover, such an approach does not comport with the overall objectives of crowdfunding, which is aimed at the masses rather than only sophisticated investors.

The SFC has clarified its intention by issuing a notice that advises participants in crowdfunding-type activities as to the potential risks involved, including the risks of default, illiquidity of the investment, platform failure and insolvency, fraud, risks associated with platforms operating outside Hong Kong, information asymmetry and lack of transparency, cyber security issues and possible illegal activities (Notice on Potential Regulations 2014).[1]

Thus, Hong Kong has adopted a strict approach towards equity crowdfunding and favoured investor protection over the economic benefits to start-ups, although more recent voices have called for the introduction of equity crowdfunding in a measured fashion (Hong Kong Financial Services Development Council 2016).

7.3.2 Carving Out Exemptions

Some jurisdictions have adopted a softer approach towards equity crowdfunding and have created specific exemptions in the regulation of public offers of securities. This seems to be the preferred strategy for regulating equity crowdfunding, with a large number of countries drawing inspiration from the Jumpstart Our Business Startups Act of 2012 (JOBS Act) in the United States.

(a) United States

Beginning with the United States, securities offerings generally require registration with the Securities and Exchange Commission (SEC) (Securities Act, s. 5(c)), a process that is both expensive and time-consuming

---

[1]   Securities and Futures Commission, Hong Kong SAR, 'Notice on Potential Regulations Applicable to, and Risks of, Crowd-funding Activities' (7 May 2014), available at www.sfc.hk/web/EN/files/ER/PDF/Notice%20on%20Crowd funding.pdf.

(Bradford 2012: 42). Although several traditional exemptions from registration exist, they are unavailable for crowdfunding as they are either aimed at offerings to sophisticated investors or are accompanied by stringent advertising restrictions. Hence, following strong bipartisan support, in 2012 Congress enacted the JOBS Act, which introduced a specific exemption under the US securities laws to permit the sale of securities through crowdfunding, thus making available a new funding option to businesses that were hitherto constrained in raising capital (Knight, Leo and Ohmer 2012: 136).

Specifically, Title III of the JOBS Act, the Capital Raising Online While Deterring Fraud and Unethical Non-Disclosure Act of 2012 (CROWDFUND Act), exempts certain fund-raising activities from the registration and prospectus requirements. This exemption paves the way for start-ups and small businesses to genuinely access the crowd. In 2015, the SEC released detailed rules to implement the CROWDFUND Act in the form of Regulation Crowdfunding,[2] which came into force in May 2016 (SEC 2015).[3]

Issuers seeking an exemption under the CROWDFUND Act may raise up to US$1 million within a 12-month period. There are limits for individual investors as well. Where the annual income or net worth of an investor is less than US$100,000, such an investor can invest up to US$2,000 or 5 per cent of the investor's annual income or net worth. Where the annual income or net worth is US$100,000 or more, such an investor can invest up to 10 per cent of their annual income or net worth. Furthermore, the CROWDFUND Act imposes obligations on portals and issuers that they must meet in order to seek exemptions from the far more stringent and onerous requirements of the Securities Act.

As one of the first statutes to regulate crowdfunding, the CROWDFUND Act created a new and largely unexplored market for fundraising (Fink 2012: 4), which has since been emulated by other jurisdictions. It sets out the primary mechanism by which a company with low share capital may offer shares to investors, whether accredited or otherwise, with reduced disclosure, registration and procedural requirements than would otherwise be required. This allows companies to access a range of investors with limited restrictions, thereby taking advantage of the diversity of the crowd.

---

[2]   17 CFR Parts 200, 227, 232, 239, 240, 249, 269, and 274.

[3]   Securities and Exchange Commission, 'Crowdfunding, Final Rule, Release Nos 33-9974; 34-76324; File No S7-09-13' (30 October 2015), available at www.sec.gov/rules/final/2015/33-9974.pdf.

(b)   Australia

Another country that follows the exemption approach to encompass some form of crowdfunding is Australia. While most forms of capital-raising require detailed disclosures in the form of a prospectus, there are carve-outs from the general disclosure rules in two specific situations, namely (i) offers made to sophisticated investors, and (ii) small-scale offerings. Offers may be made without a disclosure document to investors who can show at least AUS$2.5 million in net assets or AUS$250,000 in annual income (Corporations Act 2001 (Cth), s. 708(8)). Other investors are barred from participating in such offers. Small-scale offerings are restricted to AUS$2 million, the number of investors is restricted to 20, and they are not allowed to be advertised (Corporations Act 2001, ss. 708(8), 734(1)).

The Australian Small Scale Offerings Board (ASSOB) facilitates small-scale funding and provides for a secondary market in securities. Since 2005, the ASSOB has raised AUS$140 million in funding for more than 300 start-ups and small to medium-size enterprises through equity crowdfunding (White 2014). Arguably, neither of these exemptions serves the purposes of crowdfunding, which typically involves investors with varying net assets and annual incomes, and there are usually more than 20 investors (Vitins 2013: 108–9).

In August 2012, the Australian Securities and Investments Commission (ASIC) issued guidelines concerning crowdfunding (ASIC 2012). These guidelines reiterate the existing law on fund-raising in Australia and specifically point to certain requirements. Owners of Australia-based websites that facilitate crowdfunding may be legally considered to be the persons offering the financial products; they must apply for an Australian Financial Services License and provide a Product Disclosure Statement (PDS) to investors to whom the offers are made. Advertising and publicity restrictions also apply to offers of financial products or securities that require a PDS or a prospectus. To date, there is no specific exemption setting up a regulatory environment that is conducive to crowdfunding in Australia. However, there have been strong arguments for exempting investment crowdfunding from those parts of the Corporations Act that were designed to regulate traditional securities offerings (Vitins 2013: 123–7).

(c)   Singapore

A similar exemption is available in Singapore. Like other jurisdictions, securities offered by way of equity crowdfunding in Singapore can be deemed a 'public offering' and be required to comply with the regulations set forth by the Singapore Securities and Futures Act (SFA),[4] including the requirement to have a prospectus (SFA, s. 240). Companies that make an offer of securities to investors in Singapore must register a prospectus with the Monetary Authority of Singapore (MAS). Certain offers are exempted from the registration requirement. These include: (i) small offers of less than SG$5 million during any 12-month period made on a personal basis (SFA, s. 272A); (ii) private placements of securities with less than 50 persons (SFA, s. 272B); and (iii) offers made to institutional and accredited investors (SFA, ss. 274 and 275). The SFA stresses the importance of not advertising such offers. For these reasons, crowdfunding is not viable under the regulatory regime in Singapore (Hu 2015: 66–71). However, the MAS floated a consultation paper in February 2015 on facilitating securities-based crowdfunding (MAS 2015), which suggested that participation in crowdfunding activities be restricted to accredited investors and institutional investors only. It also reinforced the SFA's stand on advertising restrictions and suggested that exempted offers should not be subject to any mass solicitation, advertising or canvassing. As a result, if a crowdfunding platform were to allow unrestricted access to the general public as to the details of offers of securities published on its platform, such as information about an offeror and the terms of the offer, it could be in breach of the advertising restrictions.

Hu (2015: 63–4) suggests that the Singapore crowdfunding proposal is restricted to accredited and institutional investors, and also subject to advertising restrictions, which would considerably narrow the market for crowdfunding in Singapore and fail to realize the potential of the crowd. However, in June 2016 the MAS announced that appropriate amendments would be carried out in the SFA to ease the process of making small offers of less than SG$5 million to retail investors. Additionally, crowdfunding platforms would be subject to reduced base capital and lower operational risk requirements (MAS 2016). It may be surmised that Singapore will gradually open up its crowdfunding markets.

Thus, we find a wide variety of regulatory strategies deployed by jurisdictions that follow an approach of carving out exemptions from securities regulations for crowdfunding. Clearly, the US regime under the CROWDFUND Act is most accepting of crowdfunding as it permits offers of securities to non-accredited investors and on a wider basis. However, the exemptions in jurisdictions such as Australia and Singapore

---

[4]   Cap. 289, 2002 Rev. Ed. Sing.

are arguably restrictive. While there is considerable momentum for creating a conducive environment for crowdfunding, the regulators are unwilling to expose non-accredited or unsophisticated investors to the risks emanating from crowdfunding. While economic compulsions in the United States have motivated the legislature to favour economic growth for small businesses and start-ups, Australia and Singapore have maintained a continued focus on investor protection.

7.3.3 Comprehensively Legislating

A smaller number of jurisdictions have created tailor-made regulations, which seek to encourage equity crowdfunding while at the same time focusing on investor protection. Italy was one of the first jurisdictions to pass a comprehensive regulation on equity crowdfunding. New Zealand is another example of a country with specific regulations governing crowdfunding.

(a) Italy

Law 221/2012[5] specifically allows for crowdfunding to support the development of 'innovative start-up companies'. That the law refers specifically to innovative start-ups underscores that it is targeted at businesses strongly linked to innovation and technology, and not just at any new enterprise (Government of Italy 2012). This was further crystallized in a set of regulations issued by the Commissione Nazionale per le Società e la Borsa (CONSOB), Italy's securities regulator, which provides for 'the collection of risk capital on the part of innovative start-ups via on-line portals' (CONSOB Regulation 2013).[6] Much of the onus on shareholder protection has been placed on the portal. Portals must register themselves with the CONSOB and must comply with integrity and professional requirements on a continuous basis (CONSOB Regulation 2013, arts 4–11).

The portal is made primarily responsible for information circulated to potential investors and must adequately warn non-professional investors as to the risks of crowdfunding activities (CONSOB Regulation 2013, arts 13, 15, 16). While the portal is responsible for the publication of the offer information, the issuer is solely responsible for the completeness and truth of such information (CONSOB Regulation 2013, annex 3). Other investor protection measures include the requirement for at least

---

5   Law 221/2012 (12G0244), in force since 13 January 2014.
6   No. 18592 of 2013.

5 per cent of the offer to be underwritten by professional investors and the right of investors to withdraw from the company in certain circumstances (CONSOB Regulation 2013, arts 4–11).

(b) New Zealand

In New Zealand, the Financial Markets Conduct Act of 2013 governs how financial products are created, promoted and sold, and the ongoing responsibilities of those who offer, deal and trade in them. It specifically allows intermediary service providers such as portals to be licensed under the Act (Financial Markets Conduct Act 2013, s. 390). This licensing regime is intended to facilitate suitably regulated crowdfunding services operating in New Zealand. Offers made through licensed intermediaries do not require disclosures.

The Financial Markets Conduct Regulations 2014 provide for definitions of crowdfunding services (reg. 185) and set out eligibility criteria for portals to seek a licence to carry out such services (regs 186–7). The regulations also set up detailed disclosure and procedural requirements, mandatory warning statements and other obligations for such service providers. With regard to the issuer, the upper limit for raising funds is capped at NZ$2 million in any 12-month period (Financial Markets Conduct Regulations 2014, reg. 186). It is interesting to note that the crowdfunding provisions in New Zealand do not provide for upper limits on individual investments, nor do they create a distinction between sophisticated and retail investors, thereby making it one of the most crowdfunding-friendly jurisdictions (Chandrasekhar 2016).

The advantage of comprehensive regulation, as witnessed in Italy and New Zealand, is that it can seek to address the specific features of crowdfunding. These include the fact that securities representing small amounts can be offered and issued to a large body of investors, requiring advertising using the Internet and new-age media, with limited restrictions. In that sense, they capture the essence of crowdfunding more directly.

In concluding this section, we find that regulators across different jurisdictions have followed different strategies for regulating crowdfunding. Certain jurisdictions, such as Hong Kong, have maintained a strict focus on investor protection with limited room for crowdfunding activities. Countries such as the United States, Australia and Singapore have opened the doors for crowdfunding to varying degrees through the use of exemptions, some expansive and others limited. The final set of countries such as Italy and New Zealand have embraced crowdfunding more directly with a view to stimulating that activity further. This comparative analysis will enable us to discuss the situation in India within the broader global context rather than in an isolated fashion, a matter to which we now turn.

7.4 EQUITY CROWDFUNDING REGULATION IN INDIA

In this section, we first assess the nature and scope of the crowdfunding market in India, discuss the existing regulation surrounding equity funding, and then analyse SEBI's consultation effort (SEBI 2014) aimed at introducing a specific regulatory regime governing equity crowdfunding.

7.4.1 Nature and Scope of the Crowdfunding Market in India

Following US-based crowdfunding portals such as Kickstarter and Indie-gogo, a number of similar portals have established themselves in India as well. Ketto, Fuel-A-Dream and BitGiving are key players in donation crowdfunding, while Wishberry and Igniteintent are involved in rewards crowdfunding. Milaap and Rang De are involved in peer-to-peer lending. There are also a few quasi-equity crowdfunding platforms such as LetsVenture, termsheet.io, Investopad and Catapoolt, which showcase start-up companies to eligible institutional investors (MyOnlineCA 2015).

However, the market for crowdfunding in India is yet to substantially take off. Milaap, arguably India's largest donation and lending platform (Patnia 2013), is said to have raised INR705 million, while Rang De, another social lending platform, is said to have raised US$3 million (Ashta *et al.* 2015). In comparison, Catapoolt and LetsVenture are said to have raised, respectively, INR13 million (The Hindu Business Line 2015) and US$17 million (Krishnamurthy 2015). Contrast this with INR728.49 billion invested by Venture Capital Funds and Foreign Venture Capital Investors (SEBI 2015) and investments worth INR140.31 billion made by Alternative Investment Funds as of December 2015 (*ibid.*). It seems that crowdfunding has a long way to go before it becomes a credible alternative to more established forms of corporate finance.

7.4.2 Current State of Regulation

The current state of regulation in India renders equity crowdfunding a non-starter. More so, the trajectory of regulatory developments has led it towards tighter control and restrictions on offers of shares by companies, thereby moving it in a direction that is antithetical to the needs of a favourable regulatory regime for crowdfunding. The design of the current Indian regulations is such that the goals of investor protection overshadow the promotion of the crowdfunding market. In order to highlight our argument, we briefly outline major recent developments in Indian securities regulation.

In India, an offer of securities by a company is governed by the provisions of the Companies Act as well as regulations issued by SEBI under the SEBI Act, 1992. Under the pre-existing Companies Act, 1956, a company was permitted to make an offer of securities to the public only by means of a prospectus, with the securities to be listed on a recognized stock exchange so as to provide liquidity to the investors. This required companies to undertake an extensive public offering process that could last several months and be prohibitively expensive, especially for small companies.

Private placements of securities did not have to comply with these onerous requirements so long as they were targeted offers made to specific persons, with the number of offerees not exceeding 49 persons (Companies Act 1956, s. 67). By this, any offer made to 50 persons or more effectively became a public offering. Hence, crowdfunding in its usual form was not permissible within the realm of that regime.

While the Companies Act was in the process of being reformed, India was struck by several scandals involving illegal offerings of securities by certain companies, which had the broader impact of intrinsically shaping the reform process on securities regulation. Two unlisted companies belonging to the Sahara Group distributed information memoranda through which they raised 'over USD 3 billion from nearly 30 million investors from amongst their intricate network of associated companies, employees and other related individuals' (Chandrasekhar 2016). This can be considered a form of crowdfunding, although it was never termed as such.

(a) *Sahara* case

Several companies failed to comply with the prospectus and other requirements necessary for a public offering of securities. Upon discovering this, SEBI initiated investigations, clamped down on such arrangements and ordered the Sahara companies to refund the amounts raised to the investors along with interest. Sahara challenged SEBI's actions, and the litigation went all the way up to the Supreme Court of India. Ultimately, the Supreme Court found that Sahara's actions were in breach of securities regulations and affirmed SEBI's sanctions (*Sahara* 2013).[7] In its zeal to ensure the refund of monies to the investors, the Supreme Court even ordered that the high-profile chief of the Sahara Group be held in prison until all obligations were honoured. A crowdfunding effort that was brazenly undertaken in utter disregard of the regulations received a forceful judicial rap on the knuckles.

As the Sahara episode was being played out before the regulators and the judiciary, another scandal broke in the form of the Saradha Group of companies in the state of West Bengal, which had raised billions of dollars' worth of deposits from 1.7 million people in what turned out to be a Ponzi scheme (Datta 2013). This too caused a considerable political and popular uproar that resulted in the arrest of the personalities behind the group. Over the years, several other scandals involving fund-raising through illegal collective investment schemes have been investigated and dealt with by SEBI, but none as high-profile as the ones discussed above.

While the regulators and judiciary have sought to firmly deal with the perpetrators of fraud in these instances, what is more relevant for our purposes is the broader impact of these scandals on regulatory reforms. Unsurprisingly, they have caught the attention of the regulators, who have acted swiftly and firmly to impose additional checks and balances on fund-raising by Indian companies. The unfortunate, and perhaps unintended, effect of such a reaction is that it paints fraudulent acts such as those undertaken by groups such as Sahara and Saradha, and fund-raising efforts by honest and genuine small business and start-ups, with the same brush. As a result, activities such as crowdfunding have been constrained even further.

(b)   '*Sahara* effect' on regulation

More specifically, the '*Sahara* effect' reverberated during the enactment of the Companies Act, 2013. As a result, the government introduced a new provision in the legislation to deal with such situations. Section 42 of the Companies Act, 2013, provides that whenever a company makes an offer to 50 or more persons (or such other higher number as may be prescribed by the Government of India) in any financial year, the offer should be treated as a public offer requiring compliance with full-blown prospectus and related requirements. The government has since increased the maximum number of offers to 200 persons in each financial year (Companies (Prospectus and Allotment of Shares) Rules 2014,

---

[7]   *Sahara India Real Estate Corp. Ltd* v. *Securities and Exchange Board of India* [2013] 1 SCC 1.

r. 14(2)(b)). However, this limit excludes offers to qualified institutional buyers (QIBs), such as banks, insurance companies and other institutional investors, as well as offers to employees under a scheme for employee stock options.

This scenario is intended to ensnare the very type of situation witnessed in the *Sahara* episode. Hence, while it is possible for small businesses and start-ups to make offers to up to 200 investors each financial year, this limitation severely restricts their ability to widely disseminate their offer, particularly because private placements are accompanied by prohibitions on advertisements. Such an absolute cap on the number of offers that can be made each year is not only unusual, but it also operates as a severe dampener to fund-raising efforts. Hence, such businesses cannot seek investments of small amounts from a larger number of investors, an aspect that is inherent in crowdfunding. Instead, s. 42 permits the converse, namely, raising large amounts from a few investors, which is conducive to non-crowdfunding options of financing such as private placements, venture capital and angel investments.

In this milieu, equity crowdfunding is impermissible and cannot be undertaken unless the legal regime is altered. As the preceding discussion would indicate, the legal reforms have been moving in the direction of tighter control over offers of securities by companies in the interests of investor protection. At the same time, given the rapid growth of crowdfunding as an attractive fund-raising option, and the Indian government's drive towards promoting small business and start-ups in India, it is impossible to turn a blind eye to the need for such reforms. In this context, SEBI in 2014 initiated a debate for such reforms by issuing a consultation paper seeking to explore the possibility of introducing crowdfunding in India. SEBI's consultation paper (SEBI 2014) constitutes the single most detailed effort in considering crowdfunding regulation in India. Hence, we now examine SEBI's proposals and analyse them in the context of the discussion so far.

7.4.3 SEBI Consultation Paper on Crowdfunding

At a broad policy level, SEBI's consultation paper identifies the need to 'strike a balance between retail investor protection and capital market access' to small businesses and start-ups, and that if regulatory provisions geared towards investor protection are excessive, they will stifle the crowdfunding market (SEBI 2014: para. 9.0.4). In designing proposals for crowdfunding in India, SEBI also considers the legal regime in several other jurisdictions, thereby seeking to learn from their experience.

Here, we set out some of SEBI's key proposals and analyse their effectiveness in striking the appropriate balance.

(a)   Restricting eligibility for issuers

At the outset, SEBI has identified that crowdfunded companies are typically early stage start-up companies that either have limited access to capital or have exhausted available avenues for raising finances (SEBI 2014: para. 9.2.4). Any regulation must ensure that the crowdfunding mechanism is not misused by companies that have reasonably evolved businesses or that have access to other sources of finance. Hence, SEBI has stipulated certain criteria for companies that can avail themselves of the crowdfunding option. These include that the issuer must be unlisted and less than 48 months old; that it should not be part of a larger industrial group or conglomerate; and that the aggregate size of the offering should not exceed INR100 million. Several other conditions for disqualification are prescribed, including that the issuers or their controllers must not be in breach of corporate and securities regulations. These conditions are understandable and help achieve the requisite balance between promoting crowdfunding and protecting investors.

(b)   Nature of investors

When it comes to the eligibility of the investors or the composition of the crowd, SEBI has adopted a rather stringent approach (SEBI 2014: para. 9.1.4). Under its proposals, crowdfunding is restricted to 'accredited investors', who are (i) QIBs; (ii) companies with a minimum net worth of INR200 million; and (iii) high net worth individuals (HNIs) with a minimum net worth of INR20 million (excluding primary residence). These are essentially wealthy investors who are capable of taking the risks arising from crowdfunding.

A residual category of Eligible Retail Investors (ERIs) has also been added into the category of accredited investors. ERIs are those with a minimum annual gross income of INR1 million, and who have filed income tax returns for the last three financial years. Moreover, in order to qualify as an ERI, such an individual must have received investment advice from an investment advisor, availed themselves of the services of a portfolio manager, or passed an appropriate test. Such ERIs must further ensure and certify that they do not invest more than INR60,000 in any particular crowdfunded issue and not more than 10 per cent of their net worth (excluding the value of their primary residence) in crowdfunding activities.

(c) Investment and offer limits

SEBI's proposals also impose individual investment limits for crowd-funding (SEBI 2014: para. 9.1.5). Consistent with the Companies Rules (2014), SEBI has imposed minimum funding limits in multiples of a minimum value of INR20,000. For example, a QIB is required to purchase at least five times the minimum value, a company at least four times, a HNI at least three times and an ERI at least the minimum value. However, the maximum investment by an ERI is not to exceed INR60,000 and the total of all investments in crowdfunding by such a person cannot exceed 10 per cent of their net worth. Moreover, in order to ensure the quality of the offering, all QIBs must collectively hold a minimum of 5 per cent of the securities issued. An adoption similar to the Italian model, such a requirement has an important signalling effect for the crowd.

An additional condition is that a crowdfunded offering shall not be made to more than 200 HNIs and ERIs. However, offers can be made to any number of QIBs. This is ostensibly in view of the numerical restrictions on offers imposed by the Companies Act, 2013 (s. 42) and the Companies (Prospectus and Allotment of Shares) Rules 2014. In other words, any crowdfunded offering ought to remain within the confines of a private placement within the meaning of company law (Iyer 2016).

(d) Procedures and disclosures

A company that meets the eligibility criteria for crowdfunding is required to apply to a crowdfunding platform to undergo screening and due diligence. Once approved, the company's details along with information about the requirement of funds may be displayed on the crowdfunding platform. The platform is then accessed by accredited investors who analyse and evaluate the company and its funding requirements. If there is adequate interest in the company, the company may then proceed to circulate a private placement offer letter to the interested investors.

In terms of disclosures, companies are required to circulate information similar to a private placement offer letter under the Companies Act, 2013 (s. 42). These disclosures include a description of the venture for which the funds are being raised; the specified target offering amount and intended usage of the funds; a description of the valuation of the securities offered; past funding history, if any; basic financial information regarding the company; ownership and governance structures; and principal risks to the issuer's business.

Upon the circulation of the private placement offer letter, accredited investors may choose to invest in the company or may decide to withdraw their commitment. The crowdfunding platform acts as an escrow agent, collecting investment amounts and disbursing them to the fund-raising company upon the issue of securities to the investors. In terms of end-use restrictions, funds raised through crowdfunding cannot be used to provide loans or investments in other entities. Companies are prohibited from using multiple crowdfunding portals in a 12-month period, and crowdfunding portals used must be recognized by SEBI.

7.4.4   Analysing SEBI Proposals

An analysis of SEBI's proposals would indicate that they are unlikely to stimulate a market for crowdfunding. The conditions imposed are too onerous, making it too restrictive and expensive for small businesses and start-ups to utilise crowdfunding. Here we discuss some of the constraints.

(a)   Investor eligibility restrictions

The first constraint concerns the participation of investors in crowdfunding, and the availability of the mechanism only to 'accredited' investors. Crowdfunding is restricted to investors who are (i) knowledgeable or have experience in investments, or at least have access to investment advice; or (ii) able, due to their wealth, to absorb losses arising from crowdfunding. Such investors are few and far between in comparison with the larger numbers of retail investors constituting the 'crowd'. Restricting crowdfunding activities to accredited investors is simply another way of making the traditional mechanism of venture capital and private equity investment more efficient through the use of the Internet. It only repackages the traditional mechanism without creating a new one. The higher entry barriers for retail investors only exacerbate the removal of the crowd from crowdfunding (Ibrahim 2015: 571).

Even though SEBI's cautious approach might diminish the scope of investors that small businesses and start-ups can access, it would protect vulnerable investors from risks they may not be capable of managing. To that extent, SEBI has preferred to stay in line with the cautious approach adopted by jurisdictions such as Singapore rather than to embark on the more expansive stance taken by jurisdictions such as the United States and New Zealand, which do not impose sophistication requirements on investors who wish to access crowdfunding investment options.

While crowdfunding at its very core is meant to engage with investors who would otherwise be unable to participate in capital markets in the conventional sense, the high thresholds for accreditation or even eligibility as a retail investor in India means that participation in crowdfunding remains isolated from large sections of potential retail investors. Additionally, investments in crowdfunded companies in India are ultimately subject to the Companies Rules, 2014, which mandate that the size of each investment must not be less than INR20,000.

Even with the inclusion of qualified retail investors, it would be impossible for a start-up to be truly crowdfunded. SEBI's consultation paper suggests that, in order for an offer to succeed, at least 5 per cent must be taken up by QIBs. Hence, if QIBs are not attracted to a particular start-up, a crowdfunded issue would fail. Given that QIBs are likely to have access to greater resources, skill, expertise and experience in investing in start-ups, and therefore are more likely to identify start-ups which would have a likelihood of success, this seems to be an effective mechanism to ensure that only those companies or projects worthy of their attention succeed. While this has the effect of protecting retail investors from risky start-ups, it also forecloses the ability of start-ups that are unable to access QIBs from raising funds in the market.

(b)   Retaining the status quo?

In a number of ways, the proposed regulations on crowdfunding simply reinforce the existing Indian law on corporate fund-raising. The entire exercise of applying to a crowdfunding platform and having its funding requirements showcased for accredited investors remains a precursor to the standard private placement mechanism under s. 42 of the Companies Act, 2013. Consistent with this approach, companies seeking crowdfunding are prohibited from directly or indirectly advertising their offerings to the public in general or soliciting investments from the public.

The requirement of treating crowdfunding as a private placement for the purposes of s. 42 of the Companies Act with a cap on the number of offers is somewhat baffling. Admittedly, SEBI does not possess the power or the jurisdiction to alter company law. But, without recommending changes to company law to relax or remove these numerical offer limits, crowdfunding cannot be a feasible option. Even jurisdictions such as Singapore, which limit crowdfunding to accredited investors, do not impose a maximum number of offerees who can be approached. With this restriction, SEBI's proposals are merely reiterating what is already set out as the legal position in company law.

Even without SEBI's intervention, crowdfunding in the form proposed by SEBI can still be undertaken as a private placement under s. 42, and hence it is not clear what value is being added by the proposals, which only constrain further what is currently permissible under law. If crowdfunding is to be a viable option, then SEBI must coordinate with the Ministry of Corporate Affairs to introduce necessary changes either in the

Companies Act, 2013 or the Companies Rules, 2014 to obliterate a cap on the number of offers for crowdfunding. Failing this, all of the other detailed proposals discussed in SEBI's consultation process are of no avail.

The procedures needing to be adopted by crowdfunding platforms would also lead to increased transaction costs for crowdfunded share issues. The SEBI consultation paper suggests that crowdfunding platforms must conduct screening and basic due diligence, including background and regulatory checks on the company, its promoters, directors and shareholders holding in excess of 20 per cent of the equity of the company. Platforms must also filter out good business plans which, in their opinion, would be worthy of listing on the platform. This filtering mechanism takes place through a screening committee set up within the platform.

Given that sophisticated investors who express an interest in the company seeking funds would carry out a detailed due diligence and background check on the company, its promoters, directors and employees, this additional requirement would not only increase the burden on the company seeking funds, but also reduce the efficacy of crowdfunding platforms.

Ultimately, crowdfunding under SEBI's proposals seems to suffer from an identity crisis of sorts. As Soni and Bagchi (2014: 15) eloquently point out, 'it is apparent that on the spectrum of finance-raising mechanism[s], where each of the public offer and private placement routes lies on the opposite extremes, the crowdfunding mechanism stands in the middle'. Therefore, from a regulatory perspective, it would be necessary to treat crowdfunding as a separate and distinct fund-raising model, and outside of conventional capital markets activities (Heminway and Hoffman 2011: 941).

However, the crowdfunding proposals in India pay short shrift to these conceptual distinctions. While crowdfunding ought to be treated as a much less restricted form of public offer of securities so as to genuinely access the crowd (similar to its treatment under the CROWDFUND Act in the United States), the Indian scenario has been moving in exactly the opposite direction by treating it as akin to a private placement. Not only does this abrogate from the core tenets of crowdfunding, but the entire regulatory exercise does nothing more than merely embrace the existing regime on private placements, but with additional restrictions that will virtually destroy any possibility of an equity crowdfunding market in India.

7.5 CONCLUSION

Equity crowdfunding has gathered steam in recent years. Given India's gigantic population, the potential for crowdfunding in the country is unlimited. On the demand side, India's reliance on technology and innovation can only make the start-up sector much more dominant in the years to come. Any regulatory intervention can either boost or destroy crowdfunding. Ultimately, regulators have to walk a tightrope by balancing growth in small businesses and start-ups on the one hand, and investor protection on the other.

As we have seen in this chapter, India's Parliament, as well as its securities regulator, SEBI, have erred on the side of caution and overwhelmingly favoured investor protection, thereby stifling any possibility of equity crowdfunding. This is not at all surprising given the massive scandals that preceded the latest round of regulatory reforms. Even though SEBI has provided some signalling towards a market for crowdfunding, the message in its favour is rather ambiguous. At the outset, SEBI has clarified that its consultative process may not necessarily result in the introduction of a favourable regime for crowdfunding (SEBI 2014: para. 1.2). Even if it does, its current form is too restrictive to make it viable.

At one level, it may be possible to argue that SEBI must relax some of the stringent conditions it has imposed for crowdfunding, including limiting its availability to accredited investors, setting minimum and maximum amounts regarding crowdfunding, and imposing restrictions on advertisements (Chandrasekhar 2016). However, in our view, marginal adjustments to SEBI's proposals can only go so far. We do not believe there is sufficient political or regulatory momentum to open the doors fully for crowdfunding of the kind witnessed in other jurisdictions, such as through the CROWDFUND Act in the United States.

In these circumstances, we are compelled somewhat to conclude on what crowdfunding enthusiasts may consider to be a pessimistic note. As India's legal system has gradually moved in the direction of tightening its noose on offerings of securities by companies on a wider scale, equity crowdfunding is not a viable option. SEBI's proposals, detailed and lengthy as they may be, do not alter the fundamental situation in any way. However, more recently, reports indicate that SEBI may be considering its crowdfunding proposals afresh (Laksar 2017).

In any event, there is no certainty that the proposals will fructify into law any time soon. Yet, we must be realistic that the emergence and growth of a crowdfunding market in India is problematic, at least in the near future. In the meantime, small businesses and start-ups may be better served by tapping into other existing forms of funding through venture capital, angel investments and the like. As for the crowd, it will be deprived of the mouth-watering prospects of participation and financial returns from the next big idea, but at least they can save their fingers from being badly burnt.

REFERENCES

Agrawal, A.K., C. Catalini and A. Goldfarb (2013), Some Simple Economics of Crowdfunding, National Bureau of Economic Research Working Paper 19133, available at www.nber.org/papers/w19133.pdf

Ahlers, G.K.C., D.J. Cumming, C. Guenthner and D. Schweizer (2015), 'Signaling in Equity Crowdfunding' 39 *Entrepreneurship Theory and Practice* 955

Ashta, A., D. Assadi and N. Marakkath (2015), 'The Strategic Challenges of a Social Innovation: The Case of Rang De in Crowdfunding' 24 *Strategic Change* 1

Australian Securities and Investments Commission (2012), *12-196MR ASIC Guidance on Crowd Funding* (13 August), available at http://asic.gov.au/about-asic/media-centre/find-a-media-release/2012-releases/12-196mr-asic-guidance-on-crowd-funding/

Black, B.S. (1998), 'Information Asymmetry, The Internet, and Securities Offerings' 2 *Journal of Small and Emerging Business Law Review* 91

Bradford, S.C. (2012), 'Crowdfunding and the Federal Securities Law' *Columbia Business Law Review* 1

Chandrasekhar, S. (2016), 'Equity-Based Crowdfunding as an Early-Stage Financing Alternative: Critique of the Regulatory Proposals in India', *India-CorpLaw Blog* (27 March), available at http://indiacorplaw.blogspot.sg/2016/03/equity-based-crowdfunding-as-early.html

Choi, S.J. (1998), 'Gatekeepers and the Internet: Rethinking the Regulation of Small Business Capital Formation' 2 *Journal of Small and Emerging Business Law Review* 27

Datta, R. (2013), 'Saradha raised deposits from 1.7 mn people, probe finds', *The Mint*, 20 June

Fink, A.C. (2012), 'Protecting the Crowd and Raising Capital Through the CROWDFUND Act' 90 *University of Detroit Mercy Law Review* 1

Garside, J. (2014), 'Regulator's 10% spending rule set to "take the crowd out of crowdfunding"', *Guardian*, 6 March

Government of Italy (2012), 'Guidelines, the Italian Government's Policy for Attracting Innovative Foreign Entrepreneurs', available at www.esteri.it/mae/visti/linee%20guida%20italia%20startup%20visa%20en.pdf

Hazen, T.L. (2012), 'Crowdfunding or Fraudfunding? Social Networks and the Securities Laws—Why the Specially Tailored Exemption Must be Conditioned on Meaningful Disclosure' 90 *North Carolina Law Review* 1735

Heminway, J.M. and S.R. Hoffman (2011), 'Proceed at Your Peril: Crowdfunding and the Securities Act of 1933' 78 *Tennessee Law Review* 879

Hong Kong Financial Services Development Council (2016), *Introducing a Regulatory Framework for Equity Crowdfunding in Hong Kong*, FSDC Paper No. 21, available at www.fsdc.org.hk/sites/default/files/Final_Report.pdf

Hu, Y. (2015), 'Regulation of Equity Crowdfunding in Singapore' *Singapore Journal of Legal Studies* 46

Ibrahim, D.M. (2015), 'Equity Crowdfunding: A Market for Lemons?' 100 *Minnesota Law Review* 561

Iyer, A.K. (2016), 'Pennywise: A Crowdfunding Critique', *IndiaCorpLaw Blog* (9 February), available at http://indiacorplaw.blogspot.sg/2016/02/penny-wise-crowdfunding-critique.html

Khan, T. (2016), 'Tight government regulation, paucity of innovation limiting crowdfunding start-ups in India', *Economic Times*, 10 May

Kirby, E. and S. Worner (2013), *Crowd-funding: An Infant Industry Growing Fast*, Staff Working Paper of the IOSCO Research Department, available at www.iosco.org/research/pdf/swp/Crowd-funding-An-Infant-Industry-Growing-Fast.pdf

Knight, T.B., H. Leo and A.A. Ohmer (2012), 'A Very Quiet Revolution: A Primer on Securities Crowdfunding and Title III of the Jobs Act' 2 *Michigan Journal of Private Equity and Venture Capital Law* 135

Krishnamurthy, K. (2015) 'LetsVenture brings on Ratan Tata and Mohandas Pai as advisors, investors', *Economic Times*, 26 October

Laksar, A., (2017), 'SEBI Taking a Fresh Look at Crowdfunding Norms' *Live Mint* (17 March), available at http://www.livemint.com/Politics/G3YYOr UfWwA5PgprhWDdlN/Sebi-taking-a-fresh-look-at-crowdfunding-norms.html

Lin, M., N.R. Prabhala and S. Viswanathan (2013), 'Judging Borrowers by the Company They Keep: Friendship Networks and Information Asymmetry in Online Peer-to-Peer Lending' 59 *Management Science* 17

Ministry of Commerce and Industry Government of India (2016), 'Action Plan: Start-Up India', available at http://startupindia.gov.in/actionplan.php

Mollick, E. (2014), 'The Dynamics of Crowdfunding: An Exploratory Study' 29 *Journal of Business Venturing* 1

Monetary Authority of Singapore (MAS) (2015), *Facilitating Securities Based Crowdfunding*, Consultation Paper P005-2015 (February), available at www.mas.gov.sg/~/media/MAS/News%20and%20Publications/Consultation% 20Papers/Facilitating%20Securities%20Based%20Crowdfunding

— (2016), 'MAS to Improve Access to Crowd-funding for Start-ups and SMEs' (8 June), available at www.mas.gov.sg/News-and-Publications/Media-Releases/ 2016/MAS-to-Improve-Access-to-Crowdfunding-for-Startups-and-SMEs.aspx

MyOnlineCA (2015), 'Crowdfunding Sites in India: Opportunities and Facts' (6 May), available at www.myonlineca.in/startup-blog/crowdfunding-sites-in-india-opportunities-and-facts

Patnia, A. (2013), *Crowdfunding: An Indian Perspective* (19 November), available at http://yourstory.com/2013/11/crowdfunding-indian-perspective/

Schwartz, A.A. (2015), 'The Digital Shareholder' 100 *Minnesota Law Review* 609

Schwienbacher, A. and B. Larralde (2010), 'Crowdfunding of small entrepreneurial ventures' in *Handbook of Entrepreneurial Finance* (Oxford University Press)

Securities and Exchange Board of India (SEBI) (2011), 'How Households Save and Invest: Evidence from NCAER Household Survey' (22 May), available at http://www.sebi.gov.in/cms/sebi_data/attachdocs/1326345117894.pdf

— (2014), *Consultation Paper on Crowdfunding in India* (17 June), available at www.sebi.gov.in/cms/sebi_data/attachdocs/1403005615257.pdf

— (2015), *Handbook of Statistics 2015* (22 May), available at www.sebi.gov.in/cms/sebi_data/attachdocs/1462441113708.pdf

Securities and Exchange Commission (SEC) (2015), 'Crowdfunding, Final Rule, Release Nos 33-9974; 34-76324; File No S7-09-13' (30 October), available at www.sec.gov/rules/final/2015/33-9974.pdf

Securities and Futures Commission, Hong Kong SAR (2014), 'Notice on Potential Regulations Applicable to, and Risks of, Crowd-funding Activities' (7 May), available at www.sfc.hk/web/EN/files/ER/PDF/Notice%20on%20Crowd funding.pdf

Soni, J. and K. Bagchi (2014), 'Crowdfunding in India: A Tale of Misplaced Regulations' *Economic and Political Weekly* (29 November)

The Hindu Business Line (2015), 'Crowd-funding platform Catapooolt looking to raise up to $1 mn' (5 November), available at http://www.thehindubusiness line.com/info-tech/crowdfunding-platform-catapooolt-looking-to-raise-up-to-1-mn/article7846265.ece

Vitins, M. (2013), 'Crowdfunding and Securities Laws: What the Americans are Doing and the Case for an Australian Crowdfunding Exemption' 22 *Journal of Law, Information and Science* 92

White, K. (2014), 'The Solution to Equity Crowdfunding Lies with ASIC' (22 September), Startup Smart, available at www.startupsmart.com.au/growth/the-solution-to-equity-crowdfunding-lies-with-asic/2014092213259.html

8. A critical examination of crowdfunding within the 'Long White Cloud' (New Zealand)*

Trish Keeper

8.1 INTRODUCTION

When the first tranche of provisions of the Financial Markets Conduct Act 2013 ('FMC Act') came into force on 1 April 2014, a new licensing regime for Crowdfunding Service Providers (CSPs) was introduced into New Zealand law – a regime that is one of the most progressive and innovative operating in the world today. The regime operates on the basis that an offer of financial products to an investor is exempted from the disclosure requirements for a regulated offer in Part 3 of the FMC Act, if the offer of financial products is by, or through, a licensed CSP and the offer is pursuant to the market service licence held by the CSP (FMC Act, Schedule 1, cl 6).

The chapter starts with an overview of the nature of equity crowdfunding and how it impacts securities law. It then briefly outlines how this activity was regulated in New Zealand previously and discusses how the new regulatory framework operates. The final part of the chapter outlines how the crowdfunding markets have developed in the last two years and identifies future developments and potential threats to the operation of New Zealand's crowdfunding regime.

---

* The translation of the Māori name for New Zealand, '*Aotearoa*', is 'Long White Cloud'.

8.2   WHAT IS CROWDFUNDING?

8.2.1   Social Media Phenomenon

Crowdfunding as a means of raising funds for not-for-profit or for-profit enterprises has received a great deal of attention globally in recent years. The advantage that crowdfunding has over more traditional models of financing is that it uses social networks as the medium for attracting financing:

> Social networks have the potential for using crowdfunding to reach large numbers of people. Since crowdfunding is designed to reach a large number of people, limiting the fundraising request to a small amount from each donor can provide meaningful funding. (Hazen 2012: 1736–7)

Crowdfunding has been recognized in New Zealand, as it has been elsewhere, as a potentially rich source of financing for charitable, social or business projects and ventures. Bellaflamme *et al.* (2014: 586) observed that it is a concept that originates in the 'broader concept of crowdsourcing, which refers to the "crowd" to obtain ideas, feedback and solutions to develop corporate activities'. In contrast, with crowdfunding the objective is to collect money for a specific venture, project or business through a variety of financing models that use the Internet, generally through social networks (Twitter, Facebook, LinkedIn and other specialized blogs). Accordingly, the term 'crowdfunding' encompasses a variety of business financing models that all use the Internet.

8.2.2   Types of Crowdfunding Sites

There is growing international literature on crowdfunding, and the following is a summary of the different types of this form of fund-raising. Bradford (2012) identified five types of crowdfunding activities, which are distinguished by what investors are promised in return for their investment or contribution. These are (1) the donation model; (2) the reward mode; (3) the pre-purchase model; (4) the lending model, sometimes referred to as peer-to-peer lending; and (5) the equity model. Bradford (2012) observed that while the first three of these models have not attracted the attention of financial market regulators, the same cannot be said for peer-to-peer lending and equity crowdfunding.

What equity crowdfunding enterprises offer investors, in return for their investment in a business or enterprise, is something of value. This may include shares in a new company or a right to a share of profits and it is this characteristic that brings the activity to the attention of regulators and policy-makers. Worldwide, equity crowd fund-raising has been slow to develop due to the possibility that this form of capital raising may implicate wider primary market securities law, which in general strictly regulates, through various registration and disclosure hurdles, the raising of funds from the public. However, some countries have moved to encourage equity crowdfunding, recognizing that it provides the opportunity for small and medium enterprises (SMEs) to access capital that may not otherwise be available.

The IOSCO Committee for the Regulation of Market Intermediaries published in 2015 a report on the responses to a survey it had carried out to gauge members' current or proposed crowdfunding regulatory programmes. The IOSCO Committee observed a 'variety of approaches to regulate crowdfunding' (IOSCO 2015: iii), although there were some high-level similarities. An identified common objective was to achieve a 'balance between risks/investor protection related concerns and the positive role securities markets can play in supporting economic recovery and growth through the promotion of crowdfunding' (IOSCO 2015: 28).

Kirby and Worner (2014), in an earlier IOSCO Staff Working Paper, identified three regulatory responses to crowdfunding. The first is where the regulator bans equity crowdfunding. In the second option, equity crowdfunding is legal but there is regulation that creates high barriers to entry – in these jurisdictions, there is no equity crowdfunding market. Under the third regime, equity crowdfunding is permitted, but there are strict limits on who can invest, the number of investors that are allowed to invest, the size of the company issuing equity, or other similar regulatory requirements. The crowdfunding regime in New Zealand falls within this third category of regulatory responses, although, as outlined in this chapter, the level of controls on investors and issuers are relatively light-handed (Minister of Commerce Cabinet Paper 2011).

8.3 CROWDFUNDING REGULATION IN NEW ZEALAND

8.3.1 Policy Objectives and Crowdfunding

In New Zealand, before 1 April 2014,[1] the Securities Act 1978 controlled the raising of funds from the public, who, in exchange for their investment, acquired an interest in certain identified forms of securities. Any entity wishing to offer securities to the public for subscription was required to comply with the disclosure requirements of the Securities Act. These included the preparation of extensive disclosure documents encompassing both a lengthy and heavily prescribed prospectus and an investment statement. Furthermore, the drafting of certain definitions in the Securities Act, together with a number of amendments to the disclosure rules and the addition of a number of new exemptions, had combined to create uncertainty as to which fund-raising arrangements were subject to the Securities Act and which offers were not (Ministry of Economic Development 2010). These factors, together with the serious potential consequences for noncompliance, had resulted in an environment where the permitted exemptions were interpreted very narrowly, a consequence that was considered counterproductive to the development of New Zealand's capital markets.

A government review of New Zealand's securities law in 2010 observed that 'narrow exemptions … harm investors by preventing them from participating in private securities offers' (Ministry of Economic Development 2010: 47) and also harm businesses seeking funding (*ibid.*). The review recommended that significant changes be made to New Zealand's securities laws, including reforms to free up private markets and for securities law to build stepping stones from private fund-raising to public share markets. The recommendation reflected the very tight commercial lending market that existed in New Zealand at the time.

However, the Securities Act 1978 did not prohibit equity crowdfunding. Instead, this form of fund-raising, together with peer-to-peer lending, simply triggered the disclosure requirements of the Securities Act, which was not a viable option for early-stage businesses seeking small amounts of capital (Barrett 2012). Exemptions from the disclosure requirements of the Securities Act were possible if the securities were

---

[1] While the part of the Financial Markets Conduct Act 2013 that governs crowdfunding licensing came into force on 1 April 2014, the majority of the Act came into force on 1 December 2014.

only offered to eligible persons (wealthy and/or experienced investors),[2] professional or large investors[3] or other persons with close association to the issuer.[4] Barrett (2012) observed that none of these exemptions were conducive to equity crowdfunding. Furthermore, although the Securities Commission and its successor the Financial Markets Authority (FMA)[5] had authority to grant individual exemptions to issuers from the Securities Act's disclosure rules, exemptions for fund-raising via crowdfunding were unlikely to be granted given the courts' narrow interpretation of the exemptions generally (Barrett 2012). The interpretation had its origin in the view that the predominant policy objective of the Securities Act was consumer protection, and this could be best achieved through full disclosure to consumer investors.

However, the express purposes of the Financial Markets Conduct Act 2013 as set out in ss. 3 and 4 make it clear that consumers are only one of the parties whose interests need to be considered. Section 3 provides:

3. The main purposes of this Act are to:

(a) promote the confident and informed participation of businesses, investors, and consumers in the financial markets; and

(b) promote and facilitate the development of fair, efficient, and transparent financial markets.

The objectives of having confident and informed participants in financial markets which are fair, efficient and transparent are supplemented by additional purposes in s. 4:

---

[2] The Securities Act 1978 defines an eligible person as wealthy if the person has certified net assets over NZ\$2 million (s. 5(2CC)) or gross annual income of at least NZ\$200,000 (s. 5(2CD)). Section 5(2CE) sets out the requirements for a person to be considered experienced in investing money or experienced in the industry or business to which the security relates.

[3] Under Securities Act 1978, s. 3(2)(a)(iia)–(iib), an offer to persons who are each required to pay a minimum subscription price of at least NZ\$500,000 or have previously paid a minimum subscription price of NZ\$500,000 is not an offer to the public for the purposes of the Act.

[4] Under the Securities Act 1978, s. 3(2)(a)(i), an offer only to relatives or close business associates of the issuer or a director of an issuer is not an offer of securities to the public for the purposes of the Act.

[5] The Financial Markets Authority Act 2011 came into force on 1 May 2011, on which date the Securities Commission was disestablished and replaced by the Financial Markets Authority.

4. This Act has the following additional purposes:

(a) to provide for timely, accurate, and understandable information to be provided to persons to assist those persons to make decisions relating to financial products or the provision of financial services;

(b) to ensure that appropriate governance arrangements apply to financial products and market services that allow for effective monitoring and reduce governance risks;

(c) to avoid unnecessary compliance costs;

(d) to promote innovation and flexibility in the financial markets.

Gibbons (2014: 16) observed:

[O]ne of the key things achieved by the purpose provisions of the FMCA is that the various purposes of securities law are given better relativity, and investor protection is made less central. This is important in creating the right incentives, both for issuers and for investors. It also avoids the simple (perhaps simple-minded) approach that some case law seems to support, where investor protection is everything, and other purposes of securities law are subservient or ignored. It is submitted that a simplistic approach is the wrong approach: under the FMCA, different aspects of purpose must be weighed and balanced more evenly.

The fourth policy in s. 4, the promotion of innovation and flexibility in the financial markets, is one that permeates the approach taken to crowdfunding regulation in New Zealand. Regulatory flexibility is achieved by the design of the framework regulating crowdfunding in New Zealand. First, the FMC Act contains a number of mandatory requirements that apply to all regulated intermediaries (which include CSPs). The requirements include record-keeping and reporting obligations, and FMA has oversight and enforcement powers. There are also specific requirements that apply only to CSPs, which are supplemented by more detailed requirements in the Financial Market Conduct Regulations 2014 ('FMC Regulations'). Finally, FMA is able to stipulate additional conditions for particular types of service providers. Conditions can be modified by FMA at any time innovations in financial products occur or to address any perceived gaps in the regulatory framework.

The approach taken in New Zealand is to regulate through licensing persons who undertake crowdfunding services. Minister of Commerce Cabinet Paper (2011), while recording the government's approval of a new licensing regime for regulated intermediaries, stated that the regime will:

[a]llow new intermediaries to be authorized by FMA to provide certain types of services. A person licensed as a regulated intermediary would be able to

take on responsibility for meeting certain regulatory requirements, such as disclosure, record keeping etc, on behalf of an issuer. This regime would be used where it is impractical for an issuer to meet the requirements of securities law and a supervised intermediary is better placed to do so.

Section 390(1) of the FMC Act provides that a person may hold a market services licence to act as a CSP or peer-to-peer lending intermediary, although the FMC Act is drafted to allow other forms of intermediary service to be added by later regulation. FMC Regulations, reg. 185 defines a CSP as a person who provides a facility by means of which offers of shares[6] in a company are made, and the 'principal purpose of the facility is to facilitate the matching of companies who wish to raise funds with many investors who are seeking to invest relatively small amounts'. Therefore, the form of crowdfunding authorized under the FMC Act and the FMC Regulations is limited to equity crowdfunding. Below, the eligibility requirements are discussed in more detail.

8.3.2 CSP Licensee Criteria under the FMC Act and the FMC Regulations

One of the most important criteria for any service provider seeking a licence from FMA is to be registered under the Financial Service Providers (Registration and Dispute Resolution) Act 2008 ('Financial Service Providers Act'). Any financial service provider wishing to operate in New Zealand must be registered under this Act. Details of the entity, its business and management are then available to be searched on an online public register. In order to be registered, the provider must also be a member of an approved dispute resolution service, details of which are shown on the online register. In terms of the specific requirements for intermediary services such as CSPs, under the Financial Service Providers Act, the regulator, namely FMA, is required to undertake an assessment of the applicant's suitability to operate as a CSP. As part of this process, an applicant's directors and senior managers must certify that they are fit and proper persons to hold their respective positions. Furthermore, FMA must be satisfied that the applicant is not likely to contravene its licence obligations and that the applicant is 'capable of effectively performing the service' (FMC Act, s. 396(1)).

---

[6] Shares, for the purpose of crowdfunding, do not include a financial product that will be converted, or may become convertible, into another financial product.

FMC Regulations, reg. 186 details additional eligibility conditions for a CSP. These include that the provider has an adequate policy and procedures for identifying and managing the risk of fraud by issuers using the service. The policy should also operate to exclude any issuer that a provider considers is unlikely to comply with the obligations imposed on it under the service. Accordingly, the regime places the responsibility for conducting due diligence and vetting offerors on each CSP, who must disclose their selection criteria to potential investors at the time such investors sign up with an individual CSP. There is no requirement for a CSP to make publicly available its selection criteria, although the websites for the leading crowdfunding providers in New Zealand (Snowball Effect, PledgeMe and Equitise) do provide general guidance to potential issuers seeking to undertake equity crowdfunding on how their respective selection processes work. The most successful CSP at the time of writing (Snowball Effect) had reported that less than 2 per cent of the companies that expressed interest in raising funds on its platform made it to the marketplace (Daniell and Rose 2016), which suggests that, at least at the top end of the market, rigorous screening of potential issuers occurs.

All licensed CSPs are also required to make sure there are certain mandatory warnings on their respective websites, and to have in place adequate disclosure arrangements to enable investors to readily obtain timely and understandable information in relation to any share acquisition decision, including initial disclosure or question-and-answer forums. A CSP must also have an adequate fair dealing policy and procedures for excluding an (existing) issuer from using the service if the provider has reason to believe that the issuer has engaged in conduct that is misleading or deceptive, in contravention of ss. 22 and 23 of the FMC Act.

In addition, all CSPs must have adequate systems and procedures for ensuring that an issuer does not raise more than NZ$2 million in any 12-month period. This is the only financial limit in the FMC Act and FMC Regulations as, unlike regimes in other jurisdictions, there is no limit on how much an individual investor can invest through equity crowdfunding in any year or in total. There is also no rescission, cancellation or cooling off period as found or proposed in other jurisdictions (IOSCO 2015). There are also no limits on the size of the issuer, although to date only small and medium-sized entities have undertaken equity crowdfunding to retail investors. As discussed later in the chapter, the lack of limits on the amount an individual investor can invest or on the size of an issuer has meant that some CSPs are able to develop new services by providing the infrastructure for issuers to raise funds exclusively from private or wholesale investors. These initiatives are likely to assist some CSPs to become more financially viable as they develop their business models (Smylie 2016a).

8.3.3 FMA's Standard Licence Conditions and Specific Conditions for Individual Licensees

The final layer of regulation in the licensing of a CSP is the power given to FMA under the FMC Act to impose conditions on any licensee and to revoke, add to or alter such conditions at any time (ss. 402–403). FMA has adopted a two-step approach to laying down conditions. First, it has published, and recently amended, a document setting out the standard conditions for crowdfunding service licences. These conditions are described by FMA as the minimum standards that FMA expects providers to meet. While a number of the standard conditions simply explain FMA's expectations as to conditions imposed by the FMC Act or the FMC Regulations, others provide an insight into FMA's concerns about the risk of platform failure, as evidenced by the requirements to disclose to FMA any negative net tangible asset (NTA) calculation and the need for independent audit of such processes. The standard conditions were updated in March 2016 after FMA had undertaken consultation at the end of 2015. The major change was to the financial resources standard condition, which now details how CSPs must calculate their NTA and notify FMA as soon as practicable if it is negative. This calculation is required to be undertaken monthly and on other dates if there is a reason to suspect that a CSP's NTA is not positive.

There have also been changes to the condition clarifying that a qualified auditor must be appointed to prepare a report in respect of the calculation of the NTA during the accounting period. This report is required to be sent to FMA at the end of each accounting period. As discussed later, one CSP has already closed in New Zealand owing to increasing competition in the market. FMA also has the power to impose specific conditions on individual licensees. All eight crowdfunding providers licensed to date have had special conditions imposed for their registration under the FMC Act. The most common conditions are that service providers must not provide any secondary market for the equity securities offered through their service unless and until FMA approves that secondary market, and that the provider will maintain the same or better standards of capability, governance and compliance as it did when FMA assessed the provider's application.

8.3.4   Reporting and Record-Keeping Obligations and Enforcement

The FMC Act also specifies a number of reporting and record-keeping
requirements that apply to all licensees under Part 6 of the FMC Act.
First, there is a general requirement for all licensees to report to FMA
that is triggered by certain events such as insolvency, or bankruptcy of
directors, senior managers and key personnel; or civil, criminal, regulatory or disciplinary proceedings being taken against the licensee, an
authorized body, director, senior manager or key personnel (FMC Act,
s. 412 and FMC Regulations, reg. 191). Also, any changes in directors,
senior managers, key personnel or the auditor; a change of name or legal
structure; entry into a major transaction; or if a person obtains or loses
control of the licensee or an authorized body, must be reported. In
relation to crowdfunding licensees, FMC Regulations, reg. 195 requires
service providers to notify FMA if they know or suspect that an issuer
has committed a significant contravention of the fair dealing provisions
of the FMC Act or a contravention of the NZ$2 million limit.

FMA has a range of powers in the event of a material contravention or
likely contravention of a licensee's obligations, a material change in the
circumstances of the licensee, or if the licensee has provided materially
false or misleading information in the licence application or any application to amend the licence. Section 410 of the Act defines a material
change of circumstances as a change that adversely affects the licensee's
capacity to perform the market service covered by the licence or a change
that means the requirements of the FMC Act as to the conditions and
requirements of a licensee are no longer met. FMA's enforcement powers
include censure, requiring licensees to submit an action plan of corrective
measures, and giving directions. In addition, FMA may suspend a licence
in such circumstances or revoke, vary or substitute any conditions of a
licence (FMC Act, s. 414(1)–(4)). A suspension can be for a specified
period or until a specified requirement is met. A licence can be
suspended or cancelled under s. 408 if the licensee requests FMA to do
so, or if FMA is satisfied that the licensee or an authorized body has
died, ceased to exist or become incapacitated, or has become subject to
an insolvency event; or as a result of enforcement action by FMA.

8.4   DISCLOSURE OBLIGATIONS OF CSPS

As stated above, the FMC Act places the responsibility on individual
CSPs in terms of the protections for consumer investors. This is mainly
achieved through three disclosure requirements in the FMC Act and

Regulations. First, each CSP must ensure that on its website platform there is a warning statement about the risks of crowdfunding. The warning statement must be on the site's homepage, and shown before the investor uses the site to apply for a product, and also on all application forms. FMC Regulations, reg. 196 requires that the following wording be used on the warning statement:

Warning statement about crowdfunding

Equity crowdfunding is risky.

*Issuers using this facility include new or rapidly growing ventures. Investment in these types of businesses is very speculative and carries high risks.

(*Omit these sentences if the facility is confined to issuers for whom the sentences would be inapplicable.)

You may lose your entire investment, and must be in a position to bear this risk without undue hardship.

New Zealand law normally requires people who offer financial products to give information to investors before they invest. This requires those offering financial products to have disclosed information that is important for investors to make an informed decision.

The usual rules do not apply to offers by issuers using this facility. As a result, you may not be given all the information usually required. You will also have fewer other legal protections for this investment.

Ask questions, read all information given carefully, and seek independent financial advice before committing yourself.

Accordingly, the warning statement only addresses generic risks that may arise out of equity crowdfunding. It does not address the risks of individual issuers, such as any unique risk to any individual issuer or increased risk associated with particular industry types. FMC Regulations, reg. 197(1) also provides that a provider must obtain, from investors, confirmation that they have seen the warning statement and understand that the investment is risky on the following terms:

I confirm that I have seen the warning statement about crowdfunding and –

- I understand that equity crowdfunding is risky and I may lose my entire investment; and
- I confirm that I could bear that loss without suffering undue hardship; and
- I understand that the usual legal protections do not apply to this investment; and

- I understand that I may not be given the same information as is usually required by New Zealand law for investments.

The confirmation must be obtained in writing in a separate document or, if it is obtained by electronic means, through a process by which it is obtained separately from the agreement to use the service. Furthermore, the confirmation must be obtained by the provider before the investor is authorized to use the service (FMC Regulations, reg. 197(2)–(3)). It is concerning to note that there is no requirement to warn investors that selling shares may be difficult given that the shares are not usually listed on a stock exchange. It is likely that many retail investors may not appreciate the difficulties if they need to divest themselves of shares at a later stage. A warning to this effect is present on the FMA website, and some of the licensed platforms include statements warning of on-sale problems.

Second, licensed CSPs are also required to provide a disclosure statement to retail investors (FMC Act, s. 423). The stated statutory purpose (FMC Act, s. 425) of a disclosure statement is to provide information that is likely to assist a retail investor in deciding whether to proceed with the service provided by the CSP or to change any instruction in relation to the service. A disclosure statement must be given before the investor enters into a client agreement. A disclosure statement for a crowdfunding service is called a Service Disclosure Statement or SDS, and FMC Regulations, reg. 215(a)–(h) prescribe that it must contain a brief description of all of the following matters:

- The nature of the service provided.
- How investors apply for and obtain access to the facility and the eligibility criteria that apply. Accordingly, individual service providers are able to impose criteria on investors who use the site.
- How issuers apply for and obtain access to the facility and the eligibility criteria that apply.
- How investments are made and financial products are issued under the service.
- How investor money is received and dealt with.

In addition, the SDS must state the nature and extent of the checks and assessments made by the provider of the following:

- Each issuer that offers financial products under the service.
- The directors and senior managers of those issuers.
- The risks involved in those financial products (or, if checks and assessments of those risks are not made as part of the service, a statement to that effect).

The SDS must also set out any fees that an investor will have to pay to a CSP as well as contact details for the provider, how investors may complain about the service to the provider, and details of the compulsory dispute resolution scheme for all intermediary services. Finally, an SDS must be accompanied by any required documents and comply with all other requirements of the FMC Regulations (relating to content, form, presentation and similar matters).

If a disclosure statement contains a statement that is false or misleading or is likely to mislead, or there is an omission from the disclosure statement of any required information and the statement or omission is materially adverse from the point of view of the retail investor, the contravention may give rise to civil liability under the FMC Act (ss. 427 and 449(3)). If FMA seeks to impose a civil pecuniary penalty for such contravention, the maximum fine will be the highest of: consideration for the relevant transaction; three times the amount of the gain made or loss avoided; and NZ$1 million in the case of an individual or NZ$5 million in any other case (s. 449(2)). There are also criminal sanctions under s. 511 if a person or entity knowingly or recklessly provides a false or misleading disclosure statement, which includes an SDS, or one that contains an omission of required information, where the misstatement or omission is materially adverse from the point of view of an investor. It is also an offence to provide a service to a person who has been provided with a false or misleading disclosure statement.

The third document regulating the relationship between an individual service provider and an investor is a contract called a client agreement (FMC Act, s. 430, FMC Regulations, regs 224, 225, 227). In general, the agreement must provide adequately for the use and operation of the facility, including how investors and issuers apply for and obtain access to the facility and the eligibility criteria in each case. In addition, it must state how investments are made, how financial products are issued under the service, and how investor money is received and dealt with, to the extent that this is part of the service.

8.5 REGULATORY FRAMEWORK: OTHER RULES

There are no specific rules regulating the disclosures to be made by issuers seeking equity crowd fund-raising, either in relation to the material disclosed to potential investors interested in acquiring shares in the issuer or requiring ongoing or periodic disclosures to any new shareholders if the campaign is successful. Issuers are, however, bound by the following general rules of the FMC Act and the Companies Act 1993, which regulates corporate disclosures.

8.5.1 Fair Dealing

Part 2 of the FMC Act introduced a new principles-based, fair dealing regime applying generally to all financial products and services supplied under the FMC Act or other financial markets regulations, unless exempted. The key section, FMC Act, s. 19, sets out a broad prohibition against false and misleading statements about financial products and financial services. There are additional sections prohibiting the making of false or misleading statements and unsubstantiated representations (ss. 20–23). Therefore, the fair dealing regime applies to any statements, projections or representations to potential shareholders made by an issuer seeking crowdfunding equity. However, one of the exemptions to these rules is conduct that contravenes s. 427 of the FMC Act, since such conduct is subject to separate liability under that section itself. Section 427, discussed above, prohibits a licensed service provider from providing an SDS, or providing the service to a person who was required to be provided with or has been provided with a disclosure statement, that contains a false or misleading statement or omits required information.

However, a contravention of any of ss. 19 to 23 of the FMC Act will only give rise to civil liability. Under subpart 3 of Part 8 of the FMC Act, FMA has the ability to seek pecuniary penalties for breach of certain provisions, including these sections.[7] For FMA to seek a pecuniary penalty order, the High Court must first make a declaration that the person contravened a civil liability provision. The declaration of contravention can also be used by any person, such as an investor who has suffered a loss because of the contravention, to make a compensation order in favour of such a person (FMC Act, s. 494(1)). At the time of writing, FMA has not taken any actions against corporate crowdfunders, but it is clear that the regulator is monitoring such disclosures. One issue that media articles have highlighted is the perceived self-assigned valuation of assets and future forecasts (Smylie 2015a). While FMA's response to date has been to warn investors to do their own research or seek the

---

[7] Financial Markets Conduct Act 2013, s. 489. Also see s. 38(2), which provides that a pecuniary penalty awarded for any contravention of ss. 19–23 must not exceed the maximum of the greatest of the consideration for the relevant transactions; three times the amount of the gain made or the loss avoided; and NZ$1 million in the case of an individual or NZ$5 million in any other case.

advice of financial advisers, it is unlikely that investors do understand the risks involved, especially with respect to valuation methods and the instability of start-up businesses.

8.5.2   Companies Act 1993 and Financial Reporting Requirements

One of the fundamental obligations of an issuer who makes a regulated offer under Part 3 of the FMC Act is that the issuer is then classified as an FMC reporting entity. As an FMC reporting entity it is subject to the reporting and disclosure requirements of the FMC Act. The only exception is when the entity has fewer than 50 shareholders (FMC Act, s. 452). All FMC reporting entities (which include licensed service providers) are required to prepare general purpose financial statements and have them audited by a qualified auditor within four months of the end of the financial year ('balance date'). In addition, copies of the statements and audit report must be lodged with the Registrar of Companies (FMC Act, s. 461H). Corporate issuers under the Companies Act 1993 are also bound to include the audited financial statements and the auditor's report in the annual report that is sent to shareholders prior to the annual meeting. Furthermore, if the issuer is also listed on the New Zealand Stock Exchange (NZX), it also subject to additional periodic disclosure requirements and the continuous disclosure rules contained in the NZX Listing Rules.

Small-medium 'private' companies have lesser reporting and ongoing disclosure requirements, although, as discussed below, some companies that have increased the number of shareholders through equity crowdfunding will have identical disclosure and reporting requirements to those applying to an FMC reporting entity. Under Part 11 of the Companies Act, there are five categories of companies that may trigger the requirements to prepare end of financial year general purpose financial statements that comply with Generally Accepted Accounting Principles (GAAP). However, only two are potentially relevant to crowdfunding issuers. The first is if the company is classified as 'large'. A company is large if in any accounting period either its revenue is greater than NZ$30 million or its assets exceed NZ$60 million.[8] The second category, which is more likely to apply to crowdfunding issuers, is any company with 10 or more shareholders. However, if a company has 10 or more shareholders (and is not a large company or a public entity), and where the

---

[8] These figures include assets and revenue of any subsidiaries, as defined in Financial Reporting Act 2013, s. 45.

constitution does not preclude it from 'opting' out, then 95 per cent of shareholders who are entitled to vote, and voting at any meeting within the opting period, may vote to opt out of all or any of the requirements to prepare financial statements that comply with GAAP and to appoint a qualified auditor (Companies Act 1993, ss. 201, 206).

At first glance the higher level reporting rules would appear to apply to most companies that have undertaken successful equity crowdfunding campaigns, as it would be unlikely that such companies would be able to muster the 95 per cent vote necessary to opt out. However, a significant number of the campaigns have offered non-voting shares to their new investors and the voting shares remain controlled by the original founders or substantial investors. In such cases, the original shareholders may be in a position to opt out of these requirements. Finally, any company that is caught by the Companies Act requirements for large companies as outlined above is also required to prepare an annual report that must be sent to shareholders in the same manner as for FMC reporting entities.

All companies incorporated under the Companies Act are required to call an annual meeting within six months of balance sheet date and not later than 15 months of the previous annual meeting (Companies Act 1993, s. 120). However, it is possible to waive the requirement for calling an annual meeting if 75 per cent of shareholders sign written resolutions covering all matters that need to be passed at such a meeting (Companies Act 1993, s. 122). Accordingly, most equity crowdfunded companies will need to call an annual meeting, although, as discussed above, some issuers may be able to avoid this requirement, especially if they have issued non-voting shares to their new investors.

8.6 NEW ZEALAND REGIME: AN ANALYSIS

8.6.1 Platforms

In New Zealand, just over two years since its crowdfunding legislation came into force, the equity crowdfunding space is already becoming crowded, as eight crowdfunding service providers currently are licensed.[9] The first two CSPs to be licensed have continued to dominate equity

---

[9] As of 10 March 2017, licences for the following crowdfunding service providers are listed on the FMA website: PledgeMe, Snowball Effect, Crowdsphere, Equitise Pty Ltd,, Equity Crowdfunding Ltd (previously Liftoff Ltd (suspended)), Crowd88 (formerly Propellar New Zealand Ltd), AlphaCrowd Ltd, Fulqrum Limited, Collinson Crowdfunding

crowdfunding activity in New Zealand. These are Snowball Effect[10] and PledgeMe.[11] The financial statements for both companies indicate that neither made a profit for the financial year ending 31 March 2015, although it is reported that Snowball Effect forecasts a small profit for the 2016 financial year (Boot 2016). PledgeMe was an established donation and reward funding platform (Murray 2015) that extended its operations to equity crowdfunding. Its website, accessed on 15 June 2016, stated that it had successfully undertaken 12 equity fund-raisings, with one of its early campaigns raising NZ$500,000 for a craft brewer, the Yeastie Boys, in 30 minutes. Snowball Effect has been the most successful of the CSPs (Murray 2015) and it reports that it has 70 per cent of the crowdfunding market in New Zealand (Boot 2016).

Murray (2015) argued that Snowball Effect and PledgeMe are serving distinct market segments with larger, more established companies seeking larger amounts use Snowball Effect. Snowball Effect was also the first service provider to run a campaign open only to wholesale investors,[12] who were offered convertible notes. Offers to wholesale investors are also exempted from complying with the standard disclosure requirements for regulated offers under the FMC Act (Sch. 1, cl. 3). Accordingly, while convertible notes do not fall within the definition of shares and cannot be offered to retail crowdfunding investors, Snowball Effect is diversifying the services it provides by offering its facilities set up for retail crowdfunding to companies seeking wholesale investors. These facilities include technology to verify investor identity in order to comply with anti-money laundering obligations, electronic signing of legal documents, and managing payments through the online platform (Smylie 2015c).

Other service providers are also endeavouring to carve out distinct markets. Equitise Pty is an Australian company registered in New Zealand and promotes itself as a trans-Tasman investment platform.[13] It was set up pending crowdfunding legislation in Australia being enacted.

---

[10]   Snowball Effect crowdfunding platform, www.snowballeffect.co.nz/.

[11]   PledgeMe crowdfunding platform, www.pledgeme.co.nz/.

[12]   A wholesale investor must meet one of a number of criteria. The criteria for investors are: (a) having net assets exceeding NZ$5 million for the two most recent financial years; or (b) having a portfolio of financial products exceeding NZ$1 million in the two most recent financial years; or (c) having entered into transactions to acquire financial products worth this amount; or (d) the investors' principal business is investing in financial products; or (e) they are advisers or brokers in relation to financial products; or (f) they are eligible investors as certified by an independent lawyer, accountant or financial adviser; or (g) they are investing NZ$750,000 or more.

[13]   Equitise crowdfunding platform, https://equitise.com/.

Currently, Australian companies are raising funds on Equitise Pty's New Zealand platform under the trans-Tasman Mutual Recognition Scheme, which is regulated by both the Australian Securities and Investment Commission (ASIC) and FMA.

Crowdsphere Ltd (formerly trading as Crowdcube) is a New Zealand company that was originally set up as a joint venture between Armillary Private Capital and UK-based Crowdcube. AlphaCrowd states that it is going to focus on digital and technology companies and at the time of writing had launched two campaigns. It has also reported that it intends to focus on targeting Chinese investors. Another platform, Crowd88 (previously Propellar), has significant Hong Kong-based support. The latest CSPs to receive licenses are Fulqrum Limited and Collinson Crowdfunding. However, one CSP, 'My Angel Investment Ltd', which was licensed in March 2015 to target science and engineering companies, has already ceased to operate. It announced in March 2016 that for financial reasons it was not able to continue and had run only one unsuccessful campaign in 2015. Another CSP, Equity Crowdfunding Ltd (previously Liftoff) which had a specific Maori, or indigenous, business focus and promoted itself as providing a partnership model, was suspended in September 2016 by the FMA. The closure of My Angel Investments Ltd and the suspension of Equity Crowdfunding Ltd does raise the question as to how many licensees can operate in the New Zealand crowdfunding arena.

In addition to competition within the CSP market, there is potential for competition from other providers, such as a licensed exchange. The only licensed exchange in New Zealand is the NZX, which in 2015 set up a new exchange, NXT, aimed at medium-sized issuers that have a market capitalization of between NZ\$10 million and NZ\$100 million. NXT has reduced governance and disclosure rules compared to issuers listed on the NZX, which is the main board. It is still too early to see if there is any competition between the equity crowdfunding market and NXT (Murray 2015), although it is more likely that equity crowdfunding will provide a stepping stone for small and medium issuers to raise funds before seeking to list on NXT.

8.6.2 Ongoing Issuer Disclosures

Equity crowdfunding has certainly experienced rapid growth since it was introduced into New Zealand's financial markets in 2014, although it is likely that the honeymoon period is over. Although at the time of writing there have been no recorded corporate failures of companies that have successfully raised equity through crowdfunding, there have been com-ments in the media from investors and from CSPs that crowdfunded companies need to improve their post-fund-raising communications. As discussed above, most crowdfunding companies need to share their financial statements with their shareholders at the end of the financial year, but are not subject to the more rigorous disclosure requirements of listed entities, which must release interim financial statements as well as comply with the continuous disclosure regime.

It is unlikely that many investors understand the distinction between the disclosure requirements placed on listed issuers and crowdfunded companies. For companies whose statements in their crowdfunding prospectuses regarding potential growth and profit forecasts were viewed as overly ambitious, the ongoing lack of disclosure has been a particular focus of media criticism (Smylie 2016a and 2016d). Both Snowball Effect and PledgeMe have reported becoming aware of investor concerns that some crowdfunded companies are failing to disclose information on their performance to shareholders. Snowball Effect has started publishing a quarterly report containing company updates as a response. Simeon Burnett, Snowball Effect CEO, was quoted as stating that '[a]s a result of discussions with investors in recent months it has become apparent that the level of engagement that we hoped to facilitate hasn't occurred in some instances' (Smylie 2016a).

8.7 CONCLUSION

Barrett (2012: 306) observed that if equity crowdfunding was to be introduced into the SME sector in New Zealand, four fundamental requirements would need to be meet:

> Firstly, a sufficiently large number of SMEs with high growth potential that are able to present useful information to potential investors must be present. Secondly, a pool of informed micro angel investors, who are prepared to take the risk of investing in start-up companies, must be available. Thirdly, intermediaries who are knowledgeable and reliable, and have the skills to act as share nominees, perform due diligence, trusteeship and so forth, should be willing to enter and stay in the market. Finally, a regulatory framework needs to be established that is nimble and flexible enough to calibrate, possibly at short notice, the appropriate balance between investment risk and consumer protection.

While equity crowdfunding for small and medium-sized companies is now part of New Zealand's capital markets, this has occurred very

Global capital markets

rapidly and without all four of these requirements firmly in place. First, the fact that some issuers released statements with overly ambitious forecasts and inflated valuations at the time of their crowdfunding campaigns and are failing to keep investors updated on progress may undermine investor confidence in crowdfunding. Many of the crowd-funded companies would have operated as closely held 'private' companies in the past and have yet to adjust their communication strategies to meet investors' expectations about ongoing disclosures and corporate updates. While CSPs can encourage crowdfunded companies to improve their practices in this regard, the relationship between a CSP and a company is contractual and once a company has successfully raised equity via the CSP, that contract is performed. Unless a company undertakes a second round of crowdfunding in the future, the CSP will not necessarily have any future dealings with the company. Accordingly, in the future there may need to be legislative reform to close this expectation gap between investors and the crowdfunded companies.

There is also some doubt as to whether many retail investors understand the risks of investing in crowdfunding companies. In the early-to-mid 2000s, a large number of retail investors suffered substantial losses when a number of finance companies collapsed, demonstrating that many investors do not understand the basic principles of risk and return. In addition to the risk of corporate failure, many investors may not appreciate the liquidity risk as there is still no secondary market for shares in crowdfunded companies in New Zealand. As to Barrett's third requirement of having knowledgeable and reliable intermediaries, the equity crowdfunding market has already become crowded in New Zealand and one platform has already failed. While some of the CSPs are carving out distinct market shares and diversifying the services they provide, there is an ongoing risk of portal failure. Overall, any crowdfunding regime has to balance investment risk and consumer protection. Although the New Zealand experiment appears to be successfully achieving this balance, issues relating to disclosure, both at the time of the fund-raising and about ongoing progress, may undermine investor confidence in the future.

REFERENCES

Barrett, J. (2012), 'Crowdfunding: Some Legal and Policy Considerations' 18 *New Zealand Business Law Quarterly* 296
Bellaflamme, P., T. Lambert and A. Schwienbacher (2014), 'Crowdfunding: Tapping the Right Crowd' 29 *Journal of Business Venturing* 585

Boot, S. (2016), 'Snowball Effect on Track to "Small Profit"', *National Business Review* (22 March), available at www.nbr.co.nz/article/snowball-effect-may-be-first-equity-crowd-funder-turn-profit-after-snaring-70-market-b

Bradford, C.S. (2012), 'Crowdfunding and the Federal Securities Laws' *Columbia Business Law Review* 1

Daniell, J. and N. Rose (2016), 'Crowdfunding Platforms Find Capital Markets Niche', *National Business Review* (12 February), available at www.nbr.co.nz/article/crowdfunding-platforms-find-capital-markets-niche-184645

European Crowdfunding Network (2014), 'Review of Crowdfunding Regulation: Interpretations of Existing Regulation Concerning Crowdfunding in Europe, North America and Israel', available at http://eurocrowd.org/wp-content/blogs.dir/sites/85/2014/12/ECN-Review-of-Crowdfunding-Regulation-2014.pdf

Financial Markets Authority (2015), *Consultation Paper, Proposed Variations to Standard Conditions of Market Services Licences*, available at https://fma.govt.nz/assets/Consultations/151117-Consultation-paper-proposed-variations-to-standard-conditions-of-market-services-licences.pdf

— (2016a), 'Crowdfunding', available at www.fma.govt.nz/consumers/ways-to-invest/crowdfunding/#Selling_your_shares_may_be_difficult

— (2016b), 'Standard Conditions for Crowdfunding Service Licenses', available at https://fma.govt.nz/assets/Compliance-section/Crowd-Funding-Standard-Conditions-updated-160601.pdf

— (2016c), 'Licensed Crowdfunding Services', available at http://fma.govt.nz/compliance/lists-and-registers/licensed-crowdfunding-services/

Gibbons, T. (2014), 'Purpose and principles of securities regulation' in V. Stace, T. Keeper *et al.* (eds), *Financial Markets Conduct Regulation: A Practitioner's Guide* (LexisNexis)

Hazen, T.L. (2012), 'Crowdfunding or Fraudfunding: Social Networks and the Securities Laws—Why the Specially Tailored Exemption Must be Conditioned on Meaningful Disclosure' 90 *North Carolina Law Review* 1735

Heminway, J.M. and S.R. Hoffman (2011), 'Proceed at Your Peril: Crowdfunding and the Securities Act 1933' 78 *Tennessee Law Review* 879

Hillind, H.W. (2015), 'Exploiting the Crowd: The New Zealand Response to Equity Crowd Funding' 21 *New Zealand Business Law Quarterly* 46

International Organization of Securities Commissions (IOSCO) (2015), *Crowdfunding 2015 Survey Responses Report*, available at www.iosco.org/library/pubdocs/pdf/IOSCOPD520.pdf

Keeper, T. (2014), 'The New Financial Reporting Regime' *New Zealand Law Journal* 248

Kirby, E. and S. Worner (2014), *Crowd-funding: An Infant Industry Growing Fast*, IOSCO Staff Working Paper, SWP3/2014, available at www.iosco.org/research/pdf/swp/Crowd-funding-An-Infant-Industry-Growing-Fast.pdf

Minister of Commerce Cabinet Paper (2011), *Securities Law Reform*, available at www.mbie.govt.nz/info-services/business/business-law/documents-image-library/Review-of-Securities-Law-Cabinet-paper-Feb-2011-1.pdf

— (2013), *Financial Markets Conduct Regulations Paper 4, Licensing Regimes*, available at www.mbie.govt.nz/info-services/business/business-law/financial-markets-conduct-act/regulations/financial-market-conduct-regulations-decisions-june-2013/documents-images-library/Paper%204%20-%20licensing.pdf

Ministry of Economic Development (MED) (2010), *Review of Securities Law*, Discussion Paper 2010, available at www.mbie.govt.nz/info-services/business/business-law/financial-markets-conduct-act/review-of-securities-law-discussion-document-2013-june-2010

Murray, J.M. (2015), *Equity Crowdfunding and Peer-to-Peer Lending in New Zealand: The First Year*, available at http://papers.ssrn.com/sol3/papers.cfm?abstract_id=2595354

Smylie, C. (2015a), 'Company Siphons Off IP and Founder Gets License', *National Business Review* (2 February), available at www.nbr.co.nz/article/company-siphons-ip-and-founder-gets-licence-fees-cs-p-168049

— (2015b), 'Younger Crowdfunding Platforms Fail to Gain Traction', *National Business Review* (5 October), available at www.nbr.co.nz/article/younger-crowdfunding-platforms-fail-gain-traction-cs-p-179663

— (2015c), 'Snowball Runs First Wholesale Offer for SOS Hydrate', *National Business Review* (25 November), available at www.nbr.co.nz/article/snowball-runs-first-wholesale-offer-sos-hydrate-cs-p-181881

— (2016a), 'Equity Crowdfunders' Figures Off?', *National Business Review* (10 June) 1

— (2016b), 'Equity Crowdfunding Moves Away from the Public Eye', *National Business Review* (24 March), available at www.nbr.co.nz/article/equity-crowdfunding-moves-away-public-eye-cs-p-186686

— (2016c), 'First Equity Crowdfunding Platform Closes Down as Marketplace Gets Crowded', *National Business Review* (21 March), available at www.nbr.co.nz/article/first-equity-crowdfunding-platform-closes-down-marketplace-gets-crowded-cs-p-186520

— (2016d), 'Equity Crowdfunded Companies Should Make Results Public, Investors Say', *National Business Review* (13 June), available at www.nbr.co.nz/article/equity-crowdfunded-companies-should-make-result-public-say-investors-cs-p-190287

Stemler, A.R. (2013), 'The JOBS Act and Crowdfunding: Harnessing the Power—and Money—of the Masses' 56 *Business Horizon* 271

Index

accountability
  Canada, shareholder activism in 23
  China, regulation in 131, 136, 139
accountancy *see* audits of Chinese
    RMCs by Big Four accountancy
    firms
Ackman, Bill 25
advertising 180–83, 185, 189, 193, 195
agency costs 19, 23–4, 100, 102–104,
    106, 112
Alibaba 95–6
Amit, R 108
angel investors 149–50, 151, 172, 175,
    189, 196, 217
Asian financial crisis 117
asset managers 71, 73, 76, 81
auditors, liability of 38
audits *see* auditors, liability of; audits of
    Chinese RMCs by Big Four
    accountancy firms
audits of Chinese RMCs by Big Four
    accountancy firms 7, 35–57
  accounting standards 8–9, 35,
    37–40, 42, 46, 50–51
  aiding and abetting 49
  burden of proof 41
  certification of financial statements
    39, 41
  China, number of auditing firms in 42
  China Securities Regulatory
    Commission (CSRC) 43, 54–6
  China State Administration for
    Industry and Commerce (SAIC)
    40
  China–US Memorandum of
    Understanding on Enforcement
    Cooperation 5, 9, 54–7
  Chinese law 9, 42, 44–51, 55
  class actions 39

classical theory 52
compliance 51–3
conflicts of law 56
cooperation 5, 9, 36, 46, 50–51, 54–7
corporate governance 55
criminal wilfulness 48
cross-listing on US stock exchanges
    8–9, 35, 39
cultural barriers 41
Deloitte Touche Tohmatsu CPA case
    43, 44–8
deterrence 42, 45, 50
development of an effective
    regulatory framework 5, 51–7
disciplinary proceedings 41–2, 46
disclosures 5, 9, 35–6, 40–57
documents/audit papers, refusal to
    provide 5, 9, 35–6, 40–57
  criminal wilfulness 48
  Deloitte Touche Tohmatsu CPA
    case 43, 44–8
  good faith 47, 48
  knowledge 47, 49
  recklessness 49
  Secrecy Law 44–6, 49–51
  wilful refusal 46–9
Dodd-Frank Act 36, 37, 39, 41, 49
due diligence 42
duty of care to shareholders 41
enforcement 37, 40–51, 52–3, 57
ex ante prevention 9, 52–3, 57
ex post sanctions 9, 52–3, 57
financial statements 35–7, 39–41
fraud 8, 35, 40, 43–4, 47, 49, 51, 53,
    55–7
global audit and financial reporting
    landscape 36–7
global financial crisis 37
good faith 47, 48

Hong Kong, number of auditing firms
    in 42
independence of auditors 42
inspections 39, 42–4, 51–7
internal controls 40
investigations 5, 8–9, 35–57
investor protection 5, 36, 41, 43–4,
    51, 54–5
IPOs, scrutiny of 8, 35, 39, 57
liability limitation agreements
    (LLAs) 38
listing standards 53
malfeasance 8, 35, 39–40
market integrity 36
memoranda of understanding
    China–US Memorandum of
        Understanding on
        Enforcement
        Cooperation 5, 9, 54–7
    CSRC 54–6
    Ministry of Finance (China) 54–6
    Multilateral Memorandum of
        Understanding (IOSCO) 54–5
misrepresentations 8, 35, 39
monitoring 36–7, 39–44, 54–5
moral hazard 9, 36–9, 51–3, 57
national security 57
negligence 50
practice bar 46, 50
Public Company Accounting
    Oversight Board (PCAOB) 36,
    37, 39–46, 50–7
    disciplinary proceedings 41–2, 46
    enforcement 42, 45–6, 50, 55
    foreign jurisdictions, difficulties in
        42
    gatekeeper or gatekeepers 39–44
    inspections 39, 42–4, 51–7
    mission 42
    reach and limits 41–4
    reality in China 42
    state sovereignty 43
preventive measures 53–4
public interest 42–3, 50, 52–3, 56
quality of audit work 5, 40, 43–4, 53,
    54
regulation 5, 8, 37, 51–7
reputation 36, 38–9

sanctions 51–3
Sarbanes-Oxley Act 8–9, 42–52
    section 106 (SOX 106) 35, 37,
        43–7, 49–50
    section 404 37
scienter 47
scrutiny 8, 35, 39, 57
seasoning periods 53
Secrecy Law 44–6, 49–51
Securities and Exchange
    Commission (SEC) 5, 8–9,
    35–57
Securities Exchange Act 47, 49
settlement 50–51
shareholder litigation 40–41
    challenges and hurdles facing
        plaintiffs 40–41
    enforcement of judgments in China
        40–41
    knowingly assisting a tort 41
shell companies 8, 39
state sovereignty 43
subpoenas 49–50
suspension of Big 4's China units
    35–6, 44–52
systemic risk 51
tax avoidance 40
'too big to fail' 37–8, 52
transparency 51, 55
wilful misconduct 46–8
Australia
    Australian Financial Services
        License 182
    Australian Securities and Investment
        Commission (ASIC) 216
    Australian Small Scale Offerings
        Board (ASSOB) 182
    Corporations Act 182
    crowdfunding 156–7, 182, 183–4
        Australian Securities and
            Investment Commission
            (ASIC) 216
        exemptions 182, 183–4
        New Zealand 215–16
        Product Disclosure Statement
            (PDS) 182
        secondary market 182
    disclosure 182

dual-class shares 105
New Zealand 215–16
Product Disclosure Statement (PDS)
182
prospectuses 182
SMEs 182
trans-Tasman Mutual Recognition
Scheme 215–16
autonomy 103, 104–106

Bagchi, K 194
banks *see* financial institutions
Barnier, Michel 73, 82, 86–7
Barrett, J 203, 217–18
Bebchuk, L 20, 22, 26–7, 30
Bellaflamme, P 200
Bennedsen, M 108
Berle, A 8, 17, 101–102
Bernanke, Ben 1
Big Four accountancy firms *see* audits
of Chinese RMCs by Big Four
accountancy firms
board of directors *see* directors/boards
of directors (BODs)
Bradford, CS 200
Brexit 13–14
Brin, Sergey 98
Burnett, Simeon 217

Canada
certification requirements for
financial statements 4
dual-class shares 95, 105
hedge fund activism 7
misrepresentation, statutory remedies
for 4
takeover protection 111
see also shareholder activism in
Canada
Capital Requirements Directive III
66–71, 78–9, 82
Capital Requirements Directive IV/
Capital Requirements Regulation
69–71, 78–9, 82
Carrothers, A 26
certification 4, 39, 41

chaebols, ban on cross-shareholding in
South Korean 10, 112
China
corporate control-enhancing
mechanisms 10, 98, 100–101
delisting/going private 100–101
dual-class shares 95, 105
management buy-outs 100–101
United States, firms listed in 10, 98,
100–101, 103
see also audits of Chinese RMCs by
Big Four accountancy firms;
China, legal regulation of capital
markets in
China, legal regulation of capital
markets in 5–6, 116–39
accountability 131, 136, 139
boards of supervisors (BOS) 10, 127,
136–8
effectiveness 136–7
Germany 136–7
independence 137
reports 133
business law history 10, 116, 118–21
centralization 10, 116, 131–2
China Securities Regulatory
Commission (CSRC) 120, 129,
131–2, 136
China's Stock Exchanges 118,
129–31, 139
origin and growth 129–30
Shanghai Stock Exchange (SHSE)
129–30
Shenzhen Stock Exchange (SZSE)
129–30
Western exchanges, differences
from 129–30
class actions 133–4
Company Law 117–18, 133–6, 138
concentrated ownership structure 132
conflict of interests 132
Constitution 133
contracting model 118, 119–20
corporate governance 116–39
Code 135, 138
effectiveness 116, 139
efficiency 116
financial institutions 117

improvements, proposals for
    137–9
  legal sources 121–9
  major issues 131–7
diligence, duty of 132
directors
  boards of directors (BOD) 123–5,
    127, 133, 135–7
  boards of supervisors (BOS) 137
  committees 136
  duties 118
  independence 129, 132, 135–8
  protection 118
  reports 133
disclosure 118, 135
economic growth 116, 132
enforcement 10, 138–9
experimental, trial-and-error method
    10
expropriations 10, 135
fairness 132, 136
fiduciary duties 118, 132, 135
financial institutions 117
fraud 134–5
GDP 116
good faith 135
government
  ownership 10, 119, 132
  restructuring 138
gradualism or trial and error 131–2
historical background 10, 116,
    118–21
improvements in corporate
    governance, proposals for 137–9
independent directors 10, 129, 132,
    135–8
  corporate governance 129
  Independent Directors Guidelines
    129, 136, 138
  scandals 129
  weak independence 135–6
insider control 132
insolvency 117
institutions 10, 117–18, 120, 125,
    129–33, 137, 139
judicial enforcement 139
law reform 119–21, 138–9

legal sources of corporate governance
    121–9
listed companies, growth in number
    of 129–30
major issues concerning corporate
    governance 131–7
majority shareholders, control by
    132, 134–5, 138
market capitalization 129–30
market economy 10, 120–21, 124
minority shareholders 121, 127,
    132–5
modern corporate model (1993
    onwards) 10, 118, 121
National People's Congress (NPC)
    133
non-tradeable shares 130–31
OECD Principles 139
political governance 133
private enterprise 10, 121, 130, 134,
    138
purchasing power parity (PPP)
    116
Qualified Foreign Institutional
    Investors (QFIIs) 130
re-centralization 116
recessions 117
related-party transactions 134–6
remuneration 133, 137
restructurings 117, 138
scandals 129
Securities Law 10, 117–18, 133–4,
    138
self-regulation 129
Shanghai Stock Exchange (SHSE)
    129–30
shareholders' powers 133–4
Shenzhen Stock Exchange (SZSE)
    129–30
state-owned enterprises (SOEs) 10,
    117, 118–21, 130–32,
    138
stock exchanges
  China's stock market 118,
    129–31, 139
  listing on overseas exchanges 118
  self-regulation 129

stock issuance registration system 118
supervisory boards 10, 127, 136–8
tradeable shares 130–31
traditional model (1949–84) 118–19
transitional model (1984–93) 118, 119–20
transparency 118, 136
transplants 11, 129, 137–8
United States 116, 133
Chion, Antonia 50–51
civil liability 211–12
Claessens, S 106–107
class actions 39
client agreements 211
collective investment scheme (CIS) 149, 174, 188
command and control techniques 6
Commission
    Action Plan 72–5, 76–7, 79
    comply or explain principle 75
    corporate control-enhancing mechanisms 105
    corporate governance 9–10, 62–88
        Action Plan 72–5, 76
        Green Paper 70–72
    crowdfunding 153
    Driving European Recovery communication 63–4
    enforcement 80
    European Parliament 85–7
    financial institutions 65–7
    long-term shareholder engagement, proposal for directive on 9–10, 62–3, 73–88
    recommendations 64–5, 79–80
    related party transactions 79–81
    remuneration 62–5, 73–5, 78–9, 94
    Shareholder Rights Directive 9–10, 63, 77–9, 81–8
company law
    Canada, shareholder activism in 18, 20, 27–8
    China 117–18, 133–6, 138
    crowdfunding 11–12, 160
        India 12, 174, 187, 188, 191, 193, 194
        New Zealand 211–12, 213–14

India 12, 174, 187, 188, 191, 193, 194
New Zealand 211–12, 213–14
shareholder activism 17–18
comparative perspectives on crowdfunding 179–86
compensation orders 212
competition
    competitive advantage 10, 98–100, 112, 150
    corporate control-enhancing mechanisms 10, 98, 100, 112
    crowdfunding 150, 216
    human capital 98–100, 112
    New Zealand, crowdfunding in 216
comply or explain principle 71, 75
confidentiality 163–4
conflicts of interest 66–7, 73, 76–7, 132, 157–8
conflicts of law 56
consumer protection
    crowdfunding 149, 151–52, 203, 208–209, 217
    New Zealand, crowdfunding in 203, 208–209, 217
contract
    China, regulation in 118, 119–20
    corporate control-enhancing mechanisms 103, 104, 109–10
    crowdfunding 149
    economic efficiency 4
    freedom of contract 103, 104
control *see* corporate control-enhancing mechanisms
convergence in capital market regulation 2, 3, 153
cooperation
    Chinese RMCs by Big Four companies, audits of 5, 9, 36, 46, 50–51, 54–7
    enforcement 5, 9, 54–7
    regulation 5
    United States and China, memorandum of understanding with 5, 9, 54–7
co-ownership agreements 168
corporate control-enhancing mechanisms 95–113
    academic debates 96–7

agency costs 100, 102–104, 106, 112
Chinese tech companies listed in US
    10, 98, 100–101
Commission 105
competitive advantage 10, 98, 100,
    112
contractual arrangements 109–10
corporate autonomy 103, 104–106
corporate governance 96–9,
    105–106, 112
cross-shareholdings 102, 107, 110,
    112
directors, exclusive rights to appoint
    109–10
disclosure 105
dispersed ownership 102–103
disproportionate control rights 95,
    96–7, 100, 106, 108–12
economic incentives 103
economic rights 96
efficiency 98–9, 104, 109–10
emerging economies 107
empirical evidence 106
entrenchment effect 104, 106–107,
    112
European Union
    Commission 105
    pyramid 110
    voting agreements 110
    Winter Group Report 105, 110
expropriation, risk of 10, 99, 101,
    104, 112
family firms 102, 107–108, 110, 112
founding teams 97–8
freedom of contract 103, 104
globalization 98
human capital 10, 97–101, 112
    competitive advantage 98–100,
        112
    firm-specific 98–100
    information economy 97–100
human resource management
    96–118
information economy 97–100
initial public offers (IPOs) 10, 95,
    96–8, 104, 110–11
innovation 96, 99–100
institutional investors 97

investor protection 112
ISS Report 105
law and economics movement 99
long-termism 96
market failure 111
minority shareholders 96–7, 99, 102
moral hazard 104
multiple classes of shares 109–10
multiple-vote shares 106
national economic development 97
non-participative mechanisms 10,
    109–12
one-share/one-vote principle 95–6,
    102–106
participative mechanisms 10, 109–10
policy debates 96–7
problems 100–101
proportionality 95, 96–7, 100,
    105–106, 108–12
public companies 102–103
purpose 110
pyramid structures 102–103,
    107–108, 110, 112
re-conceptualization 109–10, 112–13
regulation 10, 109–12
remuneration 111
separation of ownership and control
    102, 105
shareholder value 106–10
short-termism 96–7
social welfare 110–11
South Korea, ban on
    cross-shareholding in chaebols
    in 10, 112
takeover protection 111–12
theoretical inquiries 103
transparency 105
unequal treatment of shareholders 95
United States
    Chinese tech companies listed in
        US 10, 98, 100–101
    dispersed ownership 103
    dual-class shares 96, 105, 108–10
    IPO firms 10, 95, 98
    public companies 103, 107
    S&P Composite 1500 Index 103
voting 106–12
    agreements 102, 108, 110

ceilings 109–10
event-based 111–12
Nordic countries 111–12
risk-bearing 103
weak investor protection regimes,
    regulation in 10, 112
Winter Group Report 105, 110
see also dual-class shares
corporate governance 1–2
Canada, shareholder activism in 20–
    21, 24, 27, 29
chaebols 112
China
    regulation in 116–39
    RMCs by Big Four companies,
        audits of 55
conflicts of interest 73, 76
corporate control-enhancing
    mechanisms 96–9, 105–106, 112
costs 81
crowdfunding 12, 150, 160–69, 178,
    207, 216
disclosure 73, 76–7, 84
dual-class shares 96–9
efficiency 116, 122, 126, 135
empirical evidence, lack of 9–10, 63,
    81–3, 88
end of history 4
ex ante 18
global financial crisis 5, 9, 62, 63–5,
    75, 78, 82–3
India, crowdfunding in 178
inside effect 160–64
institutional investors 73, 76, 81
investor rights 73–4
legal sources 121–9
listed companies 9–10, 62–3, 70–88,
    117–18, 121–39
minority shareholders 121, 127,
    132–5
New Zealand, crowdfunding in 207,
    216
OECD Steering Group 105–106
proxy advisers 73, 76–7, 84
quack corporate governance 82
regulation 5
related party transactions 62–3, 73,
    75, 79–81, 84

remuneration 5, 62–70, 73–5, 78–9,
    84, 86–7
Sarbanes-Oxley Act 4
Shareholder Rights Directive 9–10,
    62–3, 72–88
shareholder value maxim 3
voting 9, 64–5, 71
corporate governance in EU 9–10,
    62–75
Capital Requirements Directive III
    78–9, 82
Capital Requirements Directive IV/
    CRR 78–9, 82
Commission 9–10, 62–88
Council of the EU 84, 85, 86
De Larosière Report 63
European Parliament 84, 85–6
expertise on boards and senior
    management, lack of 63
financial institutions 9, 63–71, 88
freedom of establishment 83
global financial crisis 9, 62, 63–5
listed companies 9–10, 62–3, 70–88
long-term shareholder engagement,
    proposal for directive on 9–10,
    62–3, 73–88
remuneration 63–70
weaknesses of EU law 9–10, 63,
    83–4, 88
*Corporate Governance after the
    Financial Crisis* 2
crime
    Chinese RMCs by Big Four
        companies, audits of 48
    financial misstatements 4
    New Zealand, crowdfunding in 211
    Sarbanes-Oxley Act 4
    see also fraud
Cronqvist, H 107
Crowd88 216
crowdfunding 145–69
    access to finance challenges 145–7
    accredited investors 156
    advisers 154
    alternative sources of finance 145–7
    angel investors 149–50, 151
    bank finance 146, 149–50, 151
    barriers to entry 155

business strategy 150
caps or limits 156–60
civil society, as an innovation of 6
convergence 3, 153
company/corporate law 11–12, 160
competitive advantages 150
complex decision-making 12, 160
concept 147–50
confidentiality 163–4
conflicts of interest 157–8
consumer protection 149, 151–2
contract 149
co-ownership agreements 168
corporate governance 12, 150,
    160–69
crowd investors 150
debt-based crowdfunding 148, 151,
    166
decision-making process 162, 168–9
digital technology 165–6
disclosure duties 12, 158, 160, 163–4,
    169
diversification 151
donation-based crowdfunding 148–9,
    151
efficiency 192, 203
electronic procedures 165–6
enlargement of scope 151
equity-based crowdfunding 148–52,
    159, 166
EU law 3, 12, 152–3, 155
    authorization 155
    directive 152–3
    harmonization 153
    Markets in Financial Instruments
        Directive (MiFiD) 155
exit strategies 12, 160, 162
forum shopping 155
France 152, 154, 164
fraud 155
Germany 157
idea protection 163–4
inside effect 11–12, 160–64
insider trading 163–4
institutional involvement,
    intensification of 149–50, 151
intermediary vehicles 167–8
investment-based crowdfunding 149

investor protection 11, 156–9
invoice trading 148–9
Italy 152, 155, 157, 159, 169
large shareholder bases, dealing with
    166–9
lending models 148–50, 152–4
licensing/approval 154–5
liquidity 160, 162–3
minimum shareholding requirements
    for voting 166
minority shareholders 166–8
nominee accounts, use of 166–7
non-accredited investors 156, 159
non-equity models 166
non-public companies 160
outside effect 151–60
platforms, regulation of 154–5
popularity 146–7, 149
Portugal 155–8, 164
prescription effect 156
private companies 12, 149, 158, 161,
    163
professional investors 150, 157
profit-sharing/revenge-sharing model
    166
prudential requirements 154
public exposure 12, 160
registration 154–5
regulation 1, 3, 6, 149, 151–60
regulations 147–50
reputational strategies 12, 160
reward-based crowdfunding 148–9,
    151–2
risk assessment 157
risk management 11, 153
secondary market functionalities 162
securities model 149
separation of ownership and control
    160–62
shareholders, participation of 165–6
Sharing Economy 147
SMEs 1–2, 145, 147–8, 158–9, 163,
    165–6
social lending models 148–50, 152–4
social movements 147
Spain 154–5, 156–8, 160, 165, 169
standardization 162
start-ups 145–6, 151, 157–63, 165

syndicates 168–9
systemic effects 11, 153–4, 156, 169
third parties 157
transparency 11, 154, 163
trust 147, 157
types 148
United Kingdom 158, 160
United States 1–2, 152, 159–60
variations 147–50
venture capital 146, 149–50, 151
voting 166, 168–9
weak party protection 152
see also India, equity crowdfunding
    in; New Zealand, crowdfunding
    in
Crowdsphere Ltd 216

De Larosière Report 63
Deloittes *see* audits of Chinese RMCs
    by Big Four accountancy firms
Deng Xiaoping 121
deterrence 42, 45, 50
digital technology 165–6
directors/boards of directors (BODs)
    appointment, exclusive rights of
        109–10
    Canada, shareholder activism in
        21–2, 28–9
    China, regulation in 123–5, 127, 129,
        133, 135–8
    composition and structure 64
    corporate control-enhancing
        mechanisms 109–10
    crowdfunding 13, 205, 208–11
    EU law 129
    expertise 30, 63
    fiduciary duties 21–2, 28–9
    good faith 21–2
    independence 27, 30, 129, 132,
        135–8
    listed companies 71, 75
    minority shareholders 29, 71
    multiple directorships, disclosure of
        66–7
    New Zealand, crowdfunding in 13,
        205, 208–11
    nomination 18, 20, 27–9, 31, 70–71

primacy 19–21, 31
    removal 20
    scandals 129
    supervision 66
    United States 129
    see also remuneration and incentives
disciplinary measures 23, 41–2, 46
disclosure
    audits of Chinese RMCs by Big Four
        accountancy firms 5, 9, 35–6,
        40–57
    Australia 182
    China, regulation in 118, 135
    conflicts of interest 76–7
    corporate control-enhancing
        mechanisms 105
    corporate governance 73, 76–7, 84
    crowdfunding 12, 158, 160, 163–4,
        169
        France 164
        India 174, 177, 179, 182, 191–2
        New Zealand 202–203, 206–207,
            210–15, 218
        Spain 169
    dispute resolution schemes 211
    dual-class shares 105
    efficiency 163
    fees 211
    financial reporting 204, 208, 213–14
    France, crowdfunding in 164
    India, crowdfunding in 174, 177, 179,
        182, 191–2
    investment strategies 73
    long-term shareholder engagement,
        proposal for directive on 73
    multiple directorships, disclosure of
        66–7
    New Zealand, crowdfunding in 185
    Portugal, crowdfunding in 158, 164
    post-funding arrangement
        communications 217, 218
    prospectuses 6, 182–3, 217
    proxy advisers 73, 76–7, 84
    remuneration 64, 68–70, 71–2, 78–9
    Spain, crowdfunding in 169
    voting practices of institutional
        investors, disclosure of 66
dispute resolution schemes 13, 205, 211

diversification 122, 138, 146, 151, 156,
    215, 218
diversity policies 70
Dodd-Frank Act (United States) 4–5,
    36, 37, 39, 41, 49
Doty, James 39
dual-class shares 1, 7, 100–103,
    106–107
  Australia 105
  Canada 95, 105
  Chinese firms listed on US stock
    exchanges 10, 98, 100, 103
  corporate governance 96–9
  disclosure 105
  East Asia 102
  endogeneity issue 108
  Google IPO 10, 95
  high-tech companies 10, 95
  Hong Kong 105
  IPOs in US 10, 95, 98
  market capitalization 103
  media firms 10, 95, 97
  multiple-vote shares 106
  one-share/one-vote principle 95–6,
    102–105
  regulation 105
  shareholder value 106–109
  short-termism 97
  unequal voting rights 10, 103
  United Kingdom 105
  United States 96, 105, 108–10
due diligence
  audits of Chinese RMCs by Big Four
    accountancy firms 42
  China, regulation in 132
  crowdfunding 176, 194, 206, 217
  India, crowdfunding in 176, 194
  New Zealand, crowdfunding in 206,
    217

Easterbrook, FH 103
efficiency
  corporate control-enhancing
    mechanisms 98–9, 104, 109–10
  corporate governance 116, 122, 126,
    135
  crowdfunding 192, 203

disclosure 163
  freedom 4
  human capital 98–9
  New Zealand, crowdfunding in 203
  regulation 2, 4
  short-termism 24
empirical evidence
  corporate control-enhancing
    mechanisms 106
  long-term shareholder engagement,
    proposal for directive on 9–10,
    63, 81–3, 88
  Sarbanes-Oxley Act 81–2
end of history 4
enforcement
  audits of Chinese RMCs by Big Four
    accountancy firms 37, 40–51,
    52–3, 57
  China
    audits of Chinese RMCs by Big
      Four accountancy firms 37,
      40–51, 52–3, 57
    judgments in China 40–41
    regulation 10, 138–9
    United States, memorandum of
      understanding with 5, 9, 54–7
  Commission 80
  cooperation 5, 9, 54–7
  judgments in China 40–41
  long-term shareholder engagement,
    proposal for directive on 83–4
  New Zealand, crowdfunding in 208
  related party transactions 80
Enriques, Luca 80
Enron, collapse of 4, 82
entrenchment effect 104, 106–107, 112
Equitise Pty 215–16
Ernst & Young *see* audits of Chinese
    RMCs by Big Four accountancy
    firms
EU law
  auditors, liability of 38
  Capital Requirements Directive III
    66–71, 78–9, 82
  Capital Requirements Directive IV/
    Capital Requirements
    Regulation 69–71, 78–9, 82

corporate control-enhancing
    mechanisms 105, 110
Council 84, 85, 86
crowdfunding 3, 12, 152–3, 155
directors, independence of 129
European Parliament 84, 85–7
harmonization 153
Markets in Financial Instruments
    Directive (MiFiD) 155
pyramid structures 110
regulation, increase in 5
voting agreements 110
weaknesses 9–10, 63, 83–4, 88
Winter Group Report 105, 110
see also Commission; corporate
    governance in EU; long-term
    shareholder engagement,
    proposal for directive on;
    Shareholder Rights Directive
expertise 30, 63, 70, 77–9
expropriations 10, 99, 101, 104, 112,
    135

Faccio, M 102
fairness
    China, regulation in 132, 136
    related party transactions 80
    New Zealand, crowdfunding in
        212–13
false or misleading statements 134, 208,
    211–12
family firms 97, 102, 107–108, 110,
    112
fiduciary duties 21–2, 28–9, 118, 132,
    135
financial institutions
    alternative sources of finance 146
    Capital Requirements Directive III
        66–71
    Capital Requirements Directive IV/
        Capital Requirements
        Regulation 69–71
    China, regulation in 117
    Commission 65–7
    composition and structure of board
        64
    conflicts of interest 66–7

corporate governance 9, 63–70, 71,
    88
crowdfunding 146, 149–50, 151
De Larosière Report 63
debates 65–70
defective implementation of
    corporate governance principles
    66
diversity policies 70
expertise on boards and senior
    management 63, 70
financial products, risks associated
    with 63
gender diversity 70
institutional investors, role of 66
multiple directorships, disclosure of
    66–7
nomination committees 70
public consultation 65–7
reform 63
remuneration 63–70
risk management 63, 66, 67–8, 70
risk profiles, information on 70
shareholders, role of 66
short-termism 66
supervise and take action, inability of
    boards to 66
voting practices of institutional
    investors, disclosure of 66
financial reporting requirements 204,
    208, 213–14
financial statements
    Canada 4
    certification 4, 39, 41
    Chinese RMCs by Big Four
        companies, audits of 35–7,
        39–41
    financial reporting 213–14
    New Zealand, crowdfunding in 215,
        217
fines 211–12
Finland 102, 107
Fischel, DR 103
fit and proper persons 205
Foreign Corrupt Practices Act of 1977
    (United States) 4–5
forum shopping 155
founders 10, 97–8

France, crowdfunding in 152, 154, 164
fraud
    audits of Chinese RMCs by Big Four
        accountancy firms 8, 35, 40,
        43–4, 47, 49, 51, 53, 55–7
    China, regulation in 134–5
    crowdfunding 155, 173, 175, 188,
        206
    end of history 4
    India, crowdfunding in 173, 175, 188
    New Zealand, crowdfunding in 206
freedom of contract 103, 104
freedom of establishment 83
Fukuyama, Francis 4
future forecasts 212–13, 218

GAAP 213–14
gender diversity 70
general meetings, voting in 62, 64–5,
    74–5, 77, 84
Germany, crowdfunding in 157
Gibbons, T 204
Gilson, R 17
global financial crisis
    audits of Chinese RMCs by Big Four
        accountancy firms 37
    corporate governance 5, 9, 62, 63–5,
        75, 78, 82–3
    Dodd-Frank Act 4–5
    India, crowdfunding in 172
    listed companies 75
    long-term shareholder engagement,
        proposal for directive on 75, 78,
        82–3
    remuneration 63–5, 78
    United States Federal Reserve 1–2
globalization 1–2, 5, 7, 9, 55, 98
Gompers, PA 107
good faith 21–2, 47, 48, 135
Google IPO 10, 95
Gordon, J 17
Green, Fred 25
Guangdong Enterprises (GDE) 117
Guangdong International Trust and
    Investment Company (GITIC) 117

Hansmann, H 4

Harrison, Hunter 25
hedge fund activism 1, 7, 8, 17–18, 24–5
Heminway, JM 178–9
high-tech companies 10, 95, 98,
    100–101
Hoffman, SR 178–9
Hong Kong 42, 105, 179–80, 185
human capital 10, 97–101, 112
human resource management 96–118

idea protection 163–4
incentives *see* remuneration and
    incentives
independence
    audits of Chinese RMCs by Big Four
        accountancy firms 42
    directors 27, 30, 129, 132, 135–8
India, equity crowdfunding in 7, 172–96
    accredited investors 176, 191–3, 195
    advertising 180–83, 185, 189, 193,
        195
    agency 178
    angel investments 172, 175, 189, 196
    Australia 182, 183–4
    barriers to entry 192
    benefits 176–7, 180
    caps and limitations 193
    carving out exemptions 180–84
    collective action 178
    collective investment schemes 174,
        188
    Companies Act, 2013 12, 174, 187,
        188, 191, 193, 194
    Companies Rules, 2014 191, 193,
        194
    comparative perspectives 179–86
    comprehensive legislation 184–6
    corporate governance 178
    costs 178–9
    crowdfunding, definition of 172
    decision-making 176
    disclosure 174, 177, 179, 182, 191–2
    donation crowdfunding 172, 186
    due diligence 176, 194
    economic growth 173
    eligibility restrictions 12, 190–93

Eligible Retail Investors (ERIs)
190–91
exemptions 179–85
factors inhibiting growth 12, 175, 193
fraud 173, 175, 188
global financial crisis 172
growth 12, 173–6, 179, 184, 189, 195
high-net-worth individuals (HNIs)
12, 190
Hong Kong 179–80, 185
innovation 173
investor protection 3, 178–80, 184–5,
187, 189–90
investors, nature of 190
Italy 184–6, 191, 195
legislation 184–6
limits on investments 12, 191
minimum net worth, companies with
190
monitoring 176, 178
nature and scope 186
non-accredited investors 178, 183–4
peer-to-peer funding 172–3, 186
primary markets 175
private placements 174, 183, 187,
189, 191, 193–4
procedures 191–2
professional investors 180
prohibiting crowdfunding 179–80
prospectuses 187–8
qualified institutional buyers (QIBs)
189–91, 193
refunds to investors 12, 187–8
registration 181
regulation 173–96
balancing role 176–9, 189–90
current state 186–9
reward crowdfunding 172, 174, 186
risks 177–8
Sahara effect 12, 188–9
Sahara India Real Estate case 12,
187–9
Saradha Group scandal 188
scandals 174, 188
secondary markets 175–6, 182
Securities and Exchange Board of
India (SEBI) 174–5, 186–95
securities regulation 187, 195

Singapore 182–4, 185–6, 192–3
SMEs 175, 179, 182, 184, 196
Start Up India 178
start-ups 172–4, 176–8, 184, 195–6
transparency 180
types of crowdfunding 172–3
United States 180–81, 183–4, 185–6,
194–5
venture capital 172, 175, 186, 189,
191–2, 196
individualism 3–4
Indonesia 102–103
information economy 97–100
inspections 39, 42–4, 51–7
initial public offers (IPOs)
audits of Chinese RMCs by Big Four
accountancy firms 8, 35, 39, 57
corporate control-enhancing
mechanisms 10, 95, 96–8, 104,
110–11
dual-class shares 7, 10, 95, 98
scrutiny 8, 35, 39, 57
United States 10, 95, 98
innovation
corporate control-enhancing
mechanisms 96, 99–100
India, crowdfunding in 173
information economy 98
New Zealand, crowdfunding in 13,
204
policy 1
prospectuses 6
regulation 1
insider trading 163–4
insolvency 117
institutions
China, regulation in 10, 117–18, 120,
125, 129–33, 137, 139
crowdfunding 149–50, 151, 189–91,
193
investors 8, 66, 71, 73, 76, 81, 97,
189–91, 193
voting practices of institutional
investors, disclosure of 66
intermediaries
capability 204
client agreements 211

crowdfunding 13, 167–8, 185, 199,
    205–11, 214–18
  eligibility 13, 203, 205, 211
  institutional investors 17–18
  investor protection 73–4
  investor rights 73–4
  knowledge and reliability 217–18
  licensing 13, 199, 204–10
  New Zealand, crowdfunding in 13,
    185, 199, 201, 204–11, 214–18
  number of service providers 214–15
  warnings 206, 209–10, 212–13
investor protection
  audits of Chinese RMCs by Big Four
    accountancy firms 5, 36, 41,
    43–4, 51, 54–5
  corporate control-enhancing
    mechanisms 112
  crowdfunding 11, 156–9
    India 3, 178–80, 184–5, 187,
      189–90
    Italy 184–5
    New Zealand 13, 203
  India, crowdfunding in 3, 178–80,
    184–5, 187, 189–90
  intermediaries 73–4
  Italy, crowdfunding in 184–5
  New Zealand, crowdfunding in 13,
    203
  rights of investors 73–4
invoice trading 148–9
IOSCO Committee for the Regulation
  of Market Intermediaries 201
IPOs *see* initial public offers (IPOs)
Italy
  crowdfunding 152, 155, 157, 159,
    184–6
  caps 191
  CONSOB 184
  innovative start-up companies 184
  investor protection 184–5
  online portals 184
  professional investors 195
  warnings to non-professional
    investors 184
  withdrawal, right of 185
  dual-class shares 102

  financial institutions, attachment to
    155
  innovative start-up companies 184
  investor protection 184–5
  MiFID 155
  professional investors 157, 195
  regulation 159
  warnings to non-professional
    investors 184
  withdrawal, right of 185
ISS Report 105

Jensen, M 19, 102

Katelouzou, D 26
Kirby, E 201
knowingly assisting a tort 41
KPMG *see* audits of Chinese RMCs by
  Big Four accountancy firms
Kraakman, R 4

La Porta, R 106–107
Lang, LH 102
law and economics movement 99
liability limitation agreements (LLAs)
  38
liberal democracy, triumph of 4
libertarianism 4
liberty 3–4
licensing of crowdfunding 13, 154–5,
  185, 199, 204–10, 212, 214–16
Lins, KV 107
Lipton, M 20, 22, 27
liquidity 160, 162–3, 218
listed companies
  asset managers 71
  Capital Requirements Directive
    70–71
  China
    corporate governance 117–18,
      121–39
    delisting/going private 100–101
    regulation in 129–30
  Commission Action Plan 72–5, 76
  Commission Green Paper (2011)
    70–72
  comply or explain principle 71, 75

corporate control-enhancing
  mechanisms 95–6, 98, 101, 103,
  105
corporate governance 9–10, 62–63,
  70–88, 117–18, 121–39
cross-border listings 1–2, 8, 35, 103
crowdfunding 12, 187–8, 210, 213,
  216–17
delisting 100–101
dual-class structure 95
global financial crisis 75
India, crowdfunding in 12, 187–8
institutional investors 71
long-term shareholder engagement,
    proposal for directive on 9–10,
  62–3, 70–88
minority shareholders 71
New Zealand, crowdfunding in 210,
  213, 216–17
proxy advisors 9, 71–2
remuneration 9, 63–5, 71–2
  disclosure 71–2
  voting 71
risk management 71
shareholder identification 71–2
Shareholder Rights Directive 9–10,
  62–3, 73–88
shareholders, role of 71
short-termism 71
standards 53
structure and functioning of boards
  71, 75
see also audits of Chinese RMCs by
  Big Four accountancy firms
long-term interests 24, 27, 30, 96 *see
  also* long-term shareholder
  engagement, proposal for directive
  on
long-term shareholder engagement,
  proposal for directive on 73–88
asset managers, engagement of 73,
  76, 81
Capital Requirements Directive III
  78–9, 82
Capital Requirements Directive IV/
  CRR 78–9, 82
Commission 9–10, 62–3, 73–88
  Action Plan 72–5, 76–7, 79

enforcement 80
European Parliament 85–7
seriousness of proposals 81–3
conflicts of interest 73, 76
corporate governance 9–10, 62–3,
  73–88
costs 81
Council of the EU 84, 85, 86
criticisms 9–10, 63, 77–9, 81–7
design, criticism of 81
disclosure 73, 76–7, 84
empirical evidence, lack of support
  from 9–10, 63, 81–3, 88
enforcement 83–4
European Parliament 84, 85–6
explanatory memorandum 73
freedom of establishment 83
global financial crisis 75, 78,
  82–3
impact assessment 73
institutional investors, engagement of
  73, 76, 81
investor rights, difficult and costly
  rights of 73–4
lack of theoretical and empirical basis
  9–10, 63, 81, 88
listed companies 9–10, 62–3, 70–88
mandatory regulation 81
overreaching 81
proxy advisers, transparency of 73,
  76–7
quack corporate governance 82
Reflection Group 77, 79, 80
related party transactions, oversight
  of 62–3, 73, 75, 79–81, 84
remuneration policies 62–3, 73–5,
  78–9, 84, 86–7
Shareholder Rights Directive,
  proposal to amend 9–10, 62–3,
  72–88
  Commission criticisms 9–10, 63,
    77–9, 81–8
  criticisms 9–10, 63, 77–9, 81–8
  freedom of establishment 83
  listed companies 9–10, 62–3,
    73–88
  seriousness of proposals 81–3
  trivial, revision as 83–8

shareholders
  activism 76
  communications, improvements in
    77
  identification 71–2, 77–8, 84
  short-termism 77
  single, coherent framework, lack of
    9–10, 63
  structure of the board 87
  suboptimal regulatory strategies 81
  tax reporting requirements 85
  under-inclusive rules 81
  weaknesses of EU law 9–10, 63,
    83–4, 88

Ma, Jack 98
majority shareholders
  control 99, 132, 134–5, 138
  China, regulation in 132, 134–5, 138
  voting 20–21, 111–12, 168
management buy-outs (MBOs)
    100–101
market capitalization 103, 129–30
Markets in Financial Instruments
    Directive (MiFiD) 155
Masulis, RW 109
Maury, B 107
May, Theresa 13
Means, G 8, 17, 101–102
Meckling, W 19, 102
media
  firms 10, 95, 97
  New Zealand, crowdfunding in 217
  social media 200
micro angel investors 217
minority shareholders
  Canada, shareholder activism in 27
  China, regulation in 121, 127, 132–5
  corporate control-enhancing
    mechanisms 96–7, 99, 102
  corporate governance 121, 127,
    132–5
  crowdfunding 166–8
  directors, nomination of 29, 71
  hedge funds 8, 17
  listed companies 71

long-term shareholder engagement,
    proposal for directive on 71–2
misrepresentation 4, 8, 35, 39
money laundering 215
monitoring *see* scrutiny; supervision
    and monitoring
moral hazard 9, 36–9, 51–3, 57, 104
Murray, JM 215
My Angel Investment Ltd 216

national security 57
negligence 50
New Legal Realism (NLR) 7
New Zealand, crowdfunding in 7,
    184–6, 192, 199–218
  annual meetings 214
  Australia 215–16
  awareness of investors 13
  barriers to entry 201
  cancellation/cooling off 206
  capability 13, 207
  caps and limits 185, 201
  civil liability 211–12
  client agreements 211
  Companies Act (1993) 211–12,
    213–14
  compensation orders 212
  competition 216
  compliance 13, 202, 207
  consumer protection 203, 208–209,
    217
  convertible notes 215
  corporate governance 207, 216
  criminal sanctions 211
  Crowd88 216
  crowdfunding, definition of
    200–201
  Crowdfunding Service Providers
    (CSPs) 199, 205–11, 214–18
  Crowdsphere Ltd 216
  directors
    Crowdfunding Service Providers
      (CSPs) 208–11
    self-certification 13, 205
  disclosure 185, 202–203, 206–207,
    210–15

dispute resolution schemes, details
        of 211
    exemptions 199, 202–203
    false or misleading statements 211
    financial reporting requirements
        204, 208, 213–14
    fees 211
    post-funding arrangement
        communications 217, 218
    Service Disclosure Statements
        (SDSs) 210–12
    wholesale investors 215
dispute resolution schemes,
    membership of an approved 13,
    205, 211
diversification 215
donation crowdfunding 200, 215
due diligence 206, 217
efficiency 203
eligibility 13, 185, 203, 205, 211
enforcement 208
Equitise Pty 215–16
equity crowdfunding 199, 200–203,
    209, 211–17
facilitation of fund-raising 3, 203,
    205, 217
failures 216–17, 218
fair dealing 212–13
false or misleading statements 208,
    211–12
fees, disclosure of 211
Financial Markets Authority (FMA)
    13, 203, 205, 207–13, 216
Financial Markets Conduct Act 2013
    (FMC Act) 13, 185, 199, 203–15
Financial Markets Conduct
    Regulations 2014 185, 204–10
financial reporting requirements 204,
    208, 213–14
fines 211–12
fit and proper persons 205
flexibility 13, 204
fraud 206
future forecasts 212–13, 218
GAAP 213–14
growth 13, 216–17
innovation 13, 204
intermediaries 185, 201, 204–11

capability 204
client agreements 211
Crowdfunding Service Providers
    (CSPs) 199, 205–11, 214–18
eligibility 13, 203, 205, 211
knowledgeable and reliable
    217–18
licensing 13, 199, 204–10
number of service providers
    214–15
warnings 206, 209–10, 212–13
investor protection 13, 203
IOSCO Committee for the
    Regulation of Market
    Intermediaries 201
knowledgeable and reliable
    intermediaries 217–18
large companies 213–15
lending crowdfunding 200
licensing of intermediaries 13, 185,
    199, 204–10, 212, 214–16
    criteria 205–207
    false or misleading applications
        208
    specific conditions 207
    Standard Licence Conditions 207
    warnings 206, 209–10
liquidity risk 218
listed companies 210, 213, 216–17
Listing Rules 213
Maori/indigenous focus 216
market service licences 199, 205
media 217
micro angel investors, availability of
    217
misleading or deceptive conduct 206
money laundering 215
My Angel Investment Ltd 216
number of service providers 214–15
ongoing issuer disclosures 216–17
peer-to-peer lending 200
platforms, analysis of 214–16
PledgeMe 215, 217
policy objectives 202–205
post-funding arrangement
    communications 217, 218
pre-purchase crowdfunding 200
record-keeping 208

registration 205
regulation 13, 201, 202–208, 211–14
retail investors, understanding of 218
reward crowdfunding 200, 215
risks/investor protection, balance
    between 201
secondary market 207
Securities Act (1978) 202–203
self-assigned valuation of assets and
    future forecasts 212–13, 218
self-certification 13, 205
senior managers 13, 205, 208
size of issuers 206
SMEs 206, 213, 216–18
Snowball Effect 215, 217
social media phenomenon,
    crowdfunding as 200
Standard Licence Conditions 207
start-ups 213, 217
Stock Exchange (NZ Stock
    Exchange) 213, 216
  disclosure 216
  NXT 216
transparency 13, 203
trans-Tasman Mutual Recognition
    Scheme 215–16
types of sites 200–201
valuation of assets 212–13, 218
voting shares, control of 214
warnings 206, 209–10, 212–13
wholesale investors 215
Nielson, KM 108
Nilsson, M 107
Nordic countries 102, 111–12
Nourse, V 7

OECD (Organisation for Economic
    Cooperation and Development)
  Principles 139
  Steering Group 105–6
offensive activism 17
one-share/one-vote principle 95–6,
    102–105
oppression or unfair prejudice 20

Page, Larry 98
Pajuste, A 107

Parmalat 82
participative mechanisms 10,
    109–10
Partnoy, F 52
passive investors 8, 17
pension funds 8
PledgeMe 215, 217
Portugal, crowdfunding in
  caps and limits 156–7
  conflicts of interests 158
  disclosure 158, 164
  MiFID 155
PriceWaterhouseCoopers *see* audits of
    Chinese RMCs by Big Four
    accountancy firms
private sector
  crowdfunding 12, 149, 158, 161, 163
  delisting 100–101
  economic efficiency 4
  optimal outcomes 4
proportionality 38, 95, 96–7, 100,
    105–106, 108–12
prospectuses
  Australia 182
  disclosure 6, 182–3, 217
  doctrinaire approaches 6
  extreme ideologies 6–7
  India, crowdfunding in 187–8
  Joint Stock Companies Registration
      and Regulation Act 1844
      (England) 6
  market excesses, checking 6
  market innovations 6
  public policy 6
  regulation 6
  Securities Act of 1993 (United States)
      6
  United Kingdom 160
proxy advisers 9, 71–3, 76–7, 84
proxy contests 24–6, 28
public companies *see* listed companies
Public Company Accounting Oversight
    Board (PCAOB) (China) 36, 37,
    39–46, 50–57
public offers *see* initial public offers
    (IPOs)
public policy 1–2, 4–6, 82, 160
public regulation *see* regulation

PwC *see* audits of Chinese RMCs by
    Big Four accountancy firms
pyramid structures 102–103, 107–108,
    110, 112

Qihoo 360 101

Reagan–Thatcher era 4
Reflection Group 77, 79, 80
registration
    China, regulation in 118
    crowdfunding 154–5, 181, 205
    New Zealand, crowdfunding in 205
    United States 180–81
regulation 1–6
    Chinese RMCs by Big Four
        companies, audits of 37, 51–7
    command and control techniques 6
    corporate control-enhancing
        mechanisms 10, 109–12
    corporate governance 5
    crowdfunding 1, 3, 6, 149, 151–60
        India 173–96
        New Zealand 13, 201, 202–208,
            211–14
    dual-class shares 105
    efficiency 2, 4
    EU law 5
    events, impact of 3
    evolution of ideas 3
    facilitative regulation 6
    India, crowdfunding in 173–96
        balancing role 176–9, 189–90
        current state 186–9
    New Legal Realism (NLR) 7
    New Zealand, crowdfunding in 13,
        201, 202–208, 211–14
    opposition 3
    prospectuses 6
    self-regulation 77
    suboptimal regulatory strategies 81
    United States 14, 180–81
    see also China, legal regulation of
        capital markets in
related-party transactions
    China, regulation in 134–6
    Commission 79–81

enforcement 80
exemption regime 80–81
fairness 80
general meetings, prior approval by
    75
long-term shareholder engagement,
    proposal for directive on 62–3,
    73, 75, 79–81, 84
materiality test 84
public announcements 75
quantitative restrictions 84
Reflection Group 80
reports from independent parties 75
voting 80
remuneration and incentives
    approval of AGMs 65
    Canada, shareholder activism in 23
    Capital Requirements Directive III
        66–9, 78–9
    Capital Requirements Directive IV/
        CRR 69–70, 78–9
    China, regulation in 133, 137
    Commission 62–5, 73–5, 78–9
    committees 67–8
    corporate control-enhancing
        mechanisms 111
    corporate governance 5, 62–70, 73–5,
        78–9, 84, 86–7
    De Larosière Report 63
    disclosure 64, 68–72, 78–9
    experts, opinions of 79
    financial institutions 63–70
    general meetings, approval of 79
    global financial crisis 63–5, 78
    listed companies 9, 63–5, 71–2
    long-term shareholder engagement,
        proposal for directive on 62–3,
        73–5, 78–9, 84
    performance, insufficient links with
        63, 73, 78–9
    reform 63–4
    reports 74–5, 79, 84
    reviews 68
    risk-taking 63–4
    shareholder say-on-pay 9, 79, 86–7
    short-termism 63–4
    structure of boards 69–70
    United Kingdom 111

unproven assumptions 79
variable and fixed parts, balance
    between 64, 68, 74
voting 64–5, 71, 74–5
reporting obligations 85, 204, 208,
    213–14 *see also* disclosure
reputation 12, 36, 38–9, 160
reverse merger companies *see* audits of
    Chinese RMCs by Big Four
    accountancy firms
risk management
    Canada, shareholder activism in 30
    corporate governance 63
    crowdfunding 11, 153
    De Larosière Report 63
    financial institutions 63, 66, 67–8, 70
    listed companies 71
Romano, Roberta 81–2
rugged individualism 3–4

Saradha Group scandal 188
Sarbanes-Oxley Act (United States)
    audit committees 4
    Chinese RMCs by Big Four
        companies, audits of 8–9, 35, 37,
        42–52
    corporate governance, securities law
        intervention in 4
    criminal consequences for financial
        misstatements 4
    empirical evidence 81–2
    Foreign Corrupt Practices Act of
        (1977) 4–5
    scandals 4
Savitt, W 20, 27
scandals
    China, regulation in 129
    crowdfunding 174, 188
    India 174, 188
    Sarbanes-Oxley Act 4
scienter 47
scrutiny
    audits of Chinese RMCs by Big Four
        accountancy firms 8, 35, 39, 57
    initial public offers (IPOs) 8, 35, 39,
        57
    see also supervision and monitoring

Securities and Exchange Commission
    (SEC)
    audits of Chinese RMCs by Big Four
        accountancy firms 5, 8–9, 35–57
    crowdfunding 180–1
securities law
    Canada 18
    China 10, 117–18, 133–4, 138
    New Zealand 202–203
    United States 6, 181
separation of ownership and control 17,
    102, 105, 160–62
Shaffer, G 7
Shanghai Stock Exchange (SHSE)
    129–30
shareholder activism
    advocacy roles 17–18
    consolidation of shareholding
        amongst institutional investors 8
    corporate governance 17–18
    corporate law 17–18
    defensive activism 17–18
    hedge funds 8, 17
    information circulars 18
    institutional shareholders 8
    monitoring corporate management 8
    offensive activism 17
    pension funds 8
    proxy forms 18
    separation of ownership and control
        17
    see also shareholder activism in
        Canada
shareholder activism in Canada 17–31
    accountability 23
    agency costs 19, 23–4
    Business Corporations Act 18, 27–8
    Canadian Pacific Rail 8, 24–6
    corporate governance 20–1, 24, 27,
        29
    corporate law 18, 20, 27–8
    directors
        expertise 30
        fiduciary duties 21–2, 28–9
        good faith 21–2
        independence 27, 30
        primacy 19–21, 31
        nomination 18, 20, 27–9, 31

removal 20
discipline 23
dispersed shareholders 24
divergent interests 19
exit 23
fiduciary duties 21–2, 28–9
good faith 21–2
groupthink 30
hedge fund activism 18, 24–5
information circulars 18
long-term interests 24, 27, 30
management 19–20, 23, 27–31
meaningful shareholder participation 18
minority shareholders 27
monitoring 22–7
nomination of directors 18, 20, 27–9
Ontario Securities Commission 21
oppression or unfair prejudice 20
proxy access and its dimensions 27–31
proxy contests 24–6, 28
reform 18, 20–21, 27
remuneration of executive 23
risk management 30
scandals 30
Securities Act (Ontario) 18
separation of ownership and control 19
shareholder democracy 18–22, 29, 30–31
shareholder primacy 19–20
short-termism 22, 24–7, 30
takeovers 21–2, 26
United States 21–2
value of firm 23, 30
voice 23
voting 20–21, 23
shareholder empowerment as instrument for corporate governance in Europe improvements in corporate governance 7
Shareholder Rights Directive
amendment 9–10, 72–3
Commission criticisms 9–10, 63, 77–9, 81–8
comply or explain principle 75

corporate governance 9–10, 72–88
criticisms 9–10, 63, 77–9, 81–8
freedom of establishment 83
listed companies 9–10, 62–3, 73–88
long-term shareholder engagement, proposal for directive on 9–10, 62–3, 72–88
seriousness of proposals 81–3
trivial, revision as 83–8
shareholders
audits of Chinese RMCs by Big Four accountancy firms 40–41
China, regulation in 133–4
corporate governance 5
cross-shareholdings 102, 107, 110, 112
crowdfunding 165–6
dispersed shareholders 24, 102–103
dual-class shares 106–109
financial institutions 66
identification 71–2
listed companies, role in 71
litigation 40–41
remuneration say-on-pay 9, 79, 86–7
unequal treatment 95
United States 133–4
value 3–4, 106–10
see also majority shareholders; minority shareholders; shareholder activism; Shareholder Rights Directive
shares *see also* dual-class shares; shareholders
Sharing Economy 147
shell companies 8, 39
Shenzhen Stock Exchange (SZSE) 129–30
short-termism 18, 22, 24–7, 30, 63–4, 66, 71, 77, 96–7
Singapore 102–103
accredited and institutional investors 183, 193
crowdfunding 182–4, 185–6, 192–3
exemptions 182–4
public offers 183
Monetary Authority of Singapore (MAS) 183
Securities and Futures Act (SFA) 183

small and medium-sized enterprises
(SMEs)
Australia 182
crowdfunding 1–2, 145, 147–8,
158–9, 163, 165–6
India 175, 179, 182, 184, 196
New Zealand 206, 213, 216–18
disclosure 163
India 175, 179, 182, 184, 196
New Zealand 206, 213, 216–18
Snowball Effect 215, 217
social welfare 110–11
Soni, J 194
South Korea 102–3
chaebols, ban on cross-shareholding
in 10, 112
corporate governance 112
cross-shareholding 112
family firms 112
Soviet Union
collapse 4
totalitarian economic model, move
away from 4
Spain, crowdfunding in 154–5, 156–8,
169
accreditation criteria 158
caps 156, 160
conflicts of interest 157–8
disclosure 169
licensing 154–5
registration 154–5
shareholder participation 165
Standard & Poor (S&P) Composite
1500 Index 103
start-ups
India, crowdfunding in 172–4, 176–8,
184, 195–6
New Zealand, crowdfunding in 213,
217
Spain, crowdfunding in 145–6, 151,
157–63, 165
state-owned enterprises (SOEs) (China)
10, 117, 118–21, 130–32, 138
state sovereignty 43
stock exchanges
China, regulation in 118, 129–31, 139
origin and growth 129–30

Western exchanges, differences
from 129–30
New Zealand, crowdfunding in 213,
216
Shanghai Stock Exchange (SHSE)
129–30
Shenzhen Stock Exchange (SZSE)
129–30
Strand, Therese 80
suboptimal results in absence of clear
rules and regulation 5
supervision and monitoring
audits of Chinese RMCs by Big Four
accountancy firms 36–7, 39–44,
54–5
Canada, shareholder activism in 22–7
corporate management 8
directors 66
financial institutions 66
India, crowdfunding in 176, 178
related party transactions 62–3, 73,
75, 79–81, 84
supervisory boards 10, 127, 136–8
Sweden 102, 107
Switzerland 102
synthetic approaches *see* New Legal
Realism (NLR)
systemic effects 11, 36–7, 51, 56,
153–4, 155–6, 169

Taiwan 102–103
takeovers 21–2, 26, 111
tax
audits of Chinese RMCs by Big Four
accountancy firms 40
avoidance 40
reporting 85
tech companies 10, 95, 98, 100–101
Thatcher–Reagan era 4
'too big to fail' 37–8, 52
transparency
audits of Chinese RMCs by Big Four
accountancy firms 51, 55
China, regulation in 118, 136
corporate control-enhancing
mechanisms 105
crowdfunding 11, 154, 163, 180

India, crowdfunding in 180
New Zealand, crowdfunding in 13,
    203
proxy advisers 73
voting 9
transplants 11, 129, 137–8
trans-Tasman Mutual Recognition
    Scheme 215–16
Trump, Donald 13–14

United Kingdom
    Brexit 13
    Companies Act (2006) 38
    corporate control-enhancing
        mechanisms 111
    crowdfunding 158, 160
    dispersed ownership 102–103
    dual-class shares 105
    Joint Stock Companies Registration
        and Regulation Act (1844) 6
    liability limitation agreements
        (LLAs) 38
    pound, fall in value of 13–14
    prospectuses 6, 160
    Reagan–Thatcher era 4
    remuneration 111
    shareholder primacy 4
United States
    American Revolution, values of 3
    asset managers 76
    Canada, shareholder activism in 21–2
    China
        listing of tech companies 10, 98,
            100–101
        regulation in 116, 133
    corporate control-enhancing
        mechanisms
        Chinese tech companies listed in
            US 10, 98, 100–101
        dispersed ownership 103
        dual-class shares 96, 105, 108–10
        IPO firms 10, 95, 98
        public companies 103, 107
        S&P Composite 1500 Index 103
    crowdfunding 1–2, 152, 159–60
        CROWDFUND Act 181, 183,
            194–5

        economic growth 184
        JOBS Act 181
        prospectuses 181
        registration, exemptions from
            180–81
        regulation 180–81
        SEC 180–81
        Securities Act 181
    Delaware 21–2
    directors, independence of 129
    dispersed ownership 102–103
    dual-class shares 96, 105, 108–10
    enforcement cooperation,
        memorandum of understanding
        with China on 5, 9, 54–7
    Federal Reserve 1–2
    fiduciary duties 21–2
    GDP 116
    good faith 21–2
    institutional investors 76
    prospectuses 181
    Reagan-Thatcher era 4
    regulation
        crowdfunding 180–81
        rollback 14
    Securities Act 6, 181
    Securities and Exchange
        Commission (SEC) 180–81
    shareholders
        activism 8, 21–2
        powers 133–4
        primacy 4
    takeovers, defensive tactics against
        21–2
    see also audits of Chinese RMCs by
        Big Four accountancy firms;
        Sarbanes-Oxley Act (United
        States)

venture capital
    finance gap 146
    India 172, 175, 186, 189, 191–2, 196
    institutional involvement 149–51
Villalonga, B 108
voting
    agreements 102, 108, 110, 168–9
    asset managers 76

Canada, shareholder activism in
    20–21, 23
ceilings 109–10
corporate control-enhancing
    mechanisms 10, 103, 106–12
corporate governance 9, 64–5, 71
crowdfunding 166, 168–9, 214
disclosure 66
dual-class shares 10, 103
event-based 111–112
general meetings 62, 64–5, 74–5, 77,
    84
information on policies 73, 76–7
institutional investors 66, 76
majority shareholders 20–21,
    111–12, 168
minimum shareholding requirements
    166

New Zealand, crowdfunding in 214
Nordic countries 111–12
related party transactions 80
remuneration 71, 74–5
risk-bearing 103
takeover protection 111
transparency 9
unequal voting rights 10, 103

warnings 184, 206, 209–10, 212–13
wilful misconduct 46–8
Winter Group Report 105, 110
Worner, S 201

Young, D 50

Zuckerberg, Mark 98